HOSPITABLE HOSTS 2

INSPIRING & MEMORABLE STORIES FROM AIRBNB HOSTS AROUND THE WORLD TO EDUCATE & MOTIVATE

Stirling
Publishing House

First published in 2023 by Stirling Publishing House

Stirling Publishing House

Jodie Stirling has asserted her right to be identified as the author of this Work in accordance with the Copyright, Designs and Patents Act 1988.

ISBN: 978-1-7393520-0-4

Editing and design by Fuzzy Flamingo
www.fuzzyflamingo.co.uk

A catalogue for this book is available from the British Library.

CONTENTS

WHAT'S IT LIKE THEN, BEING A HOSPITABLE HOST?

What's it like then, you ask, being a Hospitable Host?
Turning my home into something to boast.

A gentle touch, a hammer swung,
No detail left undone.

A painting here, a mural there,
Little figurines to fill the air.

I open my home and invite them in,
To enjoy the comfort and beauty within.

I strive to make their stay a delight,
With a clean and cosy space that feels just right.

I offer them treats, amenities and books to read,
And make sure they have everything they need.

A place to eat? Maybe a nice view to sit and idle?
Don't fear, our guidebook will be your Bible.

I am a host with a passion for sharing,
The joys of home and the pleasures of caring.

I love to see my guests happy and content,
And leave with memories of a place well spent.

I am a host, provider of rest,
A friend to travellers on their journey's quest.

I offer them a home away from home,
A haven of peace and a place to roam.

This is what it means, to be a Hospitable Host,
Bringing joy and comfort to those who need it most.

– Vinci Sevilla Jr

ACKNOWLEDGEMENT

I would like to express my sincere gratitude to all those who have contributed to the creation of this book. With a special mention to Jen, my editor, for her insightful feedback, guidance and expertise. Without their support, this project would not have been possible.

I would like to extend my heartfelt thanks to the co-authors who have generously shared their stories. Your diverse perspectives and collaborative spirit have been instrumental in shaping the content of this book. Your valuable insights and experience have added depth and richness to this work, and I am deeply grateful for your contributions.

To our wonderful sponsors, I would like to acknowledge your belief in my vision and your willingness to invest in this project. Your sponsorship has played a crucial role in bringing this book to life and helping hosts with their businesses.

I would also like to thank the readers for their interest. Your encouragement has been a source of inspiration throughout this journey. I would love to know who is reading – please send me an email to say a Hospitable Hello to Jodie@hospitablehosts.com

Finally, I would like to acknowledge my family and friends for their unwavering support. Your love and encouragement have been the driving force behind this project, and I am grateful for all that you have done to help me bring this book to life.

Enjoy and Happy Hosting!

Jodie Stirling

INTRODUCTION

Welcome to *Hospitable Hosts Volume 2*, a multi-authored book that celebrates the passion, hard work, and heart-centred approach of short-term rental hosts from around the world. Being an Airbnb host is not just about setting up properties and sharing spaces, it's creating memorable experiences for guests and being a hospitable host. In this book, you'll meet professional hosts from various countries, who share their unique stories of how they found themselves doing what they love – to be a *Hospitable Host.*

Each host has written a chapter from the heart, detailing their journey into the short-term rental industry and what inspires them to continue being hospitable hosts. Their stories aim to inspire and empower others to achieve what is important to them and their loved ones, despite the challenges of life. Most of these hosts have simply found themselves doing what comes naturally to them – caring for people and wanting to be of service to others.

In this volume, we delve deeper into the world of short-term rentals and showcase the amazing hosts who make it all possible. We feature hosts from Australia, South Africa, the United Kingdom, Sweden, the USA and Canada, and each one brings a unique perspective and approach to the hospitality industry.

Whether you are a seasoned host or someone who's considering entering the industry, this book is a must-read for anyone who values the importance of creating meaningful connections through hospitality. Join us on a journey around the world and discover the joys and challenges of being a *Hospitable Host*. Volume 2 is sure to inspire and uplift, as we continue to showcase the best in the industry.

FOREWORD

MARK SIMPSON AND JULIE GEORGE

Being a short-term rental host can be lonely. There are days when you just wish you had someone you could reach out to and have a chat, rant, share a win, or all the above.

Writing a book is even more lonesome.

When I put together *The Book Direct Playbook*, I locked myself in a room and wrote down 50,000 words. There were so many steps along the way where I wished I could have had an accountability buddy or someone to reach out to, to ask how they were getting on.

When Jodie Stirling mentioned to me on a call that she had an idea of putting together a multi-author book, I instantly knew it was going to be a success. I signed up before she could finish her "pitch" to me!

I then watched how Jodie jumped on countless calls, Clubhouse rooms and Zoom calls to promote the idea to convince forty other hosts to join her on the journey. The goal was to put together a book that shared stories from all over the world of hospitality.

I will be honest here and let you know that there were certain days when I didn't think it was going to happen. However, Jodie's determination and passion shone through and, at the start of 2022, we had a crew of forty strangers all on a Zoom call.

Jodie explained what we were going to do, what was expected of all of us and what the outcome was going to be. Neither I nor the other authors of *Hospitable Hosts* could have envisioned what was going to happen next, and I think Jodie too!

A few months later and the book was ready to publish. All the hosts and co-authors got together on a Zoom to celebrate and to start to plan book launch parties and the next steps. Everyone had contributed a chapter in what would become a worldwide best seller, raising money for charity.

We are now a community, a tribe, an online family and, when I'm at an event or conference, the people I look for most are my fellow authors.

At an event in Nashville in June 2022, thirteen of the authors went on stage in front of 1000 people and posed with our copies of the book. To this day, it was one of my favourite memories of the year.

And now we are back, ready to do it all over again for 2023 and I couldn't be prouder to be back. The stories you're going to read will have an impact on you more than you realise. Who knows, it may make you want to tell your story (side note: email Jodie as 2024 preparation is already underway!).

I wanted to take a minute to say how proud I am of Jodie for doing this. Launching a business or an idea is the hardest thing to do because you have to convince others (and yourself) to buy into it. Consistency and determination are crucial, and Jodie has that in strong supply.

I've had the pleasure to work with Jodie on many projects and this is the one that I know will leave a lasting legacy.

Thank you, Jodie x

Mark Simpson

Hospitable Hosts Volume 2 is the brainchild of Jodie Stirling who approached forty short-term rental hosts from around the world, encouraging them to share their stories to inspire and educate others. What resulted from this collaboration was an incredible community of hosts supporting and championing each other, a best-seller badge of honour and a second book, which you are now reading!

The stories you will read in this book are unique and impactful, and we hope will give you an insight into the world of hosting from around the world. No matter what part of the globe you are on, you will find that the short-term rental hosts face similar challenges and, in turn, similar rewards. Creating financial freedom for themselves and their families is a common reward that inspires readers to take the leap to self-employment. Guest interactions that create powerful and lifelong memories is another reason our authors love this industry so much.

This collaboration of authors from around the globe have chosen to filter all profits of the book sales through to Great Ormond Street Hospital and War Child charities. We thank you for purchasing this book and, in turn, helping the little people of this world in the challenges they face.

Enjoy reading this book and get ready to be inspired... Perhaps you too one day may become a *Hospitable Host*?

Julie George

ALEX DECAMP

WHO YOU ARE AND HOW YOU GOT INTO HOSTING

As with many things in life, I got into short-term rentals because of a woman. From the moment I laid eyes on her at a fundraiser, I was mesmerised. I had no idea what was said at that event because the only thing I could think about was how I was going to approach her. Imagine my surprise when she actually walked over towards me! Our mutual friend thought she would make a great connection. She was intelligent, inquisitive, beautiful, with a profound interest in urban and community development. And she wanted to talk to me about neighbourhood investments. Little did I know meeting her would change the trajectory of my life.

My name is Alex DeCamp and I am the owner of Great Stays, a short-term rental (STR) manager and operator in the Southeast Michigan area. I founded this company in 2021 to exclusively focus on short-term rentals after having developed and managed long-term rental real estate for the previous decade. Like many people, I liked the consistency and reliability of annual leases. However, I am also a curious person, and wanted to know more about the potential impact STRs could have on some of the properties I owned.

In 2018, I took the first step by converting one of my long-term units in an apartment building into a short-term rental. I hired a third-party manager who managed design, setup and guest communications. I started listening to STR podcasts (shout out to Get Paid for Your Pad) and learning more about the industry. My property was doing well, but even though Airbnb was sending more and more information about being a host, I was not seriously considering expanding. Not until I went to that fundraiser and met "her".

For the next month, I did everything I could to see her. Business meetings, social events and even more fundraisers. I was riding the whirlwind, at least until she told me that she was only in Detroit on a consulting contract and would soon be heading home to London.

"London, London?"

"Yes," she replied.

My heart sank for a moment until I remembered the Airbnb emails about a conference called Host that they were sponsoring in London the following month.

"That's funny because I will be there at a conference," I said, as I quickly scanned to see if flights were still available. They were, and just like that, I was going to London to see her, and attend a conference about STRs on the side. I was so excited, I started planning every moment I could with her. Dinner at her favourite restaurant, hot baths and dinner at the Royal Automobile Club, fireworks on London Bridge, coffee in a quaint café and a night at the city's best cocktail lounge.

The morning I arrived, I went straight to the conference, with the thought that I just needed to get through the day so I could see her. A funny thing happened, though. Visiting the booths, I saw excitement in the vendors' faces. Other attendees were talking about property management software or pricing tools. Someone showed me how their door lock software would alert the cleaners when the guest checked out and then again alert the host when the cleaner was done. Some folks were even talking about keyless entry with unique codes for each guest (trust me, this was a big deal back then). I went from wanting the day to speed up so I could see the woman of my dreams, to a strange sense of possibility about STRs. For the first time, I could see how you could scale a business using mostly technology. Even as I went back to the hotel to get ready, my mind was racing with ideas about bringing what I'd learned back to the States.

You might be wondering how the date went.

I'd like to say that we did all of those things I'd meticulously planned when we met up, but I'd be remiss if I left out the part where she brought along her tall, handsome and extremely intelligent boyfriend. It was like the end of *Sixth Sense* when all of the clues I'd missed along the way suddenly made sense, but unlike Bruce Willis's character, I was only dead on the inside.

Part of me wanted to run and bury my head in tequila, but I'm from Detroit, and apparently, we are gritty. So, over the next couple of days, I did go to her favourite restaurant with her and her boyfriend, and did see the fireworks with her and her boyfriend, and did the hot baths, well that was mostly with her boyfriend due to a men's and women's section. Instead of booze, I buried my head in the conference.

It's a funny thing when you figure out what you want to do for the rest of your life, the way the universe opens doors for you. I came home from London invigorated, and soon enough a tenant could no longer rent three of my units, so I offered to take them over. I then converted another unit, so my portfolio went from one to five in one month. I knew I needed guidance, so I signed up for masterminds and training courses and focused on growth. Four more units here, two more there, I was enthralled! I loved how nimble and tech savvy the industry was and, when lockdown hit, I quickly shifted to housing travelling nurses and provided housing for a church family.

Then, when things opened up, I grew my properties and my team. The more I grew, the more I knew I needed help. I signed up for an intensive training course that introduced me to wonderful hosts from around the world, and it was in this group that I finally grew the strength and knowledge to realise I could make this a full-

In a Detroit property currently undergoing rehab

time business. Six months later, I left my cushy VP position at one of the largest banks in the country and embraced being a short-term rental host full time.

Great Stays is currently at twenty-five listings, and we plan to be at sixty within the months after the publication of this book. Every week, my team gets together and discusses how we can improve the guest experience by enhancing service, answer questions before they are asked, and truly integrate the guest into the local business and community fabric. This city and industry changed my life and gave me opportunities I couldn't find anywhere else in the world, and we want to ensure all of our guests get a chance to experience the same. Who knows, maybe they will meet the woman that will forever change their life as well.

In order to operate and manage that many listings, I needed to create systems and processes that became the foundation of my company playbook. What this meant was any task that I did more than once I would write down to use as reference material for the next time. When I expanded the team, I realised that writing it down wasn't enough and I needed to show them. However, showing multiple people the same thing didn't make sense. So, I started using the recording app Loom to record everything I did on my computer or phone. Adding those videos to the playbook really helped eliminate unnecessary questions. Once I had the playbook in place, I started investing in people and building my team. Currently, my team consists of four groups: the guest experience team (GET), operations, maintenance and cleaning.

Our GET department mostly consists of remote workers in the Philippines who monitor the guest messaging threads twenty-four hours a day. Our team works in day and night shifts with a two-hour overlap, which corresponds with guest check-in time, i.e. the busiest messaging time of the day. The team is constantly working on the Great Stays internal playbook to improve the company's systems and processes, to make the workday more efficient. Technically, they are contract workers, but we work to make everyone truly feel like part of the team. We are even exploring benefit packages and hope to be able to offer things like health insurance in the coming year.

The operations team are the boots-on-the-ground people and are what truly allowed Great Stays to grow. Everyone always talks about the owner wanting to work "on" the business instead of "in" the business, but this is extremely difficult when your daily tasks get broken up with having to deal with a faulty furnace, or run extra towels to a guest, or assist with a lock out. Even answering questions by the guest experience team chops up the workflow. Our operations team now handles all those functions by basically becoming the escalation contact point if the GET needs further assistance than what can be handled remotely. Additionally, they continuously work on creating better systems to help avoid these issues in the first place!

Maintenance is so important. It is one of the trickier teams to build due to the sporadic nature of the issues that arise. Plus, since we manage property for multiple owners, we sometimes have to deal with multiple maintenance people. How we function is we have a point of contact for each property that generally handles small maintenance issues along with snow in the winter and lawncare in the summer. If we need to escalate, then we will use a local trade that we have experience with. Most of the time, we find these trades using a service such as Thumbtack or Task Rabbit.

Our cleaning teams are arguably the most important part of our operations, and technically they don't even work for our company! All of our cleaners are third-party contractors, and this is why it is so important for us to treat them with the respect they deserve. We have the most success with mom and pop – actually husband and wife – companies. Even though they don't work directly for Great Stays, they take pride and ownership in their jobs. They know how many towels a property needs, they know if coffee creamers are running low, they also know how long a unit will take to turnover. The first thing a guest notices (as long as check-in went smoothly) is the cleanliness of a unit and, in this regard, our cleaners are the front line of defence. It is imperative we do everything we can to make the cleaning companies feel proud to work with us, which includes paying above market rate, sending end of year bonuses for five-star cleanings and doing everything we can to enhance their role.

I should also mention the property owners. This is something I had struggled with when first starting, since I was the owner of most of our first managed properties. So, it was easy to pay myself last, but that doesn't work when we are hired to manage for others. At the time of writing, we are working on an automated reporting system as well as a better cadence of communication with our owners. It is easy to get caught up in the weeds but if the owners aren't happy then we don't have properties to manage. This doesn't mean that every month will be record earnings because they won't, but it means that we do everything we can to keep owners involved so they know what is happening with their investment.

WHAT DOES BEING A HOSPITABLE HOST MEAN TO YOU

I have an unwavering commitment to respecting my guests, my team and my community. That commitment to respect ensures that the team feels inspired and empowered to provide exemplary service.

It is critical to remember that every guest has different emotional and physical reasons for travel. Working to understand why they chose to stay with us allows us to support the guest's needs more holistically. This doesn't mean we need to be pushovers and do everything they ask; sometimes, guests will ask for things that we cannot accommodate or that could negatively affect other guests. However, it does mean that we will cater to their fundamental needs and serve them with respect.

Our team is the lifeblood of our operations. What started as one person's vision has expanded into a remote guest experience team that offers 24/7 service, a boots-on-the-ground operations team whose sole purpose is to ensure everything is functioning correctly, and cleaning teams that take real ownership and pride in the properties. My job is to make sure that the team has everything they need to serve our guests to the best of their abilities. Additionally, I do what I can to go above and beyond when possible. I pay attention to scheduling to make sure cleaners have breaks on holidays, I stay in tune with market salaries and am at or above for all of my team, and make sure that the team feels empowered to make decisions and operate. One of our sayings is that there are no mistakes, just a missing or incorrect system. If something bad happens, we use that as an opportunity to create a new entry in the playbook and move on. The team feels very comfortable in this environment.

Lastly, but just as importantly, we focus on our community. Travel is not just about checking off a to-do list. It is about creating memorable experiences that leave you feeling inspired and connected. Great Stays got its start in Detroit, and its authenticity is infused in our DNA. Our guests have a better experience because they feel integrated with local businesses, services and people. Genuinely connecting guests with the community helps bring vibrancy to local businesses and contributes to the economic vitality of residents.

We want our guests to not just have a great stay in our spaces but also feel like they can look to us to recommend places and experiences while visiting. In order to accomplish this, we work diligently to create up-to-date digital guidebooks for our guests. These not only show the guest how to check-in and use everything at the property but also provide links to our favourite retail and restaurant locations, as well as links to local experiences such as tours and exhibits. We are actively working on partnerships with these places so we can offer discounts for our guests as well. The hope is to one day have a system that easily tracks all of the business we send to the local community and support sent to the small businesses.

The best STRs invest in their communities and the people who live there year-round.

At Great Stays, we foster deep connections with each community our properties are in so we can share them with visitors. We love our communities and want to share them with the world. We don't just recommend places because they have good reviews, we do it because we love going there, know the people who own it, and feel it offers something other places cannot.

MOST MEMORABLE GUEST

We've had some great guests over the years coming from every corner of the world. We get families renting for months while waiting for a new home or job. We opened our business to travelling nurses during the lockdown, who were absolutely amazing. A lot of our properties are rented by neighbours needing extra space for their in-laws while visiting for the holidays. We even hosted an NFL player for a few months who returned to throw a birthday party half a year later. He still reaches out to see which units are available when he has friends in town to watch him play. We also now focus a lot of our efforts on repeat guests, which especially holds true for our business travellers. My team loves talking about our repeat customers and making sure the units are set up the way the guests like. One of the goals of this upcoming season is to

In a Detroit property currently undergoing rehab

increase marketing to business travellers and update our units with the amenities they need. Of course, we've had some unfortunate incidents over the years, such as parties, messy guests and other violations of the rules, but you quickly forget those and it's really just so fun to meet new people.

WHAT I WISH I HAD KNOWN

Two things I wish I had realised earlier in my business were to create systems and to value my time, and really, they go hand in hand. Basically, I needed to realise that if I did something more than once then I could create a video on how to do it and then hire someone to do it for me. Obviously, this doesn't make sense when it is one thing, but if you record enough of these day-to-day activities, you've basically created the job description of your operations manager and can then remove yourself so you can focus on growing the business. This may not make sense at a couple of properties, but trust me, once you get to twenty or so, this is vital.

HOW DO I HELP OTHER HOSTS?

I've been lucky to meet and share strategies with other hosts from across this country. I made friends with a group after attending an STR conference and, ever since that time, we've maintained weekly meetings to discuss our businesses and support each other. I am also available to local hosts who reach out to learn more about the business. But I think the best thing my company can do to support other hosts is by managing a well-respected organisation that regularly advocates for reasonable STR ordinances and illustrates the standard at which STRs should operate.

Hosting has absolutely changed my life and the need to build my company was the push that allowed me to leave my job in corporate America and truly work for myself. Every day is an adventure, and I am fully committed to building this company into a highly regarded international hospitality company. I know that as long as we stay true to our values, we will get there.

ABOUT THE AUTHOR

Alex DeCamp is the founder of Great Stays short-term rental management company and a real estate developer. He helps successful investors realise their property's potential by offering top-notch customer service and sensible amenities. Alex believes that a rising tide raises all ships and works to ensure that guests experience an organic introduction into the local small business community. Great Stays is ranked as one of the largest and highest-rated independent short-term rental operators in the Detroit market.

Alex's real estate development projects are hyper focused in Detroit neighbourhoods to create residential and business density. He believes that any great urban neighbourhood must be walkable and subscribes to the idea of the twenty-minute neighbourhood in that all of a person's needs should be able to be met in a twenty-minute walk. His passion is for turning vacant, blighted buildings into mixed-use neighbourhood destinations. One of his proudest accomplishments was restoring a long vacant building into a mixed-use development, housing a nationally recognised hair stylist and a James Beard nominated restaurant.

Alex has been recognised locally with the Vanguard Award for business accomplishments and as small developer of the year by the county. Prior to founding his own businesses, Alex was a corporate banker tasked with creating and implementing creative financial tools for people and businesses in underserved low-income markets. Two crowning achievements were the creation of a down payment assistance programme for low-income individuals and being on the creative team for the Detroit Home Mortgage programme, a programme that jump-started home lending in Detroit and was the first of its kind in the country.

Alex holds a master's in urban planning and certificate in real estate development from the University of Michigan and when not travelling resides in the city of Detroit.

Links: linktr.ee/greatstays

ALEX SABIO

FROM HOSPITAL TO HOSPITABLE

My life changed dramatically when I went from working in a hospital to creating generational wealth through short-term rentals. Although I'd been investing in real estate for almost twenty years, my big break came when I started a short-term rental business in the middle of the global pandemic in the summer of 2020.

How did I transition from hospital to hospitality? Well, it started when I was a kid. I got a glimpse of the hospitality world from my great aunts Lola Belen and Lola Tacing. They owned and managed a small motel on the Las Vegas strip. Originally named the Sombrero Motel, they rebranded it and named it Pollyanna Motel after their beloved dog. The motel was a hole-in-the wall located on south Las Vegas Boulevard, close to the "Welcome to Fabulous Las Vegas" sign. It's no longer there, however, as they sold it in the early 2000s to a wealthy developer.

I have a lot of fond memories of visiting the Pollyanna. Our family lived in southern California, and we'd drive back and forth from Oxnard to pick up my Lola Belen and drive her to Las Vegas for the weekend, where she would manage the motel. We always stayed in room thirteen because it was the largest room they had available.

The rooms were terribly outdated, but if they were around today, they'd be back in style, as 1970s fashion has made a comeback.

Owning the motel was a lot of work for my great aunts, but I always thought it was really cool that they had a piece of the Las Vegas strip. I believe creating generational wealth through real estate investing has more to do with inspiring the next generation than it does with handing down large sums of money. I'm sure, when they purchased the motel, they weren't thinking of inspiring me some forty to fifty years later. My Lola Belen and Lola Tacing never talked with me about real estate; I just observed from a distance.

My Lola Belen was extremely generous and giving. During weddings, she tossed handfuls of coins onto the dance floor as our Filipino families would line dance to "Achy Breaky Heart". The crowd would go into a frenzy and rush the dance floor to pick up as many quarters as possible. I don't know what she got out of it, but it became a tradition at family weddings, and all the cousins anticipated how much money we would take home after each one. She created a memorable experience for all of us.

My grandparents on my father's side (Lola Alice and Lolo Nick) also did well for themselves with real estate investing. They owned a few board and care facilities throughout southern California and were the most successful people I knew as I was growing up. The board and care facilities would house mentally disabled people who needed a lot of help with daily living activities.

My grandparents were extremely generous as well, always giving out bonuses to their staff during Christmas. Seeing my grandfather dressed as Santa Claus and announcing everyone's names as he passed out envelopes from a large stack at the family Christmas party was always a treat. The envelopes held cash, and they gave one to everybody – all twelve of their kids, their grandkids, and all their staff from the board and care facilities. They made everyone feel so special and they gave so much more than they received; I took that lesson to heart and still try to apply it to my personal life and in business.

My Lolo Nick worked very hard. Many nights, I saw him sitting at his desk late at night, paying the bills. I believe the harder you work, the luckier you get. When you put in the work, good things always come.

Even though my grandparents were successful in business, they pushed me into getting a career with what they thought was more security – healthcare. I think they liked the security and benefits that nurses and other healthcare professionals had. Consequently, I lived with my grandparents for the first two years of college and got my degree in respiratory therapy. Honestly, that was one of the best decisions I ever made. I met my wife Tanya in college, and we have four beautiful children together. My healthcare job has allowed me to provide for my family, and I've met some amazing people. I think a lot of people go through life with a job they hate, but not me. My career has been very fulfilling.

I've been a respiratory therapist (RT) for twenty years now. Respiratory therapists are certified medical professionals who treat lung and breathing problems. They handle respiratory issues that can stem from a wide variety of conditions or events. Many work in emergency rooms, intensive care units, nursing homes, or sleep centres. I've worked in large teaching facilities, trauma centres, and burn centres, and my speciality and passion now is working with premature babies and in paediatrics. In my field, I've done it all, but none of it prepared me for the global pandemic.

COVID's climax is long over, and we take the virus somewhat lightly now, but at its height it was extremely stressful for respiratory therapists. We were at the very front of the front line, but most people had still never heard of us. Our workloads and stress levels tripled and quadrupled overnight. Without getting too technical, I'll just say that COVID directly affects the lungs and makes them very stiff, or what we call "non-compliant". This condition makes breathing and getting oxygen to the body and its vital organs extremely difficult. When oxygen levels become that low and breathing becomes too difficult, we have to put patients to sleep and intubate them, which means putting a breathing tube

Our 2,000th transport for our NICU Transport Team. Here I am with my team stabilising and transporting a premature baby to another hospital for higher level of care.

down their throat or windpipe and putting them on life support, or ventilators. With COVID, we had to use very high pressures and high concentrations of oxygen simply to maintain adequate oxygenation and ventilation.

In our intensive care units (ICUs), we usually only encounter extremely sick patients a few times a month. I'm talking about the patients whom we can't heal no matter what we do. We throw everything but the kitchen sink at them, medically speaking, yet we can't save their lives. We always reflect as a team years later, "You remember Mrs So-and-So? We did everything we could for her..." With COVID, though, we were caring for five to ten of those kinds of patients each and every day, versus the entire team seeing only a few every month.

Because of the Health Insurance Portability and Accountability Act (HIPAA) laws, I can't go into details about any of the patients for whom I cared. I can tell you they ranged in age from very young to very old, and many had pre-existing conditions, but some didn't. Stories circulated about medical professionals contracting COVID and dying. For instance, our local news covered the story of a pregnant nurse who contracted COVID. According to news reports, doctors had to deliver the baby six weeks early when the nurse was intubated. The mother later died and never got a chance to see her baby.

I can tell you, these kinds of stories make you think twice as a respiratory therapist. There was a shortage of Personal Protective Equipment (PPE). My wife and I really started to wonder if the job was worth it anymore. We felt we were putting our lives in danger and our family at risk, and with COVID's uncertainty, we believed we needed to find a way out.

As I mentioned, I had been investing in real estate since the early-to-mid 2000s. Although my great aunts had been in hospitality, I decided to start my investing in the long-term rental space. Over time, I had amassed about a dozen homes, and each of them profited about $100 to $200 per month. That profit didn't make a huge difference in my lifestyle. When COVID hit, though, my real estate investing went from being a hobby to becoming a need.

We purchased our first short-term rental in the summer of 2020, putting almost every penny we had into a cabin 2,000 miles away in a city we'd never heard of three months previously. When I was doing research, people kept telling me about Great Smoky National Park in Tennessee. I love visiting national parks, and this was the most visited national park in the United States. I loved the idea of owning property there, so I went all in and purchased our first cabin in August of 2020. Three months later, my wife was able to retire early from her job as a respiratory therapist, which removed her from harm's way during COVID. I was able to replace my income with our second luxury short-term rental a few months later, but I still work as an RT because I love my job, and the fear of COVID has subsided significantly.

Surprisingly, the transition from the hospital into hospitality was very easy. We just applied three simple principles that I learned from my great aunts and grandparents. To be honest, I think anyone could transition into any career if they follow these principles:

> Principle #1: We will always be authentic. I'm always empathetic about guest needs and never try to pull a fast one over our guests. The truth shall set you free.

On the 14th of August, we hosted our first guest. We had no idea what we were doing and accidentally went live seven days too early. You might think that was no big deal, but our four king beds still had no bedsheets! We'd ordered them, but they weren't going to arrive for another few days. We either had to cancel our first ever guest or figure out a solution. I called Sherry, the cleaner I'd recently hired, and explained to her the awful rookie mistake I'd made. I'd met Sherry a few days prior and had a great conversation with her. The second I spoke with her I knew she would be the right cleaner for us. She offered to go to Wal-Mart and purchase sheets with her own money if I would immediately reimburse her. We learned a valuable lesson that day. Treat people with extreme kindness, and they will return the favour.

I'll give you another example. Our most memorable guest was also one of the worst guests we've hosted. If you're in hospitality long enough, you'll encounter many of these guests. Our guest was disrespectful of all our house rules and damaged our indoor pool by pouring bubble bath into it. We had other guests coming in only a few hours after that guest departed, so we told our pool cleaners to do their best, but we knew we wouldn't be able to clear out all those bubbles in time. This was Independence Day weekend, and the guests checking in were paying a premium. We decided to let the truth set us free, no matter how embarrassing it was, so I reached out to the incoming guests a couple of hours before check-in. We were completely up front with them and told them we would absolutely understand if they wanted to cancel and look for another place. The guests actually respected that we were truthful, and they stayed for the entire seven nights they'd booked. They never asked for a discount, but I sent them a one-and-a-half night refund – the amount of time our pool cleaners needed to clear all the bubbles. Those guests left us a five-star, glowing review.

> Principle #2: We will work hard for our guests. Like my grandfather sitting up late at night paying bills, we always put in the work to give our guests the best experience possible. Whenever I set up my cabins or beach homes, I'm up eighteen hours a day, getting them ready.

Being a hospitable host means going above and beyond for your guests, providing them with an amazing experience, and understanding that the money will follow. We always put the guests' safety, needs and wants first. For example, once a wildfire broke out in the area, so we monitored it closely and let our guests know that they were currently not in the fire zone or mandatory evacuation area, but if they didn't feel comfortable, we would gladly give them back their money for unused days. We also promised to give them regular updates, which we did. The fire was three miles away from them, and they appreciated our candour and communication. After a few hours, even though the fire was nowhere near our cabin, they decided to leave and cut their vacation short. We lost out on several hundred dollars, but we knew we had to do the right thing. The guest appreciated us and even though their vacation was a disaster, they left us a glowing, five-star review. A lot of other hosts stuck with their strict "no refund even in severe weather" policy, but we always feel like we have to do what's right.

In another example, one weekend a snowstorm hit the area. You would think that a "winter wonderland" would be an amazing vacation for guests, but in this case the snow was simply too much. Temperatures fell to the single digits, wind knocked out several power lines, and the roads were unsafe to travel, even for first responders. COVID was rampant at the time, and more than half of the electrician contractors were out because of it. One of our cabins was rented to guests who were staying for multiple days, and it ended up with zero power or running water because of the storm. Even though our other cabin had power, and we could have made a killing renting it out to other folks who were stranded with no running power, water, or sewer, we decided to do the right thing and move our guests to the cabin that had power. We were worried about a bad review because the cabin they had originally rented had an indoor pool with a killer view. The cabin we moved them to was more spacious, but it didn't have those amenities. However, the guests wrote a fantastic review, thanking us for our hospitality. Their reservation ended the next day, and I told our cleaners I was shutting the property down. I wouldn't force them to drive in dangerous conditions to clean. I also offered to let them and their families stay for free if they were affected by the power outages. Hospitality includes how you treat the staff who make you successful.

> Principle #3: As long as we follow the first two principles of being authentic and working hard, we must surrender to the outcome. If we treat people with kindness, are honest and work hard, we just have to be okay with the results. The vast majority of guests will respond positively if you are honest and try your best to fix any problems.

Since starting my own short-term rental business, I've decided to share what I've learned with other healthcare workers. I've helped hundreds of healthcare professionals start their own vacation rental businesses. During the pandemic, a lot of these workers became interested in starting their own short-term rental business for the same reasons I did, so I've shared all my success (and even not-so-successful) stories, told them about the systems I use and revealed what works and what doesn't. People really responded to that authenticity – you can label me the anti-guru. To make better use of my time, I started a Facebook group called Healthcare Professionals Investing in Real Estate. We have weekly meetups and bring on special guests who are experts in their respective short-term rental fields. Just like my grandparents, I'm looking to inspire other people to follow in my footsteps.

If I have inspired or helped you out in any way, I ask for two things. #1. Give me a shout out. Post on social media or text me how I helped you. This energises me and makes me feel like I'm doing something right. #2. I want you to help someone else along the way. Pay it forward without any strings attached.

My Family

ABOUT THE AUTHOR

Alex Sabio is a married father of four who lives in southern California. He is a real estate investor and has worked in healthcare as a respiratory therapist for over twenty years. He has become a respected figure in his field, working in tertiary centres, large teaching hospitals, trauma centres, burn centres and has been published on the efficiency of inhaled nitric oxide on premature infants. As a respiratory therapist, he was on the front line battling Covid-19. In 2020, he decided to pivot his real estate strategy and went from the hospital to hospitality. Replacing his income through short-term rentals became a necessity. He took a chance and purchased his first short-term rental in the height of Covid. Within three months, his wife Tanya who was also a respiratory therapist was able to retire early from her career. The hospitality industry was an easy transition from the hospital, Alex just applied his strong work ethic and passion for caring and helping others. Since 2020, Alex has scaled and grew his real estate portfolio into six luxury short-term rentals, grew his net worth to over $2.5million that generates around $500,000 in gross revenue annually. Tanya's Cabin has hosted hundreds of guests and they have been Airbnb super hosts with a 4.9 rating. This husband-and-wife duo loves creating memorable experiences for their guests.

Since becoming financially free through real estate investing, Alex now focuses on inspiring and motivating other healthcare professionals to become financially free through real estate. He created a community called Healthcare Professionals Investing in Real Estate, which has close to 4,000 active members. He takes what he has learned from healthcare by serving others and hosts weekly real estate meetups with some of the top industry experts in the short-term rental community.

Links: https://www.flowcode.com/page/alexsabio

ALYSIA CLEMENTS

TWENTY-ONE AND THRIVING: MY JOURNEY TO BUILDING A SUCCESSFUL STR AND REAL ESTATE EMPIRE

If you feel like you have something great inside you, like you were created to do amazing things, then you're going to really like our story. A miraculous story that seems almost impossible but is absolutely true! I'm Alysia Clements, I'm twenty-one years old and, together with my mom, Nicole Clements, we now own and help manage thirty Airbnbs. We built our portfolio from three to thirty doors in fifteen months. This is how we did it.

Let's start with the moment I had a mindset shift, because mindset is everything! Before we decided to start this business, I was seventeen years old and going to college to obtain a bachelor's degree in computer science. My goal was to graduate college and get a job where I would be making 100k a year. One day, as luck would have it (more like the universe pushing me in the direction I was meant to go) I was on Instagram and I happened to win a ticket to my first ever business conference. I couldn't believe it! I was so excited, but it was in Hollywood, CA and I live in Denver, CO. The event was happening the very next day. I told my mom about the ticket and the event, and she thought it was a great learning opportunity, so we rented a car and drove through the night to

California, just so I could make it to this event. This unexpected and timely opportunity was the starting point of my mindset shift. It was the Elevator Bootcamp Conference and for the first time I was introduced to the entrepreneurial lifestyle. I got to hear Ed Mylett and Lewis Howes speak, see how they moved the crowd, and the passion they had for life and helping other people. I had never heard anyone talk about these concepts before. They talked with such certainty about being able to design your own life, how to become financially free, how not to worry about money anymore, and about having the time freedom to travel and help others. All of these concepts were so alluring, this was exactly how I wanted to live my life. So, after that event, I came home and decided to drop out of college and pursue being an entrepreneur and business owner. At the time of this decision, I still had no idea what type of business I wanted to start, I just knew that I wanted to be in control of my life and my future. After doing some research and using our personal experience of moving to CO, we decided that real estate and Airbnb would be a great start.

Moving to Colorado is not easy. The housing market is so competitive, and we could not compete with the multiple offer situation at the time (this was in 2014). While we were shopping for our home, we needed a place to live. Our only options at the time were staying in a hotel or signing a one-year lease. We were a family of four with pets, so a hotel room was not an option. Signing a one-year lease on an apartment wasn't ideal either because, if the perfect house was to come on the market to buy, we'd have to break the lease, which was very expensive. So, we decided that living in a camper for a few months seemed like a reasonable solution. We ended up living in the camper for eighteen months. But we finally found a fixer-upper townhouse that we bought off market. We lived in that for a year and then we finally found our home. Homes in Colorado are expensive, so we intentionally found a home with a walkout basement with the intention of using that part of the home as an Airbnb. We finished the basement to look like a studio apartment, with its own entrance, kitchenette, bathroom and washer/dryer. We had no idea how it would do. But we stepped out in faith and put our savings into preparing this space for our guests. Before we knew it, as soon as we'd created the listing, our guests began to show up! We were nearly booked 100% of the time, we couldn't believe it. Sure enough, we started to see that we were attracting people relocating to the area. So, my mom and I decided to get our realtor's licence. Our first year as realtors, we helped four people relocate and buy homes. We couldn't believe that our business idea was working, we were so excited! The best part of it all was that the Airbnb was also paying for our mortgage.

With the money we saved from no longer having to pay our mortgage and the money we earned from our real estate transactions, we were able to buy a second home and turned our original home into two Airbnbs, the main part of the house and the walkout basement apartment. The second home that we bought had a floorplan where we could easily house hack a portion of the home and turn it into a one-bedroom, one-bathroom Airbnb. We built a wall in the foyer that partitioned the Airbnb from the rest of the house. Our guests entered through the front door, and we entered through the garage and lived in the larger portion of the house. So now we had three Airbnbs going.

Again, we were attracting people moving to the area and we were selling them homes. The business was working so well that we decided to go all in and expand as fast as we could. We began partnering up with landlords and doing something called arbitrage. This is where we would sign a one-year lease at market rent, then furnish the home and list it on Airbnb. This helped us grow even faster, to ten Airbnbs. Now we were attracting not only people relocating but also investors wanting to know more about what we were doing and how they could partner with us. This is when we started using data to help investors find high-performing Airbnbs. When we started doing this, it was like magic, we exploded and grew to thirty Airbnbs in what seemed like no time at all. Once we had control over thirty Airbnbs, it was like having thirty fishing nets out capturing more and more people relocating to Colorado.

Alysia and her mom Nicole are one of the best mother-daughter teams out there!

This led to us selling four to eight houses a month! This was life-changing money. We had created a business where the relocation clients were winning, the landlords were winning, the investors were winning and we were definitely winning. All of our hard work, our sacrifices, all of the rejection and the 'no's we had endured, all of the furniture moving and setting up of the Airbnbs, all of it came together to create something truly special. But I would be lying if I said it was all unicorns and rainbows. It was the hardest thing we have ever done. It took an enormous amount of dedication, self-control, energy and FAITH to create something this amazing. Let's back up a bit and talk about the commitment it takes to grow such a successful business so fast.

Let's start with the decisions we had to make in order to become successful mid-term rental and real estate business owners. We would've never been able to do what we did without first making a lifestyle change when it came to our health. My family got a rude awakening when we almost lost my dad to type one diabetes. It was the wake-up call we all needed to make a lifestyle change for the better. I personally had two autoimmune diseases, social anxiety and brain fog. My mom and brother were obese, had severe joint pain and food sensitivities, and my dad had type one diabetes. Also, during this time, my family was living pay cheque to pay cheque. We never went without, but the quality of life was not great, and we knew something had to change. We were so tired of working so hard and barely making ends meet, feeling so sick and tired all the time. So, all together, we decided to get our health on track. We completely changed our diet and our lifestyle. We removed all processed foods, sugar and gluten. This was no easy task and, without the support of the entire family doing it at the same time, there's no way we could've stuck with it. Our diet consisted of farm fresh meats, vegetables, healthy fats, homemade chicken broth and a series of probiotics (it's called the GAPS diet). Within a few weeks, all of us started to see some changes, physically and mentally. My two autoimmune diseases started to clear up, my dad was getting his strength back and my mom and brother began to lose weight. Not only did we start to feel a lot better, we had more energy and my brain fog lifted, I could think clearly again and my brain began to fire more quickly. Once we got our health under control, and our minds clear, all the right resources and people started coming into our lives. This is the most important part of our story – you need to heal your mind and this will change your thoughts. Change your thoughts and you'll change your life. We began to believe that we were capable and worthy of being successful business owners. This mind shift was a direct byproduct from changing our eating and exercise habits. We were now in the proper state to conquer building a business.

You know how it is said that when the student is ready, the teacher appears? That's exactly what happened next. The right books started popping up along with mentors who were willing to invest their time into us and show us how they accomplished building a successful Airbnb business. That's when Amanda the Traveling Realtor came into our life and taught us how she was combining real estate and Airbnb together. She inspired us to start Colorado Furnished Rentals, and this is when we switched from short-term rentals to mid-term rentals and started hosting guests month to month. Then Chi Tah came into our lives and taught us how to find high-performing Airbnbs. This was a game changer because we were able to apply what he had taught us to help investors buy Airbnbs. Once we started partnering with investors, our business graduated to the next level. Going to the next level came with so many incredible blessings but it also came with its own challenges, which of course was inevitable.

Through our hard work, dedication and discipline, we finally started to see everything come together. We've welcomed over 700 people to Colorado and have helped many people move. We help take the stress out of the home buying and moving process because our clients no longer have to worry about finding a home right away. They can take their time, try out different cities and really get to know different areas before buying. Our clients are always grateful and it's heartwarming to be able to help so many people find their dream home. In addition to housing relocation clients, we also helped house many of the Marshall Fire victims, where 1,100 homes were destroyed and thousands of people displaced. We are currently still housing a house fire victim in one of our Airbnbs. They were so relieved to find us and called us their angels. We had no idea the impact our little business would have on our community and the personal lives of our guests and clients.

Let me tell you about one of our guests in particular. They were in the process of selling their home in Wyoming and moving to Colorado to be closer to their grandkids. They found us on Airbnb and reached out asking to stay in one of our properties while they searched for their perfect home and explored different areas. They were able to really take their time and be selective about which house they ended up purchasing. It took a few months before they found their dream home. They stayed in one of our pet friendly units with their two dogs and even spent Thanksgiving there with their family. After seeing how seamless we made their move into their new house and the almost two hundred thousand dollars we saved them in the process (they were considering building a home, but an even better home came on the market that was much nicer, was on a lake, and was 200k cheaper than the one they were considering building. They were able to be patient and wait for this house because they were staying in one of our furnished rentals), they decided to partner with us in buying another property, this time to turn it into their very first Airbnb. We helped them locate a high-performing Airbnb, put it under contract, and get it to closing. Then once they closed, we helped them stage it, provided a checklist of everything they needed to buy for their Airbnb, we took professional photos of the property along with a video walkthrough for marketing on our social media. We created the Airbnb listing and managed the property. Their first property had tremendous success and when they saw the cash flow we were bringing in every month for them, it was a no-brainer to go ahead and buy a second Airbnb property. So now we have helped them acquire two beautiful Airbnbs in Colorado that are bringing in passive income for them every month and they're working on buying an additional five more. These individuals went from Airbnb guests to real estate clients to investors, our business partners, and then ultimately also became our really good friends. This experience led them to referring their adult child to start their Airbnb investing journey and now they are creating generational wealth. To think that this relationship all started with Airbnb! It just goes to show you what is possible if you take care of your health, surround yourself with the right community, implement what you learn and put in the hard work. This business has completely changed my family's life and is continuing to change the lives of others every day.

This is only the beginning of our journey; it's been quite the ride but we're just getting started! We continue to learn and grow every day. We have set our intention to serve others first through our business. We have been blessed to be a part of some of the most amazing communities out there. My personal goal from here on out is to help as many people as possible – especially young entrepreneurs – build their business and inspire them to get started. My hope is that my story will inspire individuals to get started and take action. To show people that success is possible at any age. It took me three years to build a successful business. That's less time than going to college for a bachelor's degree. I want to show young people that there is a different way. If you're a creative like me, who loves to solve problems, network and talk to people, and have control over your own schedule and future, being a business owner is a great option that is available to anyone willing to do the work. By making the decision to not go to college and instead start a business, I'm twenty-one with no debt, a clear vision for my life, a successful real estate business, and I'm getting ready to buy my first home, while a lot of my peers are now graduating, have over 100k in student loans and may have ended up with a degree that they are realising doesn't guarantee them a good paying job right out of college. I want to raise the awareness and introduce as many people as possible to the opportunity of being a business owner.

Even Alysia's dog Stetson helps out with the family business!

Thanks to my mid-term rental and real estate business, I'm being presented with so many life-changing opportunities. I'm surrounded by some of the most giving and genuine people. I get to help individuals on a daily basis and pursue my passion of mentoring young entrepreneurs. We are currently working on getting this business automated and passive for this next year, so that I can focus my time on teaching others how to become successful in health and wealth. I'm now stepping into the public speaking space where I hope to help and inspire as many people as possible.

Becoming successful and achieving your dreams can happen sooner than you think. You just have to be willing to put in the work, listen to your mentors and not only listen but implement. Surround yourself with the right people and community that will cheer you on and get excited for you when you win. You also have to be a decision maker and be able to make the crazy decisions, like deciding to go all in on your business or your dreams. I had to make several decisions along the way that were scary and out of my comfort zone. I had to do the things that no one else wanted to do. I had to push through the days where I just wanted to be lazy and do nothing. All so that I could get to where I am today and each day get a little bit closer to being the person I want to be and, let me tell you, it is all so incredibly worth it.

ABOUT THE AUTHOR

Alysia Clements started Colorado Furnished Rentals with her mom when she was eighteen years old. They started with one Airbnb in the walkout basement of her parents' home. They quickly expanded in a year and a half, from one Airbnb to thirty Airbnbs in Northern CO. Colorado Furnished Rentals provides fully furnished, month-to-month rentals for people who are relocating to the area. They call it a "Live Like a Local" programme, where individuals and families can try living in a city before purchasing their dream home. Alysia and her mom, Nicole, are also licensed realtors and help their relocation guests find the perfect home that fits their needs.

Alysia has raised her whole life around real estate and has always had an entrepreneurial spirit. She finished high school at fifteen and went straight into college to obtain a computer science degree. While taking college classes, Alysia won a ticket to the Elevator Bootcamp Conference in Hollywood, CA. At this event, she saw the speakers Ed Mylett and Lewis Howes. This was the first time she was introduced to the concept of being a business owner and it motivated her to start her own business. When she arrived home from the event, she dropped out of college to pursue a career in real estate, and in two years, this mother/daughter team built a six-figure a month business.

Now twenty-one, Alysia is venturing into the public speaking world, where she is being equipped to go out and motivate young individuals to become entrepreneurs. Her mission is to show others that college isn't the only way to success and to help them succeed in health, wealth and relationships. She has a heart for coaching and mentoring young individuals and wants to reach as many people as possible. She hopes that her story will help inspire people to take action and go after their dreams. to work hard and stay consistent. She wants to deliver the message that success is possible at any age. You're never too young or old to start.

Links: Linktr.ee/alysiaclements

AMY CORBETT

THERE'S MAGIC IN BEING DIFFERENT

Growing up, I never wanted to be different.

My goal was to fit in. If I could be like everyone else, I knew I'd be more liked, more known and more welcomed.

Little did I know how much "being different" would become my story.

The short version of that story is that, after undergoing infertility treatments, my husband and I became parents through two open adoptions. Our daughter lost all her hair at the age of two due to an autoimmune condition called alopecia (she now rocks it as a bald teenager!). And we've got the challenge of raising our black son as white parents.

Suffice it to say: my family is anything but typical. You can't miss us!

My life story has taught me something valuable: **there's magic in being different.** Especially in the world of hospitality.

That's not to say it's easy or our family doesn't have its own set of challenges. Over the years, it's been hard to find places where we truly fit. We've switched schools, moved neighbourhoods and stepped away from seventeen years of campus ministry to find the places we truly belong.

In 2018, we left salaries and benefits without a "what's next" plan. We had a basement apartment we'd recently listed on Airbnb along with a few long-term rentals. We decided we'd scrape by with hosting for a year while figuring out our next move.

It wasn't long before a few individuals approached me for help in renting their homes on Airbnb, and a light bulb went off in my head. I loved this new gig of hosting guests in our home. And to think: I could do it for others, too?!

The idea of helping homeowners create welcoming spaces where anyone could belong was not just a fun side gig, it was strangely therapeutic. I could take my own painful experiences of not belonging and create the welcoming world I wanted to see for my own family – one that valued diversity, empathy and unmatched hospitality.

Without realising it, our co-hosting business, All Belong Co, was born.

Word soon got out in our city and clients began flocking to get our help. As part of our services, I would create a fifteen-to-twenty-page customised consultation for their property, our team would help brand and furnish it to attract guests and then we'd begin hosting. It felt like juggling three businesses in one (which I don't recommend), but it soon became our proven process to help homeowners create successful short-term rentals.

I never expected how many would connect to our family's story and brand of diversity and belonging.

By the end of year two, we were up to twenty-five properties in our collective.

CRAZY TALK

Being different can be scary for a lot of people. We'd been renting our home from the neighbourhood we'd left behind until we were blindsided by a group of neighbours complaining before the county commission. They were upset that we were welcoming "people

My beautiful family

of all races and creeds" and that we "might be harbouring illegal immigrants."

You can imagine how frustrated we were. No one had attempted to speak with us directly. We pride ourselves on being good neighbours and a welcoming presence in our community. Sadly, their fear of differences and diversity forced the authorities to close our doors at that location.

We couldn't honour any reservations already on the calendar. What were we to do? That coming weekend, we were scheduled to host a large bridal party. And now I was supposed to tell this bride three days before her wedding she no longer had a valid reservation?! I just couldn't let a few close-minded neighbours ruin the bride's big day.

My husband Marc and I came up with a plan: we'd give the bridal party our personal home (in the city) while we camped out at the newly black-listed short-term rental (in the county).

I'm so pleased to say the weekend went off without a hitch. The bridal party loved our home and made great memories. They were so grateful for our hospitality under such extraordinary circumstances.

Meanwhile, our family used that weekend to prepare the house for sale!

Being a hospitable host means being WELCOMING to a diverse world of people. It means leaning into your differences so you can be an open door for others.

After all, what's going to help you stand out in the vast sea of online listings?

It's important to think about what sets you and your property apart. What do you offer that makes you different? Sometimes what you think is a flaw in a property (or even in yourself!) can become an asset to guests.

Here are four quick tips:

1. **Look for the beauty in overlooked places.** A fire destroyed the historic gables of a home we're currently renovating, leaving a strange-looking flat roof. We're converting what is currently an eyesore into a modern rooftop deck.
2. **Take risks and get different.** We owned land overlooking a river and train tracks. Shockingly, not everyone's a fan of train noise. So, we bought an actual train caboose (off Facebook Marketplace, naturally!) and created "James Station". Now watching trains go by below is part of the experience! Once a nuisance, the train noise is now an attraction.
3. **Be open to others' ideas.** An owner/client was determined to keep her bright red walls, so we designed the family-friendly home (the "Candy Apple") around a carnival theme, complete with kids' Skee-Ball and a candyfloss machine.
4. **Use your creativity.** Over the years, we've incorporated homeowners' unique interests into property identities: plants, pineapples and even US National Parks.

There's magic in being different. Don't be plain vanilla in a world full of flavours. Had my story NOT been so unique, we wouldn't be where we are today.

Invest in places where you can open your doors wide and give every guest the dignity they deserve.

Invest in people, and the money will follow.

Invest in being welcoming and bringing belonging into each reservation, and you'll make an even greater impact on the world.

ABOUT THE AUTHOR

Amy Corbett is the co-founder and CEO of All Belong Co, a growing collective of 30+ short-term rentals (including a train caboose!) in four states. Amy's hosted more than 5,000 guests since 2019 and coaches hosts in Thanks for Visiting's membership community.

As described in the chapter, her family's journey became the "why" for Amy and her husband Marc to begin hosting. A self-described "accidental entrepreneur", her properties have been featured in multiple publications. Her town of Lynchburg, Virginia, chose Amy's family as brand ambassadors for the city's rebranding campaign in 2022.

Links: https://linktr.ee/allbelong.co

AVERY CARL

Advice from an investor with a 250-door portfolio: always over-tip your bartender. The root of all hospitality, as well as entrepreneurialism, can be learned from working in the service industry. Particularly bartending or waiting tables. I'll circle back to this after I tell you a bit about how I ended up with 250 doors and a net worth that I don't feel comfortable putting into print, and how, if I can do it, then you certainly can too.

I could start at the very beginning of my vacation rental journey, when my entire extended family (grandparents, aunts, uncles, cousins, the whole crew) rented a house in Grayton Beach, FL every summer for ten years when I was a child. Or even further back, to 1937, the year my grandmother started taking annual trips to Destin, FL, where she stayed in vacation rentals every year until she and my grandfather bought their own. But that's probably a little further back than your attention span wants to go. So, I'll start in the Lower East Side of New York City, where I wore holes in my boots running back and forth to my various bartending jobs, band practices and, most importantly, parties, in my early twenties.

I had graduated from The University of Texas just a year and a half earlier with a BS (BSc in the UK) in corporate communication. BS is right. The softest and most useless degree in existence. I had wanted to attend the UT Business School, but I was on a soccer scholarship, and the extra special guidance counsellors who get assigned to student athletes in big athletic programmes like that don't want their students in hard majors (UT Business School was top five in the country at the time). They want easy majors so there is less to worry about with student athlete GPAs being too low for the NCAA to allow them to compete, or worse, reflect poorly on the university. So, it was "suggested" that I go for communication instead. And that was probably pretty okay advice for 2006, with none of us knowing the 2008 crash was around the corner and that, when I would graduate in 2009, there would be no jobs for soft-majored graduates such as myself. I did, however, exit college with a Big 12 Championship ring for the team winning the conference in my freshman season, so I at least had a conversation starter for my bartending gigs for the next four years.

I had been playing the guitar since middle school, and I somehow managed to tour in bands throughout college while still actually attending college, so with no job prospects on the horizon for the next several years, I decided to hit the music thing a little harder and bartend to supplement the non-existent income of a punk rock guitar player. I got to go on many tours to many places (Japan was my favourite) and eventually took a gig that required me to move to New York. I did all of the typical "small town southern girl moves to New York City" romantic comedy movie things you'd expect, so I won't go into too much detail on that. I lived in a shithole apartment, played a lot of gigs, ate a lot of great food and, most importantly, met a lot of great people. Some of my bartending regulars were Stockard Channing (only on Sundays, her off night from Broadway), Adrian Grenier and one Olsen twin. We had a door guy checking IDs, so I never did figure out exactly which one it was. But I found her drink of choice, a frozen margarita, to be weird for a New Yorker. However, the biggest and most important romantic comedy-esque thing that I did in New

York was meet my husband, Luke. And it was NOT in Central Park like all the movies. It was at a Faster Pussycat show. Those of you familiar with eighties rock might recognise the name. The sleaziest of sleaze rock. Mega sleaze. The kind of band you might see and come home with a hangover and an STD. Not typically the kind of band you see and wind up meeting the person you'll be marrying and having kids with. But apparently, we were the exception to that rule. I am here to say that the guy at the end of the bar playing air drums might just be marriage, fatherhood and building a business together material, you just never know.

Eventually, we decided to move from New York to Nashville. I thought the logical step for me was to go back to school and get a master's degree and get a "real" job. I got into the executive MBA programme at Belmont University and got an entry level "real job" sales position during the day. It was my dream at the time to start working on the business side of the music industry, which I achieved after graduation with a hefty salary (obviously, I say this tongue-in-cheek) of $37,000 a year. I asked if I could possibly get $40,000 and was told I was being ridiculous, so I, quite exuberantly, in fact, started what I thought would be my dream career. I'll spare you all the boring details, but it became apparent after a few short years that I do NOT make a good employee. The feelings of discontent and trapped-ness led me to begin looking for other income avenues, which led me to real estate investing.

Our first purchase was a long-term rental. It was a really high performer for a long-term. It cash-flowed $1,000 over the mortgage every month, which, when one makes $37,000 a year, is a lot of money. That was as much as I made at my job every month after taxes were taken out of my cheques. As soon as we received that first rent cheque, we knew that we wanted to build a business out of real estate, but the problem was that it would have taken ages to build any sort of a meaningful portfolio by continuing to buy single-family long-term rentals. So, we tried to think about what we could buy that would make us the most amount of money the fastest, so that we could take that money and buy more properties.

Avery and her husband Luke

We landed on short-term rentals, but Nashville's regulations and stance on short-term rentals were WAY too scary for us as new investors with very little capital. We could not afford to buy a property that we would eventually be regulated out of renting short-term. We had just been on vacation to the Smoky Mountains, where we had stayed in a cabin. We noticed that EVERYONE in the Smoky Mountains stayed in cabins, and someone had to own those cabins; why couldn't it be us? So, we went out and bought one. This was 2015. There were no STR influencers, there were no courses, there weren't really even property management software programmes yet. We knew we did not want to hire a property manager who would take 20-40% of our gross income, which would defeat the purpose of buying a short-term rental to begin with. So, we figured out how to self-manage remotely the old-fashioned way: trial and error. After a period of figuring out processes and procedures (which have been made EXPONENTIALLY easier with the property management tools and pricing software that has risen in popularity since then), we knew that vacation rentals were our ticket out of the grind and into our preferred lifestyle design. You may have noticed that I just switched from using the phrase "short-term rental" to "vacation rental". To me, there is a marked difference. A short-term rental is an all-encompassing term for any property in any market that is rented on average for less than thirty days by guests who may be renting for any number of reasons: business travel, conferences, leisure, etc. A vacation rental is a type of short-term rental that is in a tourism-dependent vacation market that is used primarily by guests who are on vacation. We focus on those types of properties in those types of markets because the combination of tourism dependency and friendly short-term rental regulations offered by most true vacation rental markets just make it easier to own and navigate. I don't have any interest in trying to swim upstream investing in short-term rentals in markets where the local government and its constituency does not want them.

Over the course of the next two years, we were able to scale our one little rental cabin into five rental cabins. The income from those funded the down payments for ten single-family long-term rentals, and then three more vacation rentals in Destin, 30a, and Cape San Blas, FL. During that time, I started what would eventually become my company, The Short Term Shop, a real estate agency that focuses exclusively on helping investors purchase, and learn to self-manage, vacation rentals. I wanted to open other investors' eyes to the opportunities that remotely self-managing short-term and vacation rentals present in terms of portfolio scaling. It only took the income from eight vacation rentals to scale my total portfolio to 250 doors. It started because I kept having friends ask how much our cabins were making, and once they learned, they'd ask me to help them find one and to teach them how to self-manage it. Eventually, it was friends of friends, and even more eventually, it became real clients. Our first office was in the Smokies, and today we have over seventy agents in fifteen top vacation rental markets. The Short Term Shop has had the privilege of helping over 5,000 investors purchase and learn to manage their short-term rentals, several of whom have chapters in this book as well as its previous volume. I don't mention that to toot my own horn, but to illustrate that I have the unique perspective of not only experiencing my own short-term rental journey from the driver's seat, but also experiencing the short-term rental journey of many other investors through riding shotgun on their short-term rental journey.

I give you that background so that I can now revert back to my original comments about hospitality and bartending. When you go to a bar to have a beer or a glass of wine with your friends, do you choose the venue because it's the best atmosphere for you to hang out, or do you choose it solely because of the bartender? The beer, the wine, the friends, are going to be the same in any bar, but you choose the one that has the best atmosphere. You're probably choosing based on 80% atmosphere and 20% bartender, right? You choose the bar based on the atmosphere and a great bartender is a bonus that enhances the experience. In the service industry, a great bartender, server, host, should be a part of the background, a part of the atmosphere. They are available and helpful, but they are not taking centre stage of your party and hanging out with your friends. They pour the drinks, they contribute to the atmosphere, and they understand that they are there to enhance the guest experience at a high level, without trying to become their new bestie. The same applies for running short-term rentals.

As it relates to hosting a short-term rental, many hosts try to do too many things, which gives them too many opportunities to fail the guest. I take a less is more approach. I am providing an amazing place to stay, I am available and as helpful as possible (let's face it, there are sometimes guests who just do not want a solution, they just want to complain, and that's okay!), but at the end of the day, I am providing an atmosphere for their memories to happen, and nothing more. This may sound crazy to some of you but hear me out: I do a few things and I do them REALLY well. Great properties with very thorough guidebooks and expectation setting, with clean simple systems, lead to happy guests. I have sparkling clean properties that have everything a guest will need for their stay, and I provide them an amazing place for their memories to happen. The more things you try to add to a system, the more opportunities you give yourself to fail, which results in disappointed guests.

I think that sometimes investors get caught up in wanting to provide the MOST UNIQUE experience and impress their guests SO MUCH that the property becomes more of a vanity project for their own egos rather than providing the best environment for the guests' memories to be made. Offering your guests the ability to

Not an employee.

choose what flavour of sparkling water will be in their fridge when they arrive sounds like a great idea, until the person stocking the fridge misreads the flavour and stocks the wrong thing, and the guest is disappointed. And a complimentary car washing service scheduled to come during their stay sounds SO LUXE, until something comes up with the car washer and they have to cancel at the last minute. And then the guest is disappointed. You see where I am going with this. The more creative you try to get with your extras, the more opportunities you open up to disappoint the guest. You do not have to have the most interesting or outlandish amenities to be outstanding at hospitality. People remember the things that made them sad and upset more than they remember the things that went smoothly. So, if you try to get too tricky and one of those systems fails, that's the thing the guest will remember about their trip. Let your property be the bar with the great atmosphere, and you be the helpful, cheerful bartender that's right there in the background ready to help as soon as anyone needs something. Don't be the bartender trying to juggle the glasses to be impressive who drops them all on the floor where they shatter to pieces. The stay is about giving the guest a backdrop for their fond memories with their family and friends, not about making sure the guest sees you juggling six wine glasses over your head before pouring their drinks.

I take this same approach with my long-term rentals, by the way. We put granite and nice LVP (luxury vinyl plank flooring) in all of our long-term rentals, even if they aren't in A+ neighbourhoods. One of our contractors asked my husband once, "Why do you put these in all your houses? You could save so much money with laminate counters and a cheaper, albeit less attractive, LVP." The reason is that these units are going to be people's homes. They are going to be the place that they have holidays, birthdays, good days, bad days, literally all the days. Everyone deserves to have a nice place for their life to happen.

I have the good fortune of now living in the town where my family always rented vacation rentals growing up. There were several beach houses that we rented over the years, but there is one in particular that we came back to over and over again. I remember jumping in the pool in front of the house after a long day at the beach. I remember my mom sleeping on the back porch with my baby sister (who was screaming her head off all night) to keep her from waking up the entire house. I remember running off the same porch with all my cousins with flashlights and nets trying to catch ghost crabs after dark. I remember sneak-watching Maury Povich in the same bedroom every day with my cousin after lunch. (Why Maury Povich? What a weird thing to sneak. Kids are weird.) Now, twenty years later, I have driven past that house to show my husband more than once. Twenty years later, I remember exactly how to get there from the main road. Clearly, I remember a lot of things about that house. However, the one thing about it that neither I, nor my parents, nor aunts and uncles remember about that house is who the property manager was. The key to providing an exceptional experience to guests is not always about having the slickest or most interesting amenities and experiences, it's about providing the backdrop for a family or group of friends to create new and amazing memories that will last a lifetime.

ABOUT THE AUTHOR

Avery Carl is, first and foremost, a real estate investor. She and her husband have built a real estate investment portfolio of over 250 doors (with no partners) over the course of five years through strategically investing in (and self-managing) short-term rental properties.

Avery is the author of the best-selling book on short-term rental investing, *Short-Term Rental, Long-Term Wealth: Your Guide to Analyzing, Buying, and Managing Vacation Properties*, which has sold over 40,000 copies worldwide in its first year of availability. She is also the host of top short-term rental investing podcast – with over 500,000 downloads – "The Short Term Show", where she interviews other short-term rental investors and business owners weekly.

Avery is also the CEO and founder of The Short Term Shop, the USA's premier short-term rental acquisition firm, with offices in fifteen of the top short-term rental markets in the country. The Short Term Shop has connected over 3,500 investors with cash flowing short-term rental investments since 2017. The Short Term Shop also specialises in training investor clients on how to self-manage their investments remotely, enabling them to optimise their cash flow and allowing them to expedite the scaling of their investment portfolio more quickly than other investment methodologies.

Before becoming a full-time real estate investor, Avery was a Big 12 Conference Championship-winning soccer player at The University of Texas, where she received her bachelor's degree. She then spent several years pursuing her love of rock 'n' roll, touring in bands as a guitar and bass player. She later received her MBA from Belmont University in Nashville, where she worked as a marketing manager in the music business before her real estate investing career began. Avery enjoys spending time with her family, collecting vintage guitars and running. She has been featured in *Forbes*, *The Wall Street Journal*, *Yahoo Finance* and is a regular contributor and speaker on many entrepreneurship podcasts and investing conferences.

Links: https://linktr.ee/theshorttermshop

BILL FAETH

THE AUTHENTIC HOST

The 17th of September 1989 was the first time I beat Tiger Woods in a golf tournament. This feat would only happen one more time the following year, even though I had hundreds of opportunities in tournaments, practice rounds, and just playing for fun. Yes, Eldrick (that's his real name, in case you didn't know) was the GOAT at the ripe age of fourteen, and even though I was two years older than him, I just couldn't beat him; when I did, I relished it and rubbed it in for sure. He was that good, but getting my ass kicked on what seemed like a daily basis during the summer as we travelled to tournaments together was what set the groundwork for my future success in life.

Even as a teenager, Tiger worked harder than any of us. After a tournament round, the rest of us would go back to our hotel or go to a movie while Tiger would be on the range practising until dark, and when he didn't feel like practising, his father, Earl, "encouraged" him to anyway. Sometimes that encouragement was tough, and sometimes it was just a nudge, but even when it was tough, I yearned for it, as I didn't have a father around to give me that push.

I did have an amazing mother who worked her ass off as a

teacher and many second jobs over the years to invest every last penny into my golf. She taught me the essence of working hard to achieve our goals. She taught me entrepreneurship without even knowing it at the time. She taught me the value of money and investing as she started her first business outside of being a teacher when I was twelve years old. I got to be involved as she built a private preschool from the ground up. I got to see the early struggles of entrepreneurship and then see her reap the benefits when she sold and retired. This firsthand look inside owning and operating a business, I am sure to this day, is why I have launched twenty-seven bootstrapped start-ups.

In the autumn of 1990, I started selling T-shirts in Bakersfield, CA at my high school football games out of the back of my mother's 1985 Ford Tempo. At our first game, it was just me standing in the car park at the back of the car with twenty or thirty T-shirts. By the end of the season, I had four friends (Kevin, Mike, Butch and Paul) working for me at other schools selling them and we were selling forty-to-fifty per game every Friday night at five schools. I was grossing $3,500-$4,500 a week during the football season selling T-shirts, which was more than my mother made in a month as a teacher at the time, all because I took advantage of an opportunity when I played golf with a gentleman named Jay Jacoby. I believe that we all have opportunities presented to us throughout our lives. Maybe a handful. Maybe more. The question is, do we see them when they are presented, and then do we take advantage?

I met Mr Jacoby in a Junior-Am in Los Angeles which is a golf tournament where there are three sponsors playing with one of us junior golfers. Jay owned the company American Pacific Clothing that made super cool T-shirts and athletic wear. Jay gave me four or five basketball shirts after the round and I was grateful, thanked him, and then my mother drove me back to Bakersfield. Two months later, my mom and I were at another tournament in LA where we ran into Jay again, and he asked how I liked the T-shirts; I told him I sold four of them and kept one. He asked why I sold them, and I told him because I kept the best one and we needed the money, so I sold the other four and apologised. He laughed and said that was OK.

While I was out playing in the tournament, Jay had a conversation with my mother, and after the round, we followed Jay to his home in Santa Monica as he had invited us over for dinner with his family. During dinner, Jay asked if I wanted to be his business partner. I had no clue what this meant, but he explained it very clearly so I could understand: Jay would provide me with as many T-shirts as I wanted, I would take them back to Bakersfield and sell them, and we would split the profit 75%-25%. I got 75%. DEAL!

This was my second opportunity in life. The first was golf with my big brother and thank God my mother and I took advantage of both, as they fundamentally changed the rest of my life. Golf is expensive and there is no way my mother could have afforded to send me to national junior tournaments all over the country without the income I was generating from the T-shirt business. Jay Jacoby allowed me the opportunity to become the third ranked player in the world and earn a full scholarship to UCLA. He also taught me and my mother how to run a business, which also benefited my mother in her preschool business and me to this day.

I have had plenty of opportunities put in front of me over the span of almost fifty years, but there have been four that have been huge. The fourth was meeting Reginald Booth when he had a business called GlowRange, which was Top Golf long before Top Golf existed. Brea and I bought the first franchise, ran it very successfully, and then spun it into creating the glow in the dark mini golf industry and expanded to over 100 locations in shopping malls across the country. This was a huge business with over 700 employees that brought Brea and me to Nashville in 2003.

The fifth opportunity happened by chance when my family was on holiday and having lunch in Seaside with my long-time friend William Wilson with whom I played professional golf in South America and who was a groomsman in our wedding. William owned and managed over 300 properties in Destin, Miramar,

Rosemary, and 30A long before most of you started buying down there or were even born. He was a local expert as he had been in the vacation rental business with his family since the eighties.

During this lunch was when Brea and I decided it was time to buy a beach house, and Brea wanted one in Seaside. William asked what our budget was, and we said between $600,000-$700,000 ($700K was a stretch at the time), but Brea had a couple of requirements. She wanted to see, hear and smell the ocean, and that is when William crushed our dream and told us that wasn't going to happen for $700,000, even in 2015. But he did recommend we go west and check out Orange Beach and Gulf Shores, AL.

After a few months of researching houses and the Alabama Gulf Coast market, we flew down for a day and looked at ten houses. We ended up buying the very first house we saw, which was in the best condition, the most unique, had incredible views and Brea could hear and see the water.

At this point in our life, I had plenty of experience with real estate, had built a 54,000sq ft LEED Certified commercial property, owned many houses and long-term rentals, but this was going to be our first short-term rental on our own. Like many, we went with a local property management company to manage the house for us. The relationship with the property management company didn't last long and is what was ultimately the seeding for why I started Build Short Term Rental Wealth as they sucked at marketing, didn't really do anything to make me more money and were not transparent. All of these things were why I fired them, took over self-management and doubled the rental income in less than a year before Covid. You see exactly how I did it here: https://buildstrwealth.com/bellavistacasestudy

The experience of making this investment, using a property management company and then increasing revenue from $54,000 to $90,000 in year one and to $112,000 in year two is why I started growing my short-term rental portfolio via self-management.

If you follow me, you might think I had millions of dollars or trust fund money to just start buying properties left and right.

Bill self-managing a luxury property

Well, that is not the case. I am not an ex-hedge fund manager with unlimited resources, so I had to be very calculated with my next investments; that is why I waited for almost two years to purchase number two, utilising the profit from the first investment and some additional savings. But, before I could make the second investment, I needed to be sure I had a system in place because self-managing one property was fairly easy, but adding a second could complicate things, as I wasn't using any real technology at the time except for the Airbnb and Vrbo apps. This is when I started researching property management systems; I went through all of them at the time and didn't make the leap until I found OwnerRez, which was life changing for me, and I still use it today, as I believe it is hands down the most robust platform available for short-term rental hosts and investors like you and me.

If you want to scale your STR Business, your technology is going to be the cornerstone and one you need to nail early. I chose OwnerRez because it is the most robust and provided me the ability to scale with API integrations to QuickBooks, Google, Facebook, Vrbo, Airbnb, calendar synching, ability to co-host and so much more. Today, I own eleven properties and am co-hosting sixteen;

OwnerRez has allowed me to automate the majority of the work and communication with my guests, cleaners and tradespeople in multiple states across the country. I couldn't self-manage twenty-seven luxury properties nationwide and run four additional businesses without them, that is for sure.

I have also automated my door locks, thermostats, security cameras and pool heating to save a tremendous amount of time managing the required tasks manually. Time is my biggest asset and why I switched from LTR to STR, as STR generates four-to-seven times more profit than LTR, but it used to take five-to-ten times more time until I implemented the technology and automation.

This has been very intentional, as I have a detailed business/life plan that I follow and I would strongly advise you to build one before you start investing or get too far down the path, as we all need a roadmap to follow, and without it, it is very easy to get lost on the journey of life. This is why I only invest into high value properties that will yield $150,000+ of annual revenue. Very rarely will I purchase a property that yields less because it takes me the same amount of time to manage a $300/night stay and a $1,200/night stay.

We have also diversified geographically and invested into both summer peak season markets and winter peak season markets. This allows us to create a more stabilised cash flow and mitigates risk for natural disasters. We also cluster two-to-three owned properties in each market to create economies of scale with trades and purchasing power. I believe you will get more love from your boots on the ground if you have more than one property in the market for them to work on and I have found three to be a great number.

This investment strategy has allowed me to achieve my financial goals without having to own/manage "100 doors", and I promise you I am making more money with less time invested than the influencers online bragging about adding fifty doors here and thirty there. It's crazy. Build out your desired outcome. What do you want to get out of your investments? How much time and resources are you comfortable investing? What does your end game look like? There is no right answer, but there is a wrong answer and that is not having one. We need to be able to keep score on a daily basis to ensure we drive down the field to achieve the ultimate goal of scoring a touchdown. This is exactly why I have defined what retirement means to me and my wife, how much cash flow we will need, how much debt we are comfortable with, the exact date we will retire, what expenses will look like, and what we want to do. Without all of this, we as human beings are not able to make effective decisions on a daily basis without being able to distil down from the outcome. This is WHY I invest the way that I do. Because I know what retirement will look like for Brea and me. We know how much income we will need, how much time we want to spend working, who will run the businesses, and how we will spend our money and time together. We are on the same page.

This helps with our investment strategy and execution, as we have created the framework to help guide us, and we meet every Friday to discuss the previous week and the future. Without clearly defined and unified goals, we would have nothing to discuss. Being unified with your spouse and having these types of defined goals makes it a lot easier to make investment decisions and makes them much less emotional; if we are trying to make a financially driven decision, we need to remove as much emotion as we can on each purchase.

There is a lot that goes into building a fruitful future, and short-term rental can be an excellent path to supplement incomes, replace a W2, or be a long-term investment strategy for retirement or for your children. I believe it is still the best investable asset class we have available to us, even though rents have slowed down in the autumn of 2022 and I believe 2023 will be slower than 2022 by 15%-20%. Short-term rentals are still going to outperform long-term rentals and commercial if you are implementing the right components to thrive in 2023. You will need to focus on listing optimisation, off-platform marketing and pricing optimisation.

The biggest skills that separate me from other hosts are my marketing skills. The ability to effectively run targeted Facebook

Bill self-managing a luxury property

ads to all of my properties is number one, but I have also run over $10,000,000 in Facebook ads since 2013. Running Facebook ads is easy to learn and difficult to master, and you must master them to benefit, but they are worth the time commitment to learn.

The second is listing optimisation. The days of "set it and forget it" are long gone. You need a Rankbreeze account to track your positions and updates and you must be ranked on the first page. If you are on page two or below, it is like being on Exile Island on *Survivor*, where everyone forgets about you. PRO TIP: leverage every character of copy in your listings, especially under all of your images, and be creative with your writing in your description and under images. Tell the guest a story of what they will experience, not just "there is a king bed and nightstand in the master suite". Check out Jasper.ai if you need help with creative writing. It will change your world.

The third is email marketing. If you can STOP selling and START helping your guest via email you will WIN the email marketing game. This means you need to educate your past guests and provide them information they may not know that provides them with reasons to want to come back to your properties. You need to be an expert in all things going on from compression events (conferences, concerts, sporting events) to the best restaurants, places to picnic, etc. Share this information with your guests via email. HELP them and EARN the right to sell to them every third to fourth email.

The future is bright for short-term rentals, there is no question about that. It may seem a little dark right now, but it will pass and be stranger than ever. People want experiences, and we can provide these much better than hotels, so nail your desired outcome, build a plan, get your tech set up, and work on your marketing to achieve your dreams.

ABOUT THE AUTHOR

Bill Faeth has a unique passion for helping people map out a plan for their future while leveraging short-term rental investing and hosting to achieve their desired outcome. He has taught thousands of students how to achieve financial freedom by applying twenty-seven years of business experience to the real estate industry after bootstrapping twenty-six start-ups and scaling three to $30M-plus in annual revenue.

Bill got his start at seventeen years old selling T-shirts out of the trunk of his mother's Ford Tempo at high school football games before he dropped out of UCLA to embark on a professional golf career. Now he owns a multimillion-dollar luxury short-term rental portfolio, a $2M co-hosting portfolio, and is the founder of the STR Wealth Conference, the largest host-focused conference in the industry.

If you don't want to hear the truth, then you probably don't want to ask Bill for help, as he has the propensity to educate on how to avoid the pratfalls of investing without any BS. This mentality has branded him the Mr Wonderful of the short-term rental industry, and there is no better way to experience the unbridled truths of STR investing than on his podcast STRunfilitered or in his Build Short Term Rental Wealth free Facebook group that has over 24,000 members.

When Bill isn't teaching and hosting real estate investing events, you can find him on the pitch watching his two daughters excel in travel soccer, or travelling the country with his wife and interior designer Brea, sipping fine wine and playing golf.

Links: https://linktree.com/bfaeth

BRIAN HATCHER

ESCAPING CORPORATE BURNOUT WITH A HOSPITABLE RECIPE

"Just wait until you become an adult."
– Mom

Wide-eyed and eager as a fresh college graduate, I was ready to take on the world – so I thought. Upon finishing my master's degree in accounting with a focus in data and analytics, I moved a few states away from my family and home in Alabama and found myself in Houston, Texas. Now living in such a big city, with my first real corporate job, I was certain that it was just a matter of time before I would find the right opportunities to aid me in making a name for myself. In reality, it wasn't long before I found myself in the typical rat race of working over sixty hours a week, feeling unfulfilled, burnt out and living for a weekend that lasted a mere blink of an eye. The phrase "oh just wait until you become an adult" from my parents constantly rang in my ears, but my stubbornness wouldn't let me accept that this was all that was waiting for me in adulthood. So, I did what any other millennial in a quarter-life crisis would do, and started bingeing as many personal development, investment and

FIRE (financial independence/retire early) podcasts as possible. My commutes to and from work became my planning sessions and I ultimately decided that real estate was the smart and safest place to start.

Real estate investing wasn't a new phrase to me, but it was something I always reserved for later in life, when I was older and "more established". With my work schedule and podcast hosts reminding me that "there's no time like the present", I decided to take the dive. Fortunately, I came across one of the best online communities for real estate investors, "BiggerPockets", and discovered that there were plenty of others who felt the same way I did and were also looking to use real estate as an escape! I got to networking – well, digitally – and to my surprise developed some of the most impactful relationships of my life. I found my first realtor there (shout out to you, Cheryl, if you're reading this) and began spending each weekend looking at multi-family houses. The first goal was to "house hack" – a phrase that has become more popular over the years (especially if you're listening to podcasts) where you purchase a multi-unit home with the intention to live in one unit and rent out the others to cover your housing expense. Since housing is the largest expense for most people, and was for me at the time, this seemed like a great first step towards financial freedom.

I spent months looking at different duplexes, triplexes, and quadplexes, and even got a few under contract, only for issues to come up during due diligence or an inspection that ultimately made the home not worth it. Just as I began to get discouraged and even more burnt out, I got a phone call that my job was transferring me to Atlanta, Georgia. This turned out to be one of the biggest blessings in disguise.

Because it was such short notice, I struggled to find a place to live and, knowing that I still wanted to purchase a multi-family home, I didn't want to get locked into a lease. My solution – Airbnb! I got to looking on the platform and opted to stay in a private room of a condo that was close to the city for a few months. All I had to

The home that started my hosting journey, and my Airbnb House Hack: The East Atlanta Escape.

do was show up and bring my clothes, which was perfect! At first, there was another guest in the other bedroom when I arrived at the condo, a very nice travelling nurse who was never home. But, after a week or so, he moved out and I had the whole place to myself, which was amazing! I couldn't stop thinking about how convenient it was to have the Airbnb while on my real estate hunt, and once my new "roommate" showed up – a lawyer from London – I realised that plenty of people from all over the world were in similar situations staying in these Airbnbs. While this should have been my big wake-up call to start my hosting journey, I, unfortunately, told myself I would need a nice property close to attractions or downtown for it to make sense as an Airbnb. As you'll find out later on, I was wrong!

Once again, I enlisted the help of BiggerPockets and found my then realtor – and close friend today – and fellow hospitable host Ruben Kanya. He and his team were able to assist me in finding my dream duplex that I was finally able to house hack. I quickly found some amazing tenants to occupy the upstairs unit of the home while

I occupied the downstairs. This was a fun and unique experience that served as my intro to hosting. We occasionally made each other dinners, exchanged small gifts, shared recommendations, and even gave a ride or two when needed. While this did put me in a position to eliminate the majority of my housing expense, I quickly started to realise that I would need to repeat this long process a number of times before I was able to truly get to the level of freedom I was looking for. By this time, Ruben and I had become friends and would regularly catch up and talk about real estate. He has an amazing podcast (shout out to The Real Estate Experiment) and one day called me, talking a mile a minute about how he'd just had a guest on his podcast who opened his eyes to the power of Airbnb and short-term rentals. My mind started racing. I thought back to my time staying at the Airbnb condo downtown. Could this really work, I thought? After hanging up the phone, I immediately listened to the episode with my now coach, and additional fellow hospitable host, Mike Sjogren – who also has his own phenomenal podcast that you should check out called Short Term Rental Secrets (are you noticing a trend yet? Listen to more podcasts!). I was mesmerised. My eyes too were opened as I realised this could be the solution to the freedom I was looking for.

Once my tenants' lease was up, instead of finding new long-term tenants, I converted the upstairs unit of the home into an Airbnb. I can't lie, like most of you probably were or will be when you start hosting, I WAS NERVOUS. Not so much about whether the investment would pay off, but if my guest would enjoy the experience, and if I would even get good guests. You would have thought I was a child waiting on Santa's sleigh the day my first guests pulled into the driveway. I peered out, trying to see their reaction once they opened the door. I sat anxiously by my phone waiting for a message in case they needed anything. Ultimately, all went well, and I received my first glowing five-star review! Within the first few months, I fell in love with the opportunity to be a host to so many wonderful people. Not only did this new venture get me much closer to my goal of financial freedom, but it was fulfilling. It was as if I had answered a newfound calling that aligned with both my goals and passions. I was constantly thinking of extra things I could get for my guests, do for my guests, and share with my guests. The feedback was incredible, and as the five-star reviews continued to grow, so did my love for hospitality and Airbnb. It has not only helped me develop more as a person but has also taught me so much more about people, serving, compassion and generosity.

THE RECIPE

"I've learned that people will forget what you said, people will forget what you did, but people will never forget how you made them feel."
– Maya Angelou

I remember hearing this quote as a small child and thinking just how cliché it was. Like many popular quotes from famous or prominent people, they are often repeated without much true thought or consideration. However, today – more so than ever – I not only resonate deeply with these words from Maya Angelou but am constantly reminded of them.

It is said that memories linked with strong emotions often become seared in the brain. As a self-proclaimed steak chef, I love this analogy because a perfect sear is where you get the maximum flavour out of the meat. Similarly, strong emotions are where you find the real flavour in life, and being an Airbnb host in the hospitality industry you are constantly given opportunities to add flavour to other people's lives.

Throughout the rest of this chapter, I will take you on a journey of personal experiences that have helped me find just the right mix of ingredients to get the perfect sear for my guests. My hope is that you can pick up a few of these ingredients along the way to develop your own hospitable recipe!

INGREDIENT ONE: **SERVICE**

"To give real service, you must add something which cannot be bought or measured with money."
– Douglas Adams

I had no idea at the time, but I was groomed to understand what good service was. My family didn't eat out much growing up, but when we did, we often ate for free. Partially because my parents convinced my brother and me that O'Charley's was their favourite restaurant, where kids just so happen to eat free. Other times, it was due to terrible service. I remember thinking we had some sort of curse when we would go out because of how frequently we received bad service. From cold food to incorrect orders, disappearing waiters and more, I learned exactly what was NOT good service, thus teaching me more than I could have imagined. I realised that each of these restaurants was falling short on a key ingredient for a great experience, and that was amazing service.

While service can be described in many ways, in its simplest form, it boils down to one thing: caring. And while that doesn't cost a dime, it sure does pay off! I once had a guest who booked one of the longest stays I had ever had at my home. In her details, she shared that it was a small family of three and that they would be visiting for business purposes. They seemed like nice people and I was happy to accommodate their stay. However, over the next few weeks, I began to get more and more questions from them. At first, it was just the exact address of the home, not a problem. Then, questions about the neighbourhood and the families in it – I thought this was a bit much but still proceeded to provide very detailed information to address all of her concerns. I think it's important to note that at this time my listing had over forty reviews that were all five stars. Because of this, I began to wonder if this was going to be "THE" difficult guest – the one who is impossible to please and tries to break my five-star streak. I couldn't have that!

The questions continued; she wanted to know about safety and explained to me how she was aware that certain areas within the city could be dangerous. I pointed her to a specific review left by a group of young girls who shared how safe they'd felt in the home. Next question: "Is there an HOA [homeowner association]?" At this point, as strange as it sounds, I wanted to win her over. I wanted to over-deliver in answering her questions and provided her with all the information she desired to feel comfortable staying at the home. It's easy to become annoyed and forget the real reason we are in this business, especially when you have to put in a little more effort than usual. But our goal should be to serve and provide a great experience for each guest, every time. Once they arrived, I received a message that I had never received from a guest before: "We have a gift for you!" I was shocked. Never had a guest provided me with a gift. I met them in the driveway, and to my delight, these were the most kind-hearted and generous guests I had ever met. They gifted me with not one, not two, but THREE bottles of vodka from their distillery. They owned a large company and were looking to expand their operations in my hometown of Atlanta. As I saw all the inventory and valuables they brought into the garage, I began to understand the many questions I received prior to their arrival. The wife smiled and said, "Thank you so much for your great customer service and for answering all of our questions, we can tell you are a great host, and we are happy to be staying here."

When you care, you serve your guests better and, while it doesn't cost a thing, it may just pay you three bottles of the best vodka you've ever had! ;)

INGREDIENT 2: **COMPASSION**

"If you want others to be happy, practice compassion. If you want to be happy, practice compassion."
– Dalai Lama

I had another guest who was coming into town for a few days to explore the city in the hopes of moving. I was happy to share different places to check out and give insights on potential areas to live. They arrived at the property right at check-in and, within an hour, messaged me about having a family emergency and needing to leave. This was early into my hosting journey, and I knew I likely wouldn't be able to get these dates rebooked in the event they cancelled. However, since they were already at the property, my cancellation policy would allow me to keep their full payout for the stay. I was still recouping the cost of furnishing and setting my Airbnb up so it would've really helped to keep the money, but I also thought about how I would feel in their situation. As I began to type, so did they. We both played the back-and-forth typing game, waiting for the other to message first, until I decided to extend a full refund and wish them safe travels on the way home. They were very thankful in their response, and to my surprise even more so in the five-star review they left, which I wasn't even expecting! I often think back to this experience as a reminder that compassion is the greatest currency for goodwill.

INGREDIENT 3: **GENEROSITY**

"It's not how much we give, but how much love we put into giving."
– Mother Teresa

To this day, one of my favourite experiences hosting was a wonderful family that was coming into town to celebrate their son's sweet sixteenth birthday. They mentioned it was their first time, and that their son specifically requested to spend his special day in Atlanta. Taking this into account, I wanted to do something unique and generous for them. On their day of check-in, they arrived in the city far earlier than the check-in time but let me know in advance that they would be sightseeing. I let them know as soon as the previous turnover was complete and offered them an early check-in, which they happily took advantage of. Upon arrival, I heard someone scream, "THE GREEN WALL!" with excitement, referring to the faux grass and light-up sign hanging on the wall that reads, "The

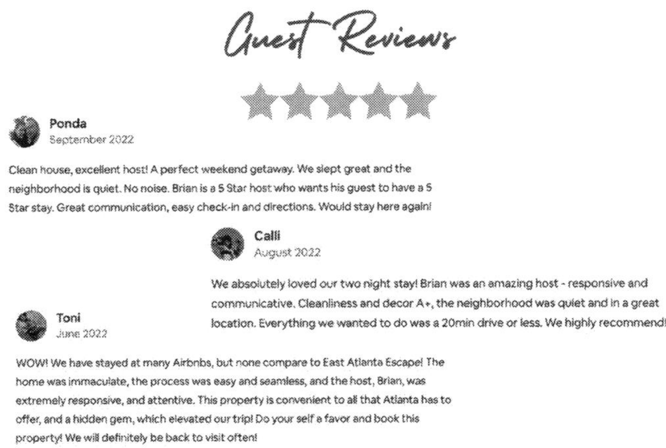

Here are a few reviews highlighting the key guest experience ingredients!

East Atlanta Escape"; always a great feeling as a host! During our initial messages, it just so happened that they shared the exact date of their son's birthday. I went down the street to the local Publix and got him a customised cake made saying "Happy Birthday & Welcome to Atlanta!" I picked up the cake and couldn't contain my excitement when they answered the door. I'll never forget the look on the mother's face, she literally burst into tears. "Oh my gosh, thank you so much, this is unbelievable!" as she wiped her face and called to the rest of the family. We moved to the driveway and their son came up and gave me a big hug with a quiet, "Thank you." The father came in with a firm handshake and said, "I really appreciate your generosity, we've never had a host who looked out and cared for us, thank you." Of course, they left an amazing, heartfelt five-star review.

Believe it or not, this moment brought me just as much joy and happiness as it did them. It also confirmed the old saying about life: "you get what you give".

I hope that you can use some of the same ingredients from these stories that have helped me become a hospitable host, and trust that you will add some of your own to create your memorable sear for your guests. A great meal isn't complete without a toast, so cheers to you and your future hospitable hosting!

One last thing, if you enjoyed this chapter, I'd love to connect with you! Feel free to reach out about anything related to hosting, real estate hacking, and even food. You can find me on social media @therealestatehacker – I look forward to hearing from you soon!

ABOUT THE AUTHOR

Brian Hatcher, aka The Real Estate Hacker, is a serial entrepreneur and investor with a background in accounting, finance and data consulting. While serving an array of multi-billion-dollar companies, he was able to learn from and assist some of the top fortune 100 businesses in developing transformative analytics, processes and initiatives to achieve their strategic goals. He now uses those same skills to help budding entrepreneurs learn unconventional ways to approach and invest in real estate to achieve financial freedom.

Beginning his journey in real estate right out of college, he purchased a duplex home to renovate, live in and rent out (house hack). While this strategy was beneficial to get started, he soon realised that he would have to acquire a large number of traditional buy and hold rentals to achieve his financial goals. After being introduced to the option of Airbnb by a mentor, he began another real estate hack by turning a single-family home into an Airbnb House Hack to not only live completely free but also cash flow over $1,000 a month! He quickly fell in love with the experience of sharing his home and knowledge of the area with guests and became a Superhost in his first three months.

In 2022, he founded Elite Escapes, a short-term rental travel company, which he was able to scale to six figures in only seven months by offering a concierge experience on discounted resort stays across the globe. As a hospitable host of over eighty resorts and 350+ units spanning the United States, Mexico, Hawaii, Canada and Fiji, he believes that amazing service and care should not be a luxury, but a standard. He always strives to not only anticipate guests' wants but to exceed their needs by curating experiences that leave a lasting memory.

Links: https://linktree.com/therealestatehacker

CALE DELANEY

FROM THE W2 WORLD TO ENTREPRENEURSHIP: THE PATH TO FINANCIAL AND TIME FREEDOM

"The heart of man plans his way but the LORD establishes his steps."
– Proverbs 16:9 ESV

You've probably heard it said that the path to success is never a straight line, but a zig-zag. That is certainly accurate in my case. You see, I wasn't one of those kids who just knew what they wanted to do. Instead, I just followed logic where it led. I had an innate ability for maths and science and so when high-school counsellors suggested that I study engineering, that's what I chose as my major in college. I didn't have a passion for it; it was a logical thing to do based on my abilities. After graduating, I began working as a commercial real estate investment broker as that seemed logical since I knew that many wealthy people gained their wealth by being in real estate. After the great recession, I ended up working a fifteen-year career as a senior project manager for large construction projects across the country, not because I had a passion for it, but simply because it was the next logical thing to do with my degree. Starting to see a pattern here?

Well, that same pattern of logic eventually led me to my own wealth and financial/time freedom through short-term rentals. Let's dive in and take a look at how it all got started.

BUT I'M NOT AN ENTREPRENEUR...

I've always been a bit of a dichotomy. I flock to safety and security, but I'm a bit of an adrenaline junkie (solo skydiving, hang-gliding, paragliding... anything to get the blood pumping). I'm naturally an introvert and keep things close to the chest, yet I want to get my story out (hence being a contributing author in this book). I'm relatively risk-averse, yet it's easier for me to invest $100,000 in a piece of real estate than it is for me to spend $10 on a meal.

All this is to say that I never thought I would be an entrepreneur, let alone a successful one. I was stuck in the rat race believing that a W2 job was the only way to be safe financially, which is why I stayed in that world for fifteen years. Yet, as I look back, all the signs for entrepreneurship were there.

We didn't have money growing up, so I had to be creative in ways to make it. As a young kid that sometimes meant picking up cigarette butts from a parking lot for a few bucks. As I got into my teens that meant working various jobs. And as I went out on my own that meant buying and selling cars/motorcycles/ATVs on the side or buying and selling used items I'd find on Craigslist or even on the side of the road. A friend joked that I was the only person who could take a paperclip and swip-swap it enough to buy a Porsche, which did actually kind of happen... but that's a story for another book. It goes so far as that anything I buy for myself I look at as an asset versus liability. As such, I guess I've always had an entrepreneurial mind, but I let the fear of the unknown tell me that the safety and security of a W2 was what I needed. Can anyone relate?

So, how did I finally make the break and flick that switch to activate my entrepreneurial powers?

WHAT IS YOUR WHY?

What is your why? What's meant by that is what is your driving force, your motivation, your no-compromise end that justifies the means. For me, it started with the birth of my youngest son, Ramses.

Ramses was born on the 8th of October 2019 and came out with a smile on his face, literally. It was such a cute and strange thing to see, as you typically expect a newborn to be crying. Not Ramses. Calm and with a smile on his face as he greeted the world. And at three years old now he still has that ever-present, infectious smile, which I hope he never loses.

It was over the next couple of months that the transformation began to take place and, in January 2020, the mental switch clicked on and I knew that I could not continue living in the W2/employee world for the next thirty-to-forty years, only to one day be able to maybe have freedom. That is all dependent upon having sufficient finances at retirement as well, for which the sad truth of the W2/401k path is that it leads most people to retire poor. According to a Bloomberg article from May 2022: "Just 22% of people approaching retirement age said they'll have enough money to maintain a comfortable standard of living..." When you see these numbers, it opens your eyes and makes you think: is following conventional wisdom really the best path to financial/time freedom, aka retirement? The short answer, as you hopefully have surmised, is a resounding NO!

Enter *Rich Dad, Poor Dad*. Around this time of my mental switch (or breakdown, whichever you prefer!), I read this famous book by Robert Kiyosaki. Suddenly, it started to become clear, and I began to realise that I actually did have the skillset to be an entrepreneur; it was right in front of me! And that's when it hit me: what I was missing was that I didn't have a business or investment. After a bit of soul-searching, I decided that real estate was going to be the investment vehicle through which I would gain that financial/time freedom. And off to the races I went!

My Why: Ramses Delaney: What's Yours?

I began voraciously devouring books and podcasts on real estate investing. I followed the steps the experts recommended to find a market and how to get the first property under contract. I was on Zillow daily looking at/analysing deals and literally walking the market I'd chosen locally, pushing an infant in a stroller. Within ninety days, I was under contract on my first property in April 2020 in the midst of the Covid pandemic: a cute 1920s quadplex in a quirky beach town. I'd partnered with my father on this first deal and our plan was to just rent it out as a long-term rental, get it stabilised and cash-flowing. And I did an excellent job at that! Within three months, all the leases had turned over, I'd implemented some cost-saving strategies to cut expenses and, within six months, had increased the net operating income (NOI) by almost 100%! This was a huge accomplishment, but I began to realise that this strategy of investing in small multi-family homes was going to take a lot longer than I wanted to achieve my goals.

At this point, I began to get a bit discouraged and was looking at all different types of real estate assets to find something that would offer a better return. The week before Thanksgiving in 2020, I happened to listen to an episode of Bigger Pockets Real Estate Rookie in which Tony Robinson was talking about how he was making amazing returns by investing in the Smoky Mountains in TN by renting them out as STRs. After listening to that episode, a light bulb switched on. Who wouldn't want to own a cabin in the mountains and make a crazy return on it?! I didn't even know where the Smoky Mountains were, though, so I researched it and discovered it was about a fourteen-hour drive away (equals seventeen hours when you have kids). So, within a couple of days of hearing that podcast, I took massive action and loaded the minivan with seven people and luggage, and we drove to the Smoky Mountains.

During this drive, on the intervals where my wife was driving, I was on the computer doing market research and trying to find a realtor. I came across someone named Avery Carl, not knowing that she was an STR superstar and is indeed a fellow contributing author in this book! I reached out and asked to meet and see some deals. And so, upon arriving, I set up appointments to look at properties, just drive around, explore and learn the area. We viewed a handful of cabins and gained some insight as to what the buy box was to look for and what kind of returns to expect for different sized cabins. The big shock, though, was the prices, as I was looking at cabins twice the price of my own house! Not only that, but the market was so hot almost every property was getting into a bidding war and going significantly above asking.

As the trip ended and we drove home, I agonised over this. Being Mr Frugal himself, I couldn't come to terms with these prices and the bidding wars. However, I was hooked on the market and knew that STRs were the ticket to financial/time freedom and needed to find a way that would work for me. So, I developed a strategy that has served me very well. Instead of getting into these bidding wars, I looked at "stale" listings that had been sitting on the market for a few weeks. I came across one cabin using this method that looked amazing. I immediately reached out to my realtor and asked about it and he came back surprised as to why it hadn't sold. The only problem was that it was listed for $700,000! Yikes. That's a scary high number. I did my conservative deal analysis and the numbers made sense. But $700,000 on your first STR property in a market almost a thousand miles away that you've just discovered, that's crazy, right? How am I going to manage this remotely while still working a demanding W2 job and supporting a family with three kids? What if this doesn't work out like I planned and I lose money? What if it doesn't rent? These are just a few of the myriad of questions and concerns going through my mind.

In situations like this, I believe you have to turn to prayer and give it up to God. And that's what I did. I sat on that property for a couple of weeks, knowing full well it was a miracle it hadn't already sold and that it could sell any minute in this super-hot market. Yet I decided I would put it up to prayer and trust God that, if it was meant to be, He'd make it happen. And so, after a couple of weeks of meditating and praying on this, I decided to make an offer at $650,000. Mind you, I was going against every norm in that market as nothing, I mean NOTHING, went below asking. To me, it was another test of whether it was God's will. I submitted the offer and... they accepted! Indeed, I was a bit shocked when I got the news from my realtor. And then the heavy weight came down upon me in realising that this was now becoming real. I was about to spend more money than I'd ever imagined and take a seemingly huge risk. No turning back now!

"And they said to him, "Inquire of God, please, that we may know whether the journey on which we are setting out will succeed"."
– Judges 18:5

The closing was stressful, but eventually happened and I had a huge 3,400SF log cabin in the Smoky Mountains that I now had to figure out how to make into a profitable STR! Thankfully, Avery's husband Luke Carl teaches you everything you need to know to get started. From there, the snowball started to grow as, during the contract period, I discovered that the seller owned the two neighbouring cabins and was looking to sell them as well. So, immediately after closing on the first one, we negotiated off-market and went into contract and closed the next two cabins and now had three cabins in a span of four months. And then the snowball really started to gain momentum. Three months later came cabin number four, then number five in January 2022, number six in July 2022, and number seven in September 2022. Back in March 2021,

I converted one of those units in the quadplex into an STR as well. So, in the span of roughly eighteen months, I now had a portfolio of eight STRs and five LTRs worth over a combined $6,000,000 and had generated over $1,200,000 in bookings!

IT'S NOT ALL SUNSHINE AND RAINBOWS...

Sounds simple, right?! However, this journey was hardly easy and has had many challenges to overcome along the way. Not the least of which was a serious medical issue with my wife that turned into a tremendous nightmare.

In March of 2021, just before closing on cabins two and three, and in the midst of converting the local LTR unit, my wife had a planned trip to Ecuador (where she is from) for two weeks. Without going into details to respect her privacy, something happened that required her to have an operation there. And what was supposed to be a relatively common procedure turned into complication after complication that ultimately led to two more surgeries in Ecuador and then two additional surgeries upon arriving back to the US after being stuck in Ecuador for six months.

Meanwhile, back home, I was all of a sudden responsible for taking care of three kids, our youngest being eighteen months, all while working fifty-to-sixty hours a week at my W2 and building the fledgling STR business that now had four properties to finish setting up and manage. Oh, and all this in the midst of the Covid pandemic. Thankfully, my wife had some great family friends in Ecuador who took care of her during that entire six months where she was basically bedridden, her elderly father flew to the US from Ecuador to help with the kids and during the summer we sent the two older kids up to New Hampshire with my father. It was towards the end of August that we were finally able to get my wife on a flight back to the US, even though she was hardly in the condition to travel. Upon arriving and seeing her condition, I immediately took her to the emergency room. To cut a very long story short, over the next six months, she endured another two surgeries, wearing a very cumbersome medical device, and being very limited in what she could do.

During this time, it would have been easy to just throw in the towel on this crazy real estate and STR investing idea and let life knock me down and keep me down. It reminds me of a quote from Rocky Balboa where he says, “You, me, or nobody is gonna hit as hard as life. But it ain’t about how hard you hit. It’s about how hard you can get hit and keep moving forward. How much you can take and keep moving forward.” So, through sheer grit, determination, discipline, prayer and an unwavering commitment towards my WHY, I kept moving forward during what was certainly one of the most difficult times of my life. And now, thankfully, we are beginning to see the fruits of all this labour. In fact, as of December 2022, less than two years after getting started, I have left my well-paid W2 career of over fifteen years to now focus solely on growing my real estate investing and STR business! I am excited for the new doors that God will open as this journey continues.

In this short eighteen-month period since my STR business officially began operating, I have certainly learned a lot! I’ve made mistakes and I’ve learned from them and have overcome many challenges along the way. At this time in the business, though, it is beginning to run much more smoothly as my systems develop and lessons learned help me navigate the inevitable challenges as they come. One of the main things I love about the real estate investing industry is that almost everyone is so open to help and share. It is one of the only industries I know that is not a cut-throat, scarcity mentality, but is one of abundance, and that is a huge reason why so many people turn to and become wealthy in real estate.

THE HOSPITABLE HOSTING SIDE

This journey has moved so much faster and successfully than I ever dreamed. In eighteen months, we’ve had the pleasure of

Cale and his family (Blanca, Gabriela, Jose, Cale and Ramses) hiking in Acadia National Park, ME, USA

hosting over 3,400 guests (including over 100 pets)! As every host experiences, there are certainly ups and downs to the business. And, yes, you will occasionally have those nightmare guests who keep you up all night stressing out or driving you crazy, but the majority of guests are great and will bring a smile to your face when they let you know how much they've enjoyed their stay. We've had a few memorable experiences with guests, both good and bad, that are a good representation of what you can expect when you get into the hospitality and STR business. Let's start with the bad, shall we?

One that comes to mind was bad not because of the guest, but because of the situation. This came just a couple of months after I'd started with my first cabin. We had a group of sixteen guests check-in only to message around 8pm (mind you, I'm usually in bed by 8pm) that the drains downstairs were backing up every time they flushed a toilet or used a shower. In my panicked new-host frenzy, I found a plumber that could come out and he supposedly fixed a clogged drain. I let the guest know, apologised for the inconvenience and started getting ready for bed again. Around 10pm, I got another message that the drains were backing up again! I immediately called the plumber who said that it must be a septic tank issue then and I'd have to call someone else. Nothing I could do at 10pm, so I gave the guest the bad news and asked them not to use the showers or toilets (easy request, right?). After hardly sleeping at all from being so stressed, come 7am the next morning I called every septic company within a couple of hours and nobody could make it out there for a few days. Regrettably, I had to inform the guest and help them find alternative accommodation. And, when the septic company came, they discovered it was just a clog and the plumber who came before didn't do his job. This was a very expensive lesson to the tune of about $3,000, but I ended up finding an excellent septic/plumbing company who I trust and use frequently now.

Now for some good! There are many that come to mind, but I'll briefly share a few special ones. First, at our little beach cottage in South FL, we had a charitable organisation make a reservation for two weeks to temporarily house an Afghan refugee family as they helped them find a permanent home. Charity is a big part of our values, and we donate 10% of all profits from our business to charity as well, so this was a great fit. We were pleased to help and, since this was during Thanksgiving, we gifted the family with a delicious smoked turkey delivered right to their door. The second is we had the opportunity to host a Make-a-Wish family at one of our cabins. Our cleaners put together a wonderful welcome basket for the young girl and delivered it, for which the family was very appreciative, and we helped them make some lasting and precious memories together as a family. And the last one I'll share is from a family who just recently stayed with us at one of our cabins during Thanksgiving. I'll let the guest's words speak for themselves:

"Thank you from the bottom of my heart for such a beautiful stay – our family had such a beautiful time – me and my daughters are nurses and with the Covid pandemic, we have worked non-stop, and

have had a little time to be together – this cabin was our sanctuary for the long weekend and we loved it so much!"

So, as said before, you'll get the good with the bad. That's the nature of the hospitality business. When it gets stressful and tough, it helps to remember to put yourself in their shoes and remember that, at the end of the day, you are helping people and families make memories. And, hopefully, it will make you a better guest as well, as you can empathise with a host if something is not perfect at your next stay in an STR!

It truly is a life-changing investment vehicle and business. In fact, I sit here typing the final words of this chapter one day after I officially left my W2 job. Never did I dream it would happen so fast. I praise Jesus for his hand of blessing on these ventures thus far and pray for His continued blessing on them to not only grow our financial/time prosperity, but also to grow our giving prosperity and the new opportunities this will provide in helping others achieve their own success. I've turned to prayer in these large decisions and during the trials and the successes and am 100% confident the Lord's hand has been the reason for my success to this point. Though I fall short constantly, I pray He can continue to grow me in being worthy of His calling and blessing. And I pray that anyone struggling to get started or gain momentum in this industry or on the verge of giving up is given strength and courage to persevere. My hope is that my story has given inspiration and encouragement to its readers.

ABOUT THE AUTHOR

Cale Delaney, who titles himself the "accidental-intentional millionaire" is a Christian, real estate investor, entrepreneur, husband and father of three. After graduating cum laude with an engineering degree from the University of Miami, he began his real estate career in 2006 working as a commercial real estate investment broker in Miami, FL where he was awarded the Pace Setter award his first year for the most number of listings and sold over $7M in multi-family and retail real estate. However, with the crash of 2008, he left that business and put real estate on hold until 2020 when he decided to go all in to start building generational wealth for his family.

Since then, his investment portfolio went from $300k in January 2020 (a previous primary home turned LTR) to over $6M less than two years later. In those two years, he acquired a total of thirteen units, including five LTRs and eight STRs, seven of which are luxury log cabins in the Smoky Mountains in TN. Due to his rapid success, he's been featured on several well-known podcasts, including Bigger Pockets Real Estate Rookie.

Cale self-manages all his properties remotely and, as of December 2022, left his W2 job to focus on his real estate ventures. In the first eighteen months, his business Mountain to Sea Cabins & Cottages generated over $1.2M in bookings and hosted over 3,400 guests (including over 100 pets!). He took his very first STR cabin from a projected revenue of $85k to an actual of $150k and converted an LTR generating $17k to an STR generating $70k.

Cale's focus now is on building his STR business with the intent to diversify into larger multi-family and/or self-storage for additional passive income streams. He also has several other projects in the works, including a non-profit, mastermind programme, co-hosting and podcast (anticipated launch in January 2023).

Links: https://linktr.ee/mtntoseacabinsandcottages

CASEY KARLEN

PERSEVERANCE IS THE KEY TO FINDING YOUR PASSION

"This is the one!" I whispered to myself as I sat in front of my computer screen at 3am on a Tuesday. My eyes felt heavy as I could feel the bags underneath them getting larger the longer I stayed up, but the excitement of finally launching my newest venture sparked this energy in me that I couldn't stop thinking about. I finally had an idea that was going to have an impact on the world that would also make me feel fulfilled. After months of work, I finished building out the e-commerce store that was going to change my life. I had launched and failed six other businesses before, but this one was different, it was special and personal. I created an online store that sold autism-related products, selling custom T-shirts and hats that displayed inside jokes within the autism community. Its sole purpose was to employ autistic adults like my brother, Brendon. Brendon was having trouble finding a good fit for him after school. It seemed like there weren't many good options out there for him. I wanted to create a space and movement where people in my brother's situation could be active in the workforce and feel a sense of purpose. Not only did I want to have an impact on the autistic adult community, but I needed extra income as well.

My wife and I had just purchased a two-bedroom condo in Glendora, California, which we couldn't afford, we had an eighteen-month-old baby with a newborn on the way. My wife, Shayla, was patient with me and stood by as I changed from business idea to business idea with energy levels going up and down like a roller coaster of emotions. She always gave me a gift that not many husbands get; she believed in me. I was employed and had a good job running operations for my dad's floor care and water damage restoration company. I loved working with my parents, but the industry wasn't a good fit for my personality and didn't line up with my goals. I felt like I could create and do more than just have a regular job. I watched as my father had the freedom to attend all my sports games and make it a priority to always be at the things that mattered. By being his own boss, he called the shots concerning his time.

I longed and craved for financial freedom, time freedom and location freedom. I wanted to be able to create a life where I could travel the world with my family and use my resources and time to help others in need. I figured going this route with e-commerce and trying to add value to the autism community was my vehicle to get there. Fast forward only one month later, and the results were not what I was hoping for. "Only two orders?" I said to myself as I looked at the results of the first week. I was astounded to see what the results of my efforts were. My advertising costs were being eaten alive; every day I would spend lots of money targeting who I thought was my ideal customer. I had only a handful of sales for the month, and the biggest sale I had was from my mom. All those people who said to me they "can't wait for the launch" and "they are going to buy" didn't purchase anything. It was not the turnout I was hoping to have or planned to have. One night, after spending $200 in ads in one day for no sales and feeling like a failure, I broke down and started crying to my wife. "This was supposed to be the idea that took off!" I said to her with tears falling down my face.

I felt defeated. I wanted to create something special, but I was $30,000 in debt and didn't know what to do to make the business better. I needed a better solution where the product itself actually solved the problem, and to create that I would need money that I didn't have.

Imagine being a young father and husband, having a significant amount of bad debt, another business idea thrown in the trash, and the little light at the end of the tunnel of hope you had was gone. It can be a difficult feeling to have. What kept me going was thinking about the phrase "entrepreneurs only have to be right once". It took Thomas Edison 1000 attempts to create the light bulb. He never viewed those attempts as failures, but rather as 1000 steps to create a light bulb. I knew I hadn't found my light bulb yet. Although I could have tried harder and endured longer on my other business start-ups, they failed for a reason, it wasn't the right path that God had for me.

One month later, after closing down the Autismy store, I was talking with my friend Sam who came over that evening with his wife and kids. Sam is an extremely likeable guy, who most would describe as a social butterfly. He is into "commercial real estate" and "multi-family investing", whatever that means. Sam's career choice to me sounded a bit boring, and he wasn't the biggest fan of long and complex spreadsheets. Sam would often say to me with a smile on his face, "You know, Casey, ninety percent of the world's millionaires are made through real estate!" I figured I would invest in real estate one day, but I thought it was something that only the rich had the luxury of doing. It made sense to me how it can build generational wealth, but words like investing, property taxes, cash-on-cash, return on investment, appreciation, depreciation and inflation were not commonly used words I heard growing up. It seemed so out of reach to me, and I didn't see myself with the title "Casey the Real Estate Investor". My personality is that of a dreamer or a visionary who has the desire to create and I often get obsessed with an idea or a project I'm working on.

Shortly after this conversation, late one night, scrolling through

Casey's Family

my phone on Instagram, I saw a video of how a guy was investing in real estate and using Airbnb to cover the mortgage. I ended up going down the rabbit hole of the Instagram algorithm and watched tons and tons of videos going from this expert to this guru until I eventually got the gist of the concept. I thought to myself, "Wait, what? You can make decent money renting out a house on Airbnb?" I knew some were doing it, but I thought it was mainly for private rooms in people's houses with just an air mattress. However, the thought of visiting potential properties or markets all over the country excited me because my true passion is travelling to new places and adventuring with my family.

My love for travelling and experiencing new places started while I was serving a mission for The Church of Jesus Christ of Latter-day Saints. I spent this time in Northern Germany for two years falling in love with the culture, people, food, chocolate, castles, and yes, again, the food. Every week I would visit a different monument, museum, or castle and explore the different amenities that Germany had to offer. After this trip, I took several holidays away with my family to places like Europe, Bali, Dubai and Central America. All those trips were a blast, being some of the best memories that I have. One could say that I had "the travel bug".

I thought to myself, “Hmm, I think I would really like this real estate Airbnb thing.” I started buying real estate investing books and listening to as many topics on the subject as I could. Instead of listening to the newest and trending music, I would listen to podcasts about short-term rentals, real estate investing and hospitality. Additionally, I researched topics on how to buy distressed properties and turn them into beautiful masterpieces that are perfect for hospitality and short-term stays. I loved the idea of buying properties in weekend getaway spots where the average family could take a trip and make amazing memories together. All this combined made me have a strong desire to be the best host I could possibly be. After weeks of research, a strategic plan was put in place. I was going to buy fixer-upper homes in holiday markets and turn them into beautiful short-term rentals. I realised I naturally had the perfect team to make this happen. I would be the host and find the properties, my dad would manage the rehab projects, and my mom and wife would handle design and furnishing. Together, we would purchase our first short-term rental in Joshua Tree, California, in December of 2021. Being just two hours away from our hometown, it was the perfect place for our first project. This was the beginning of something amazing, not just a business, or a “fun little project”, but the start of being a host, and not just any host, a hospitable one.

Being a hospitable host is no easy task, it requires patience and showing genuine kindness, but the experiences make it worth it. Before the birth of Jesus Christ, Mary, the mother of Christ, and her husband Joseph were searching for a place to stay in the city of Bethlehem. Joseph took Mary to Bethlehem for the census ordered by Caesar Augustus. Because of this event, it was crowded in the city and there wasn’t much room for outsiders. It is commonly known that they made several attempts to stay in a comfortable place fit for a woman who was expecting a baby. In Luke 2:7 it states: “there was no room for them in the inn”. This unfortunate circumstance resulted in the baby being born and placed in a manger after his birth. This is typically not the ideal scene for this type of activity. I ponder on that story and wonder how different it would be if they'd stumbled across a truly hospitable host on their search. I imagine the alternative version would sound something like this:

"Joseph and Mary eventually found one person kind enough to help them find a solution, greeting them with a positive attitude and a happy smile. Although their place was packed full of visitors, the host made it work by switching things around and finding a happy medium. The host made them feel comfortable, welcomed and that their presence was wanted. Knowing the tough situation that Mary was in, the host offered to help and make their stay as enjoyable as possible. The host spent quality time with the couple to get to know them and have meaningful conversations. After the birth of the baby and things had settled down, the host rushed in to congratulate them and meet their new baby boy. You could feel the genuine excitement booming from the host's tone. After the stay was over, they kindly said goodbye, and hoped to see each other again, knowing the positive experience they all just had would be with them for a lifetime."

In my opinion, this is how hospitable hosts would have handled themselves in a situation like this. A truly hospitable host loves and cares for human beings, they care about their guests and their happiness. Their guests are trusting them with shelter away from home and a host will ensure their satisfaction while they are in their care.

I believe that all my guests are trusting me and the space I provide to enhance their holiday experience. Holiday time is precious, and sometimes being out of your normal home can be uncomfortable. I strive to make my guests feel comfortable but also give them a great experience to be remembered. I cherish my travelling and holiday time with my family, so I know how important that must be to all my guests. Hosts care about people and the spaces they create and the service they offer is simply a reflection of that trait.

I love being able to create unique stays and then meeting the people who decided to make a reservation at my funky spaces. I have a 1976 thirty-foot Catalina Sailboat in West Los Angeles that we placed in a slip at a local marina. We remodelled the inside and made it suitable for overnight stays. It is a beautiful boat and made really cute with some paint and interior design. Not a traditional type of stay, it's an old boat with a few character flaws and has a bit of a smell, and I don't mean the salty ocean breeze. I assumed that most people would stay one to three nights max being that it's a small sailboat. On the contrary, the second booking we received was a long stay for over three weeks in the middle of winter by someone named Grant. I immediately thought to myself, "Who would book a sailboat for three weeks? This Grant guy must be crazy to stay in a boat like this for that long." As I scratched my head in disbelief, I accepted the booking request and awaited his check-in. I had the opportunity to meet with Grant in person when he contacted me with a plumbing issue on the boat. He told me how wonderful a time he was having. I asked him what he did for work to be able to stay in a boat for three weeks. He explained to me that he was a digital nomad who worked from his laptop and could work from anywhere. He worked for an advertising agency and loved his work because it allowed him to live in different Airbnbs around the country. I was impressed by how lightly he travelled – he had a small suitcase and basic essentials. He was very low maintenance and took pride in his freedom. I had this realisation that experiences are always better than material things. Having the ability to experience new places, try out new things, and go where you want to go when you want to go trumps any item you can buy at the store. As this trend continues to grow more and more desirable, the need for short and medium-term rentals will continue to be in high demand.

My hosting journey has been an amazing experience, I have enjoyed the people I have met, not only amazing guests but other hosts as well. I truly feel that I have found my "tribe" and type of people. The memories that have been made in the spaces I provide are something to be cherished and I am extremely proud of that. As someone who classifies themselves as a people pleaser, I try to make sure everyone I come in contact with is happy. I avoid

Casey and Brendon

contention at all costs and dwell on the positive side of things instead of the negative. I wish someone would have told me at the beginning of my hosting journey that not everyone will love your space or the service you provide. Some people might be going through a hard time, have above-average expectations for their stay, or are simply negative, unhappy campers. I always help my guests have a positive experience, but when a guest leaves a review that is not 100% positive, I do feel discouraged. I often remind myself that even the nicest most luxurious hotels or resorts in the world don't have all five-star positive experiences. When I got my first non-five-star review, I was up all night thinking about it. I was evaluating and trying to understand what I could have done to be better. But I came to the realisation that this is a people business, and on holiday is when one's emotions are most sensitive. Some may be excited and thrilled about the amazing location and time away from home, but others may be stressed about the work they are missing, or financially concerned, or maybe their mother-in-law is on holiday with them. Ultimately, all I can do as a host is my very best to make my guests happy; as long as I am doing all I can to be the greatest host I can be then the negative feedback should not discourage me.

It took me years to learn the things I know now. I spent hours and hours of time learning and researching how to be a good host and the best way to acquire properties. All the books I read, podcasts I listened to and events I attended brought me to where I am now. I used to wonder, "How do real estate investors buy so many properties?" and, "How do Airbnb hosts manage so many properties at once?" These types of questions kept me from starting my journey, but once I got over these hurdles, I was able to see that it was achievable. I had these moments of clarity that changed my life for the better. I thoroughly enjoy sharing the insights that I have learned and helping others have that same moment of clarity. I started a mentorship program for others that want to accomplish financial freedom, time freedom and location freedom so they too can start living their best life. I help hosts build their short-term rental portfolio by learning to use other people's money to grow. Coaching and mentorship are special to me because one of my favourite things is to see someone take value in the information that I share with them. I look forward to the short-term rental journey that lies ahead of me, and I can't wait to see what my team and I can accomplish when we work together.

ABOUT THE AUTHOR

Casey Karlen is the founder of Short Term Rental Investors LLC, an entrepreneur and real estate investing coach. His real estate investing company buys ugly houses in holiday markets and turns them into unique and creative spaces. They focus on nice, family friendly and affordable stays. He helps other short-term rental hosts grow their portfolio and achieve financial freedom, time freedom and location freedom. His property management company, Urlaub Properties, manages short-term rental units for property owners who do not have the time to be full-time hosts. In less than a year, his companies have purchased three million in real estate, manage multiple units in over six different locations, and have helped dozens of investors come closer to financial freedom.

In his youth, Casey served a two-year mission in northern Germany for The Church of Jesus Christ of Latter-day Saints. It was there he found his passion for learning new cultures, languages and creating fun experiences while being away from home. After his mission, he was determined to start a business that would help him travel more and spend time with family. He launched seven businesses that failed before finding his passion in hosting, real estate and coaching.

Casey is a big believer in goal setting and mindset. Growing up, he was a C student and would often say, "I don't like to read." After changing his mindset and creating good habits, he now reads three to four books a month that bring him closer to accomplishing his goals. He currently resides in Southern California with his beautiful wife Shayla, two young boys, Mckay and Liam, and their two dogs. His hobbies include dirt bike riding, fishing, travelling, being with family and indulging in his passion for entrepreneurship.

Links: https://linktr.ee/Casey_karlen

CHRIS BALLARD

ONE MAN, HIS DOGS AND DYZYN

Like many here, my journey to becoming a host has been a little varied. My first full-time job was as an engineer. But, no matter what I do, I have always found my way back to hospitality. With my engineering background, I take a little more of an analytical approach to hospitality than most in the industry. I believe that to be a truly hospitable host, you need to have the right systems and structure in place to enable you and your team to have the time and energy to deliver top-class service and hospitality.

At the tender age of fourteen, I first dipped my toe into the hospitality world, working in a Welsh-themed restaurant called the Celtic Cauldron opposite Cardiff Castle. I can still remember how nervous I was on my first day, a small, spotty, little me stuck out in the dish area not looking at or talking to anyone. We have all got to start somewhere, right? I worked there most Saturdays and Sundays until I was seventeen and ended up opening and closing the restaurant most weekends.

After a seven-or-so-year stint as an engineer, I eventually found my way back to the hospitality industry. I joined the Creative Hospitality Group in Cardiff. It was wild! Working in one of Cardiff's busiest and best cocktail bars, Peppermint, we worked hard and partied harder, and I met so many great people; some of them are now stuck with me for life. Good luck to you guys!

In my short ten months there, I moved from bartender to assistant manager and, after just three months, Mike and Bruno made me general manager of their tiki bar Bambu. It was a baptism of fire; taking over a failing bar that the owners were thinking of selling left no room for error. I grafted day and night for the first six months pushing myself with 100+ hours weekly. It was beyond hard but also the time I learnt the most about what I am capable of. Often pushing through the challenging times is the most rewarding.

After a whirlwind eighteen months, I upped sticks and moved to Sweden with my now-wife Angelica. It was here, whilst working at the five-star Copperhill Hotel Resort, I took my first steps into hosting. Seeing how they effortlessly provided curated stays with every detail and piece of decor thought through thoroughly really got me thinking. As many do, I started on Airbnb, heading to Cardiff during my annual leave to set up my first property, get the cleaners on board and dive in headfirst. The first few months, as usual, were a bit of a roller coaster. Having spent a few hours on YouTube, I thought I knew it all! How wrong was I?

The journey to where DYZYN Living is today has been fast and challenging. Myself and the team have been through many ups and downs as we have moved from two units to thirty and then to the fifty-three units we are on as of writing this.

There are many, many things that intertwine and grow together to help you build a successful serviced accommodation business, but for me connection is the single most important thing. No, I'm not talking about super fast wi-fi, although that's also a must. It's the personal connection between your company and your guests. When you lose that connection, or even worse never make it, you open yourself up to all sorts of issues. Building and growing DYZYN remotely has been the toughest part to get right.

We used to regularly have guests firing off complaints through emails, texts and WhatsApp. The problem wasn't the properties, it wasn't the customer support they received, it was that we were

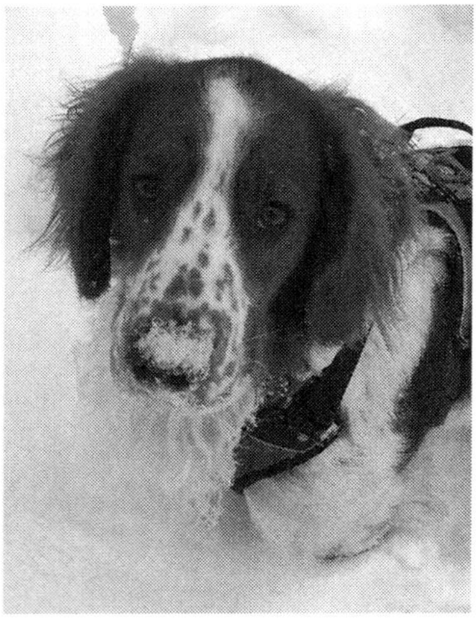

Dai – the dog behind the man behind DYZYN Living

a brand without connection, without that human touch. The change was simple but effective. We didn't stop the automations, but we added in three quick calls.

The first, the icebreaker. We make this call as soon after booking as possible, and it has two simple aims. The first and most important for us is to turn DYZYN from just a faceless online brand to the caring company with real people that we actually are. The second, which saves us so much time and headaches on the back end, we check the guests have booked the right apartment for their needs.

The last part probably seems a bit stupid to most of you, but we are trying to proactively solve future problems. I have had numerous guests in the past where they have just booked the wrong apartment for what they need. We have had penthouse apartments when they are scared of heights, groups of six turn up to a one-bedroom apartment because they thought they had booked six of them, the list goes on and on. Thankfully, since introducing this, we do not get many of any of these issues anymore.

We call this second call The Check Back call. Ever been to a restaurant and a couple of minutes after you have started your meal the waiter comes back to check if the food is what you wanted? The great servers always check how your food is! The great hospitable hosts do the same, which builds the connection, again shows that we care and gives us the chance to fix anything we may have missed. We want to be perfect, but we also know we are not; this is our way of getting one step closer to that perfect stay.

And finally the long goodbye. So simple but so effective, it's just a thank you for staying. We wish them a safe journey home and say there is an email coming out with a voucher code for them or their friends when they are next in Cardiff.

Again, this works twofold. They feel like the valued guests they are and we put the idea in their head to return to stay with us. Plus have you ever had a call to say thank you for being a guest? Me neither... and I'm a tremendous guest, as I'm sure you are.

If you are interested in the call templates we use, head over to www.dyzyn.co.uk and click the mentorship tab where you will find a free download there.

Once we got this three-call system nailed down and started creating connections between the guests and us, the business really took off. We spent less time solving problems reactively and more time creating and selling memorable stay experiences for guests. There are obviously a lot more systems and checks involved in running a successful property business, but focusing on connection and making those calls took DYZYN Living to the next level. Everyone sends an automatic email, nobody calls anymore. Zig when they zag

We never really set out with the idea of being the best property managers in Wales but, when people started to notice our success, people just wanted a part of it, and we began growing steadily, even through the pandemic. We worked hard and never compromised on what we offered, always making sure to deliver the comfortable quality stays with connection that our customers expect.

In 2019, Angelica and I welcomed our first dog into the family, Dai the Welsh Springer Spaniel. He was such a bundle of joy and happiness that we couldn't imagine going anywhere without him. Luckily, when we travelled in our camper van, this was not a problem – chuck him in with us, it was ours and nobody could say a thing. But booking a hotel or B&B, well, that was a completely different story. Something that was so simple when you booked yourself became a minefield of extra charges, properties that were not pet friendly and just poor quality places to stay.

So, after a few too many terrible stays and extra charges, DYZYN Living Pet Friendly Accommodation was born. We quickly became

Cardiff's go-to for pet-friendly business stays and started to attract the responsible pet owners we wanted. Unfortunately, whilst writing for this book, Dai the dog behind DYZYN was taken ill and quickly passed away on Christmas Day. His influence led to us at DYZYN meeting some wonderful people and fantastic pet owners.

Which brings me on to Karla Bailey. As of writing this, Karla and her cats have been staying with us for the best part of eighteen months. She came over from the USA to start a new chapter of her life in sunny South Wales. While her first few emails littered with emojis did make me a little confused, this lady brightens each and every day I get the pleasure of speaking with her. She beams happiness, love and genuine caring each and every time I speak with her. It has been my and the team's honour to have hosted Karla and, honestly, it's meeting people like her that makes hosting worthwhile.

While not every day is brightened by somebody like Karla, we have found that the more we focus on the type of person or guest avatar we want, the better results we get. By understanding that people like myself and Angelica want to bring their pets somewhere safe, quiet and secure, we are able to deliver great hospitality for guests and their pets.

It's been a long journey for DYZYN to get to where it is today, but I now work nine hours a week in my business, from anywhere I want in the world; on a beach, in a cabin or by a lake. My team, systems and proactive connection approach allow us to focus on the guest and hosting.

Do you want to increase your revenue twenty times while reducing your work week to just nine hours? Spots will fill up fast and I am not looking to work with just anyone, you will need to be willing to put the work in now to get the rewards later. If this sounds like you, then send me an email with the title 'Hospitable Hello' to chris@dyzyn.co.uk and we can have a chat to see if I can help you get to where you want to be.

ABOUT THE AUTHOR

Chris Ballard is a dog daddy, digital nomad, husband and Hospitable Host.

You'll often spot him in his camper van travelling around Europe with Angelica and Bobi. Becoming a host and taking control of his future has brought him an amazing sense of pride, as well as liberty. He can work whenever and wherever he wants, whether it's in a cabin, on the side of a mountain or relaxing on a beach after a day surfing in Portugal. Being able to build and live the life he loves is amazing – and there's no better feeling than that!

Links: https://linktr.ee/chrisballard

CHRIS MILLER

FROM BANKER TO SHORT-TERM RENTAL OPERATOR; HOW OUR NEVER-QUITE MENTALITY LED TO A LIFE-CHANGING JOURNEY

If you are anything like me, you have spent countless hours at your job wondering what it would be like to own your own business and build your own dream instead of someone else's. I never knew where to start and what type it would be, but I liked the idea of owning my own business. It wasn't until we purchased our first short-term rental that I realised this would be the vehicle for me.

I hope what I share inspires you to take the first step towards getting started in the direction of your dreams and writing your own story. If I can help you eliminate one mental roadblock or help you take the simplest of actions toward your dreams (listening to a podcast, reading a book or purchasing an audiobook, etc.) then I will consider this a success!

People often think success in real estate or business is because the successful people were well-connected when they started, had wealthy families or a had a special skill or talent. While this may be true for some, I have yet to meet any of those people in my life. Most successful entrepreneurs simply had dreams that could not be fulfilled at traditional jobs and a 'never quit' mentality. My journey as a short-term rental operator was not an overnight success, nor was it one that came easily or naturally. I had to be a student of the business, work at it and make adjustments along the way. I always enjoyed meeting new people but had to learn how to be a hospitable host.

I was an athlete my whole life. In fact, baseball paid for my college and at one time I had aspirations to play professionally. I earned a degree in exercise science and considered becoming a physical therapist. However, after graduating, I ultimately began working at a credit union as a banker in Jacksonville, FL and joined a multi-level marketing company at the same time. I learned a lot about sales and leadership in that MLM. I moved up the ranks quickly in banking using these same sales and leadership skills I had acquired. When my wife and I moved to Daytona Beach for her job as a physician assistant, I got a new job at a major bank there. I became the youngest financial centre manager in my region in 2015 and even led my branch to be in the top fifty in sales nationally out of 2,600 branches in 2016. Although I may have been perceived as successful in corporate America, my personal goals and creative thinking never fully aligned with the corporate world.

Shortly after we moved to Daytona Beach, we were looking for a house with a mother-in-law suite or separate space my brother-in-law could live in so we had our own spaces but could still save on bills by living together. We found a house that met our criteria and jumped on it. It was a three-storey house with kitchens on each floor along with separate entrances and exits to each floor, but was technically a single-family home. So, we rented out the first floor to my brother-in-law, Keri and I lived in the middle floor and we had the third floor always available to family and friends for visiting. We soon ended up renting out that floor to long-term tenants and just lived in the middle floor. We later learned the term for this is house-hacking. At the time, we were just trying to have our mortgage payment covered and get out of the student loan debt Keri had accrued. Together we made what we considered good money,

My beautiful family!

but she had nearly $200,000 in student loan debt we needed to pay off. That monthly payment alone was about $2,400 per month and our mortgage was about $1,600 per month. So, by renting out the two floors, we brought in $1,600 when my brother-in-law lived with us. After he moved out, we increased rents to $2,175 and now had our mortgage and utilities covered.

It was around this time in 2017 that we went to visit some friends in Seattle. We'd planned to stay a few days in San Francisco first, then drive up the Pacific Coast Highway all the way to Seattle (which, by the way, if you have never done this, put it on your bucket list! We made some incredible memories and saw the glory of God's creation through nature!). When we were pricing out hotels, we didn't see anything affordable, so our friend told us about this app called Airbnb and how we could rent other people's homes for short stays. Homes on there were much more affordable, so we booked an amazing place with great views of Coit Tower and the bay. It was such a cool experience that we came back to Daytona Beach after our vacation and thought, "Why don't we try this at our house?" The third floor was already furnished and all I needed to do was change some locks. We went live in July of 2017 with our little 350sq ft third-floor room and we made $2,500 – $2,600 on average each month on the third floor alone! This was life-changing for us! This new side hustle gave us an excitement and energy we had not had before because we finally saw a way out of the crushing student loan debt! At the time, we had no intention of starting a short-term rental business or quitting our jobs.

Then we get this not-so-friendly letter from the city telling us to shut down operations immediately because we are not "zoned" for short-term rentals. I thought, "Not zoned for short-term rentals? Firstly, what in the world is a zone and don't we own this property? Can't we do whatever we want here?" I went to the city with the letter to ask them what a zone is and how we can continue to operate. They explained the zoning and where we could legally operate, etc. In light of the zoning restrictions, we turned our third floor back into a long-term rental. However, seeing how successful our first humble Airbnb property had been, we were eager to find properly zoned houses to purchase. We set up searches on Zillow to alert us any time a property became available within the short-term rental zone.

At this point, I became extremely interested in real estate after seeing how quickly and effectively it could generate income. I began reading many real estate books and listening to a variety of real estate podcasts to learn as much as I could. We also joined our local Real Estate Investor Association (REIA) and took a class on something called wholesaling (assigning a real estate purchase contract for a fee). I learned so much during that bootcamp, but little did I know, I would meet a future business partner that weekend.

Shortly after that, a house finally came on the market in March in the STR zone. We put an offer on it almost immediately! It was already renovated, came furnished and was a licensed holiday rental, so it would cash flow from day one! By the end of that first full year of renting the new house, that property alone matched my annual salary at the bank (before bonuses). That same year, our son was born and returning to work after spending time with him those first couple of months of his life was difficult for both Keri and I. We knew we wanted to get to work on creating more income to buy our time back and create more opportunities to be with our family.

I then came across a YouTube video in July 2018 on a concept called "rental arbitrage" in which you rent a property from an owner with the rights to re-rent it to travellers either directly or online through Airbnb, VRBO, Furnished Finder, etc. It made complete sense to me but also made me frustrated because I had just put down $40,000 to purchase a rental property and this video was telling me I could make similar money with only $4,000 plus furniture. So, I gave it a shot and started pitching landlords and property management companies. I secured my first lease in August as a corporate lease in which my LLC was the tenant, and all travellers were my guests. I was paying $1,100 per month, which included water, for a two-bedroom one-and-a-half bath apartment and we averaged revenue of $4,200 per month, so it just added fuel to the fire!

I had learned about leveraging home equity, so we took out a HELOC (Home Equity Line of Credit) against our primary residence in 2018 for $95k, wholesaled our first property in December, then two weeks later, on New Year's Eve, purchased our first "fix and flip" property, again not knowing anything about construction and renovations, only the painting of some cabinets I did at our own house! I went on Craigslist and Facebook, hired some people, got the renovation done and we were under contract to sell it for a $35,000 profit with six weeks of work. Everything was going well. However, we would have a setback.

We went under contract to flip another house in 2019 using the HELOC funds we had available again and the net proceeds of $35,000 from our first flip. We hired a general contractor for this second flip property because we were both still working full-time jobs, had a baby, still didn't know a lot about construction and this next project was a TURD! I wired the GC $25,000 as a deposit to get started on the demo and renovation after closing while I hunted for the next flip and/or short-term rental property and worked full time. I thought things were going well until I drove by the new property that was supposed to be getting renovated and nobody was there. I drove by another day and another day and another day, still nothing. It turned out that the GC did some demo, left all the debris in the back yard, was doing shoddy work, refused to pull permits although I was adamant about it and, after finding one of the workers involved in unsavoury activities as well as living in the property, I finally fired them. That GC then took off with the $25,000 after doing $4,000 worth of "work" and refused to give me

Sunny Daytona Beach, FL

my money back. He even went so low as to call the city to tell them work was being done without a permit there, even though he was the one who refused to pull them!

Stress levels were at an all-time high for me in our business and I was completely distracted at work because I had never come across a situation like this before. I didn't have the knowledge, skillset or time to do this renovation on my own or have time to hire all of the sub-contractors on my own. "I wouldn't even know how to hold them accountable," I thought. I had to fix this. I had to make a decision. By this time, our rental business had exceeded the income of my full-time job, we had savings built up and a majority of the funds available in the HELOC still if needed. I wasn't inspired by my corporate job anymore. I knew that if I were to step away from my job, I could grow the business by giving it my full attention. I could probably also recoup some of that $25,000 by being hands on every day at the job site, learning about code, renovations, the various trades and permitting. So, I took the leap!

On the 29th of June 2019, I left my job making nearly six figures a year, just one year after having purchased our first rental property and went all in with real estate! I got that project to the finish line and learned how to manage a full renovation. Our rental business also grew and we ended up moving into that house to recoup some of the money we'd lost with the contractor and rented out all three floors of our previous house. We were excited again and so proud of what we had accomplished in that time!

The next year was 2020. In March, we leased a second rental arbitrage unit and purchased a single-family home. That same month, I got a four-unit apartment complex under contract but needed access to more capital. I contacted one of the speakers from the wholesaling bootcamp I mentioned previously, which I'd taken two years before, and asked if he wanted to partner on the deal. We came to an agreement and closed on the apartment with no money out of pocket! In the start-up process for these new properties, I depleted almost all of my cash reserves between purchasing the single-family home (down payment, renovation, furniture) and starting the new rental arbitrage unit. Keri and I had thought we would make that money back very quickly since busy season for short-term rentals started that month. Little did we know the world would come to a standstill in April due to lockdowns from the pandemic. Our business came to a screeching halt, and we lost nearly $50,000 in revenue overnight. Every single booking scheduled between the last week of March through to the end of April 2020 all cancelled. It was devastating watching my phone light up that week with cancellation after cancellation. We recorded $0 of income in April and didn't know what we were going to do. Thankfully, bookings came back in May stronger than ever, and we now have a much stronger business because of it. We learned valuable lessons about taking big risks but using wisdom in having strong reserves for our business.

Today, besides the blessing of wisdom gained in this process, we can also say we paid off the remainder of Keri's student loan debt (~$150,000), we had our second child, and Keri was able to leave her job and be a stay-at-home mom. 2021 was a great year! As of 2022, we have now automated the majority of our business, we have over twenty units in our portfolio, our homes are worth nearly $5million, have generated well over a million dollars in revenue, have begun to manage (co-host) other people's short-term rental properties and revenues next year are projected to break through that million-dollar mark.

We were blessed throughout the ups and downs and, if it weren't for the wisdom and grace God gave us during the hard times, we would not be able to have the life we have today. I'm thankful for the opportunity to now help others get started in their short-term rental journey.

So take that first step, stick your neck out there, squash that fear because, if I can do it, you can too.

ABOUT THE AUTHOR

Chris Miller is the founder of NuWave Properties & Investments LLC, is a short-term rental manager, coach and speaker. He has completely renovated dozens of homes to create unique and memorable spaces for guests. Chris also enjoys helping busy professionals and individuals get started in the short-term rental space to create secondary or even primary sources of income, regardless of whether they currently own rental properties or have any experience.

Chris believes that each person has the seeds of greatness inside of them; they just need some encouragement and confidence to take the first step, like he needed. Chris loves to share his real-life failures and successes to expedite the learning process for others, so they understand mistakes are okay and getting started is not as scary as it seems! He enjoys discussing and showing people how he had no experience or knowledge of construction, hospitality, or short-term rentals when he got started either. He has since scaled his business to over twenty properties generating over $1million of revenue, now owns multiple businesses and has created a net worth of over $5million, but believes his biggest achievement is helping others get started and have success through short-term rentals!

Chris was able to achieve financial freedom from his corporate job as a financial centre manager for a major bank through short-term rentals in just over one year after purchasing his first rental property without any prior experience. He now lives in Daytona Beach, FL with his wife, two children and dog Chipper, where they enjoy their time at the beach and have a goal to visit all of the national parks!

Links: https://linktr.ee/chris.miller

CHRISTIANNE CRUMP

FROM TAXES TO FRIENDS

Taxes and retirement – these two words sum up why my husband and I decided we should get into short-term rentals. He had been wanting a retirement strategy other than the stock market and a new accountant we'd switched to suggested we look into short-term rentals. The next thing I knew, we were remodelling our lake house and looking to buy real estate. It feels vulnerable and a little embarrassing to share the naked truth that it was a financially driven business decision for us – no warm, fuzzy story, just accounting. I'm laying all this out there on the off chance that someone else in the room – maybe you, my reader friend – can relate on some level. While it's true that the start of my journey as a host began as a business decision, it has evolved from numbers on a statement to faces, names, friends and guests.

I can clearly remember one night that now seems like a crossroads moment. It was well past midnight, and I sat in the dim light of one lamp and the glow of my laptop. My mind was flooded with emotions and questions. "How does Airbnb work? Can it really be profitable? Is it realistic to think I could be successful as a host even though I have zero real estate or hospitality experience?" I remember the feeling of my chest tightening and my pulse quickening as the stress of the project I was contemplating began to sink in and affect me physically as well as mentally. A concoction of fear, excitement and adrenaline kept me researching deep into the night.

By the next morning, I knew a few things. First, I knew I was "all in" on short-term rentals and failure was not an option. Second, I was keenly aware of how much I *didn't* know. Third, I knew I needed to create a plan for getting knowledge as quickly as possible. Fourth, I knew that to qualify for tax benefits that year, I had to get a property "in service" before the end of the year, about three and a half months away.

Thankfully, we live in the golden era of the information age and, between social media, the internet and podcasts, I was able to start bingeing content at a freakish rate. Eventually, I settled on a few favourite gurus whom I tuned into regularly, and a short time later, I joined a mastermind group run by one of them. The mastermind gave me a built-in sounding board for my questions with people I knew I could trust, and who could give me answers based on their experiences. I can say with one hundred percent sincerity that there's no way I'd be where I am today, have the knowledge I've gained, or have the network of STR friends I have, if I hadn't joined that mastermind.

OUR FIRST GUESTS

Every host dreams about what it will be like to welcome their first guests. The carefully decorated home will be immaculate. The coffee bar will be fully stocked. Perhaps a cute welcome gift, note and locally sourced snacks will be set out. Everything will be perfect! The guests will walk in and instantly be thrilled they booked your home. Their stay will come off without a hitch and they will leave a thoughtfully written, glowing review. Isn't it great to have a dream?

I am happy to report that I have had guests who have

Construction Chaos

experienced something similar to the charming scenario above, but my first guest stay was quite another story. Do you remember how I confessed we launched into our short-term rental journey for tax advantages and retirement purposes? Do you recall I discovered we needed to put a property into service before the end of the year for tax advantages? To meet this deadline, I created an LLC and immediately put our lake house into service. Did I have a listing on Airbnb or Vrbo? No. I did nothing but register an LLC, create a rental agreement, and spread the word that we were open for business. Getting a property in service before the end of the year – check!

As an aside, I do NOT recommend this to others; it was a total newbie move. I should've got our tax permits, bank accounts and rental permit lined up before we started accepting guests. Please spare yourself a headache and do it correctly.

Everything about our lake house was amazing. The whole reason we bought it back in 2014 was that we loved being on the lake all summer and having access to the ski resorts all winter. It was perfect in every way, especially if you're into commercial-grade mauve carpet, dated 1990's light fixtures, textured wallpaper, trim painted pale pink and cheap, hollow core doors. Are you getting the picture? Since we'd purchased the home, we hadn't updated a thing. Now that we were going to start renting it, I knew it needed a total interior remodel to fulfil its potential as a successful rental.

Full of enthusiasm for a new endeavour and too much time watching HGTV, I launched into taking down wallpaper, ripping up carpet, breaking down walls, removing dated tiles and generally making a huge mess of the place. The scope of our project included replacing all the flooring, replacing all the interior doors and trim, replacing lighting, repainting the whole interior, remodelling three full bathrooms, installing new countertops, repainting all the cabinetry and having a new fireplace installed with custom rock work. Have you ever done a remodel before? It's a disaster. It was in this glorious disaster that we welcomed our first guests. Why on earth would we ever consider hosting when our home was completely torn up? Well, we had a tax strategy session with our accountant, and he advised us that it was important to get two or three bookings before the end of the year to solidify our basis for the tax advantages we were hoping to capture. Ugh, there was no way our home would be done before the end of the year. Who on earth was going to want to book a stay with us?

This turned out to be a situation where the answer to our problem was found IN the problem itself. Problem – the home was torn up due to a remodel. Answer – see if any of the professionals working on our home would be interested in staying there instead of commuting to the job site. Lucky for me, the first people I extended the offer to immediately accepted! Dan, the incredibly talented craftsman I had hired to repaint all the cabinetry in our home, was more than happy to bring his wife up for a weekend.

To say things were less than ideal is a huge understatement, but we had the essentials covered: running water – yes; functioning toilet – yes (though only one out of three were still in place and working); functioning HVAC (heating, ventilation and air conditioning) – yes; a bed with clean bedding and a set of clean bath towels – yes. That's about all we had to offer at that point. Of course, I did my best to make them feel welcome and get the home as clean as possible, but it was almost the exact opposite of the picture-perfect start I'd imagined for our first guests' stay. They were such good sports about the whole thing, though. Dan, in his good-natured way, reassured me that after a long career of working on construction sites he felt completely at home in the construction chaos. Right then and there is when my hosting journey took a shift from being just about taxes and accounting to being about people and guests.

I had a lovely time hosting Dan and his wife. In fact, it worked so well that I was able to repeat the whole process twice more with other members of the construction team before the end of the year. Ultimately, it turned out to be a winning outcome from every angle. Our accountant was satisfied we'd positioned our new short-term rental business well from a tax perspective, I was able to get my feet wet as a host in a low-pressure environment, and my guests were able to enjoy the scenic beauty of our area.

While this is a fun story, it also illustrates a key trait of successful hosts – creative problem solving. I feel confident in saying that every host you'll ever meet has at least a handful of crazy stories where things went wrong and they had to work out a solution under stressful conditions: water heaters leak, appliances break, furniture gets broken, internet goes out, smart locks fail, guests get lost, toilets get clogged, issues come up with cleaners, etc., etc. Shoot, I've already dealt with almost all these issues, and I've only been hosting for a relatively short time! The key to handling these situations with grace is good guest communication and having a good team in place. Generally, guests are understanding, as long as they can see you are actively working on a solution and you're keeping them in the loop with how things are progressing.

THEN THERE WAS TWO

One of the benefits of coming into hosting from a business perspective was that we had a business plan from day one. For us, that plan was to acquire and launch at least one property a year for the next ten years. 2021 was taken care of with our lake house, but 2022 was right around the corner and we needed to set ourselves up to make a move. On the 6th of January 2022, opportunity came knocking when an agent we'd developed a relationship with sent us the listing of an ocean-front home in Gulf Shores, Alabama.

She was an adorable pale blue beach bungalow with enormous floor-to-ceiling windows and stunning ocean-front views. The original owners had only used her as a personal second home, and she glowed with the pride of ownership and a lifetime of family memories. Our purchase unfolded much like the stories filling the news during 2021 and 2022. Shortly after submitting our offer, we were informed that there were ten competing offers. Thankfully, our stellar real estate agent helped us write a strong offer and connected us with an excellent local lender. With those two things, and some heartfelt prayers, we were grateful to hear a few hours later that our offer had been accepted.

The goal with a new short-term rental (STR) property is to get the home ready and listed as soon as possible, so bookings can start paying the mortgage and expenses. For us, that meant everything from the 7th of January, when our offer was accepted, to the 22nd of March, when we welcomed our first guests, was an absolute flurry of activity. Immediately after the purchase was finalised, my boys and I flew down and spent four weeks in Alabama sorting through what was left behind in the home, bringing in new housewares, furnishings and decor, interviewing and hiring cleaning and maintenance teams and exploring the local restaurants and attractions. I did so much shopping for the home that my credit card was frozen for suspicion of fraud twice and my kids nicknamed me "two carts" because we couldn't go anywhere without needing *at least* two shopping carts. Desperate to spare ourselves two trips to the same store, we frequently crammed our little rental car to the point I couldn't see out of the rearview mirror and the boys were squished in the back, sitting on pillows and blankets with a sea of housewares packed in around them. We can all look back on those weeks and laugh, but putting together a property is a *lot* of work and only those who have been through the process can truly appreciate what it takes to make a home ready to start welcoming guests.

THE BUSINESS OF THE BUSINESS

Buying and setting up properties is only a small fraction of the total hosting journey. Once the excitement of a purchase and the fun of decorating are over, we all transition into the day-to-day operations of property management. This phase isn't nearly as glamorous, but it is where the brunt of the business occurs.

If I'd thought navigating the decision of choosing the right mattress or pillows for our property was bad, it was nothing compared to the pain of deciding what property management software to use. Did you know that there are over eighty-five different property management software companies out there? Can you imagine how much time it would take to track them down, research them, and decide which was right for your business? The struggle doesn't end there, though. Smart hosts who want to optimise their business also need to consider utilising tools for other aspects of their operations: channel management, accounting solutions, cleaning and property care, furnishing and consumable buying, digital guest guides, direct booking websites, guest vetting, third party damage insurance, dynamic pricing tools, smart home automation management, smart locks, property insurance and more!

In the early phase of my journey, I didn't have the time to properly research all the different options because I was already buried by ten thousand other decisions and tasks competing for my attention. As a result, the initial decisions I made were based on what I'd heard other people were using as opposed to my own research.

When the dust settled, and I had a chance to catch my breath, I began to second guess the decisions I'd made due to herd mentality

Offer accepted in Gulf Shores!

for a few reasons. First, as I started researching, it became apparent that I lived in an STR bubble. Most of the hosts I associated with all used the same STR tools and knew very little about the other options out there. Once I started looking, I was stunned to learn how many different options there were. Up to that point, I didn't know how much I didn't know! Second, I decided I didn't want to use tools someone else had decided were perfect for *their* business. My business wasn't their business and never would be. My goals and plans are unique to me, and I needed to make sure what I was using would move me in the direction I wanted.

Have you ever noticed that as soon as you buy a car you start noticing the same model of car all over town? In a somewhat similar way, as soon as I started seriously researching STR tools, it seemed like everywhere I turned I saw hosts asking the same questions and trying to find the best choices for their businesses as well. Conversations were sprinkled all over social media with hosts asking each other questions about what tools they were using.

"Has anyone ever used company X? Do you like it?"

"What company are you using for XYZ?"

It was obvious that many other hosts were trying to optimise their businesses, but they were going through the same painful decision-making process that I was. The more I researched, the more I realised it would be helpful if I had a way to organise and share the information I'd gathered with the STR community. That's when the concept for STRHUB.com was born.

In the months since then, I've continued my research and worked with a team of developers to create the website I wished I'd found in the beginning. We have built a space to help investors, hosts and property managers discover choices they may not have been aware of, and view side-by-side comparisons of different companies. Knowing that no matter how many product demos I watch or how much research I do, I can never find *all* the information about *every* company, and seeing how eager hosts on social media are to answer each other's questions and share knowledge with their peers, it was obvious there needed to be a way for hosts to contribute to the site as well. In that sense, STRHUB.com isn't *MY* site, it's *OUR* site – for STR professionals, by STR professionals. The goal is to help short-term rental investors, owners, co-hosts and property managers find the right tools for the unique needs of their STR business with confidence and efficiency, and create a community for them to share their knowledge and network.

When I launched into this project, I didn't fully appreciate how enormous the task would be or how dynamic the STR industry was. There have been a dozen or more times when I think I've got a handle on all the STR-related companies out there, and then someone tells me about another. With travellers spending billions of dollars on short-term rentals each year and double-digit industry growth, venture capital has been pouring into companies, and the rate of innovation and new start-ups is dizzying.

It seems fitting that my journey in the world of hospitality has been changing just as fast the industry itself. What was first about taxes and retirement, quickly became about hosting incredible people and discovering a whole new network of STR friends. While I still love serving my guests, I'm also excited to be able to help the fantastic community of investors, hosts, co-hosts and property managers around the world. With tens of thousands of new listings going live each month, those who want to maintain a competitive edge will be those who stay up to date with the latest changes and newest offerings. Thankfully, you don't need to feel like you're in this alone! We'd love to have you join the conversation and contribute your knowledge at STRHUB.com. See you there!

ABOUT THE AUTHOR

Christianne Crump is the founder of STRHUB.com, a website that connects property managers and hosts to the tools they need to succeed. She is a voracious learner who spends her days researching the latest products and companies in the STR world. She loves speaking, sharing her knowledge with others and networking with other short-term rental owners.

She started her hosting journey in the fall of 2021 and has found that it fits perfectly with her natural passion for helping others. In addition to her work on STRHUB.com, she currently owns and manages properties within an easy drive of her home and also over 2,200 miles away. With each of her properties, her focus is on creating beautiful, safe and delightful spaces. By having warm and inviting homes, she lets guests know they are welcome and appreciated the moment they walk through the door.

When she's not working, Christianne enjoys travelling and exploring new places with her husband and three boys. Like all savvy hosts, though, she knows how to maximise the tax benefits of a travel-related business, so you can be sure she's going to spend a bit of time looking at local real estate listings while she's away having fun.

Christianne's top three dream property locations are:

1. Ocean-front home on Kaui, Hawaii
2. Chateau in France
3. Riverside lodge in the Rocky Mountains

Christianne loves to connect with other short-term rental hosts, owners and property managers. Find her on your favourite social media platform!

Links: https://linktr.ee/christiannecrump

DAVE AND KIM MENAPACE

SUNNY DAYS AND SKI CHALETS

DAVE

Our love for STRs started on Cape Cod. After college, my friends and I would frequently vacation in Dennis, MA, where my friend's grandma, affectionately known as Grammy, had a house where I would crash on the floor, futon and even a tent in the backyard. Grammy was the most hospitable host that anyone had ever met, greeting us with her famous homemade peanut butter puffed rice treats upon arrival, setting up dinner for us on the back patio when we got back from the beach, letting us litter her lawn with our parked beach cruiser bikes and never once complaining of loud boys in their twenties having little to no regard for the sound they made day and night. She was just happy that everyone was together, in her company, and creating memories together.

KIM

When I entered the picture, Dave talked about us going to the Cape for the 4th of July holiday months before it was upon us. He even bought me my own beach cruiser in my favourite colour, teal. The first summer I joined him, his crew and Grammy for a Cape holiday, I got to experience Grammy's hospitality, the simple joys of drinking coffee on her front porch, playing corn hole in the yard, eating lobster rolls at the Summer Shanty, drinking mudslides at Sand Bar, and riding bikes to West Dennis Beach where the boys would play spike ball and us ladies would chat while we sunbathed. We would go to the bars at night to dance to live music at Sundancers. It was one of those places where your flip flops stick to the floor from spilled drinks due to very sloppy dancing. It was the epitome of a good time in your twenties, although Grammy, a spritely woman in her seventies, did join us on the dance floor one night, a night which we'll never forget.

DAVE

When we entered our thirties, things were looking a bit different. We were married, owned a house, two Great Danes and were expecting our first child. We decided it was time to rent our own place near Grammy. A few months before that holiday, Kim stumbled on a small cottage for sale in the area that had been sitting on the market for months. The listing stated: "strong rental history" and that the cottage was being sold fully furnished, which piqued our interest. There was an open house that weekend, so we decided to attend. Saturday came and so did a snowstorm. Kim started to get cold feet, claiming it was because of the snow, although it was also the idea of actually buying a beach house, but I insisted we still went. We drove by a number of other houses for sale to kill time before the open house. We arrived right on time for the open house and did our rounds. We found out later that we were the only people to attend the open house all day. The cottage was only 476ft, so it was a quick tour. It was quaint, in a better location and at a better price than any of the other houses we drove by. We got back in the car, and I turned to Kim and asked, "What do you think?" With a slight smile and a wave of confidence, Kim replied, "I think we should go for it!" Kim is definitely not the spontaneous one of the two of us, so her unwavering certainty gave me reassurance. We started brainstorming ideas for names for the cottage on the drive home and landed on "Sunny Daze Cottage" after our Great Dane, Sunny.

KIM

We closed on the house on the 25th of April 2019, which happened to be the first day of our third trimester with our son, Logan. We planned to "holiday hack", using the house for a couple of weeks ourselves then renting it the rest of the season to cover all expenses. I had seen a friend's parents do that themselves for the last twenty years and now they have an amazing beach house on the coast of Maine that is fully paid off that they get to enjoy themselves in their retirement. I saw the benefit of making simple and smart moves early in life paying dividends later and I wanted that for us and our kids while experiencing amazing holidays and making memories along the way.

With only a few weeks before the peak rental season, we wanted to move quickly to get some shoulder season bookings under our belt and build up both our confidence as hosts and our reviews on Airbnb. We learned that fully furnished doesn't mean rent ready. The days were long, beginning at 6am and wrapping up at 11pm with frequent trips to local stores. The sellers were kind enough to give us some tips and content to start building our listing. We took their version of the Welcome Binder and put our own, unique spin on it, trying to capture everything we wanted our guests to experience in one of our favourite places on earth. Friends booked the first few weekends in May and provided helpful feedback and then in June we had our first guests who were complete strangers.

Kim & Brooke at Sunny Daze Cottage, Dave & Logan at Logan's Lodge!

We were nervous, excited and on edge before, during and after their stay. They turned out to be a lovely young couple with two dogs on holiday from Boston, and actually were friends of a friend from work, reminding us that the world is small and hosting through Airbnb doesn't have to be impersonal.

DAVE

That first summer of hosting was a whirlwind with both getting our sea legs as hosts and welcoming the birth of our son. I'll never forget being in the hospital the day after Logan was born, messaging with a guest who had left two rings at the cottage and not believing us that our cleaners only found one. The very next week, a tornado hit Cape Cod, which was very uncharacteristic for the area. While still on my two-week paternity leave, I headed down to the cottage with a chainsaw in tow to clean up the fallen tree that had broken the door to our outdoor shower and a storm window in the kitchen, but thankfully nothing else.

The rest of the rental season went relatively smoothly, with bookings rolling in through the end of October. We scheduled some maintenance projects in November and breathed a sigh of relief as we entered the off season with enough revenue to cover all expenses until we started renting again in the spring. In fact, we had made 60% more revenue than the previous owners had renting on Airbnb!

KIM

That December, Dave and I decided to head to the cottage for a getaway weekend. Someone had given us a gift card to The Ocean House, a well-known high-end restaurant about a mile from our house and we were excited to finally use it. While driving down to the Cape on that grey December day, Dave insisted we listen to this new audiobook he had discovered, *Rich Dad Poor Dad*. I was captivated within the first five minutes. As a studious kid and young adult, I greatly valued academic success and wore it as a badge of honour. Hearing how successful the "poor dad" was in business, investments, real estate, and with only an eighth grade education, blew my mind. Dave and I strategised how we could invest more in real estate in the years to come. Our modest plan to just cover expenses started to transform into something much bigger.

DAVE

In our quest for more knowledge on real estate investing, we started to listen to the Bigger Pockets podcast and stumbled on an episode with Avery Carl, an STR investor in the Smoky Mountains, and now one of our fellow authors in this book. In that episode, we learned that you can get a holiday home loan for only 10% down. We didn't know this at the time we'd bought our house and had put 20% down. We asked our mortgage broker about it, and he confirmed and said we couldn't buy another beach house in the same market that way, but we could buy, say, a mountain house, as underwriters would find that reasonable. We had been having holidays at Kim's parents' house in Maine for years and had talked about getting one of our own as our family continued to grow. We wanted to make memories of snow-filled holidays in the mountains and get our kids on skis as soon as they could walk. We also wanted to leave our kids a number of properties as part of our legacy so they too could enjoy these beautiful places with their kids and grandkids. So, in early 2020, we started shopping around for mountain houses.

Our hunt for a mountain house didn't go far in 2020. We toured some properties and drove by others for sale to get a feel for the different areas in Maine in New Hampshire. We analysed properties, ran our numbers, talked to realtors and property managers in the area to pick their brains. We ultimately struggled with how to fund our next STR and used the exercise largely as a learning experience to tap into when we picked this back up later.

KIM

Then, in March of 2020, the COVID pandemic hit and knocked the world off kilter. We were grateful we hadn't just recently bought a mountain house with all of the uncertainty around the pandemic and how it would affect travel. We were, however, concerned about how this would affect Sunny Daze Cottage. We had reset our expectations and planned to not make money on the cottage that year. In fact, we were excited at the prospect of spending the whole summer there. Except, nobody cancelled. Instead of slowing down, Cape Cod rentals became hotter than ever. The calendar stayed booked from May through to October and the shoulder seasons had even higher occupancy than the prior year! We found ourselves in a situation where revenue increased by another 30% from the previous year, while also getting to spend sixteen days on holiday at the cottage during the busy summer season. That holiday was our favourite to date. We had sunny, clear skies every day, temperatures hovered around eighty degrees, our now one-year-old son loved playing in the sand and surf at Sea Street Beach, and we ate out at any and every restaurant that offered outdoor seating. We would bookend the day on our fantastic screened porch with coffee in the morning and wine in the evening, often having neighbours join. It was just the break we needed from the burnout we were feeling from working overtime at our jobs while caring for our infant son with day care centres being closed. The guests, friends and families we hosted that summer also echoed our sentiments and it was a true joy of ours to provide that escape for them.

The 2020 season came to a close, and on our first visit to the cottage in the off season, usually in late October, we love the feeling of picking up the guest book we leave on the entry table and reading all of the handwritten notes and stories guests left throughout the season. That year, on a rainy summer day in July we even had a marriage proposal in our kitchen! The thought of that makes me smile every time, that our cottage will always be part of that couple's love story.

DAVE

In early 2021, I became interested in learning more about long-distance investing, specifically the BRRRR (buy, refurbish, refinance, rent, repeat) strategy. With a young toddler and another baby on the way, Kim took a back seat on this endeavour, focusing on the pregnancy, Sunny Daze Cottage and advising that our life savings were off limits for real estate investing. I took six months to learn all about creative financing, how to build an out-of-state team, how to leverage equity, debt, partnerships and how to analyse markets. I leveraged equity from Sunny Daze Cottage, which had grown handsomely thanks to the worldwide pandemic, partnered with a close friend and began BRRRR-ing out of state in Chattanooga, TN. In total, we did five deals together and still hold those properties as long-term rentals. That exercise of strategic and creative financing, along with learning how to build and manage a team, became an invaluable and powerful skill set, propelling both my investing career and my role as a realtor, helping clients finance their investments.

KIM

Dave's BRRRR and long-term rental experience taught us that we are far more passionate about short-term rentals over long-term rentals. They are more personable. They are more fun. They require creativity. We find it way more enjoyable to craft amazing holiday experiences at our homes rather than providing people with primary housing. Yes, they can be more work, but they are also more lucrative in a variety of ways, which benefits our family and our long-term goals.

DAVE

I went on to get my real estate licence in the autumn of 2021, just before our daughter, Brooke, was born. It was a natural progression given my passion for investing and the various benefits that being an agent provided. With more tools in my toolbox, I picked back up our search for a mountain house and Kim was on board. I had learned how to find off-market deals from my investing in Chattanooga and started reaching out to owners who had purchased homes we were interested in back in 2020. Many owners didn't reply, but one did. These owners entertained the idea as they had personal reasons that prevented them from using their mountain home near Sunday River Ski Resort. We and the sellers came to mutually agreeable terms and, as part of the purchase, we included a free Cape Cod holiday for them with a dinner at The Ocean House on us. All parties were truly ecstatic. This home is now called Logan's Lodge. It sits on six acres and boasts a cathedral ceiling with a window wall

Logan playing at the Sunny Daze Cottage beach!

showcasing a stunning view of Sparrow Hawk Mountain. It is an amazing escape and it allows us to spread our love of hosting and offering guests amazing holiday experiences.

KIM

Venturing into a mountain house rental definitely pushed us out of our comfort zone. Deciding which cosy mugs to purchase for people to enjoy coffee by the fireplace and mounting my grandfather's antique skis from the 1940s on the wall of the Great Room was the easy part. The hard parts are the challenges that come with having a private well in the middle of one of the worst droughts on record, and the additional maintenance and upkeep for things like the hot tub, snow removal and frequent window cleaning for the window wall of the Great Room. We also had to adjust to the different types of guests you get at a larger house in a different market. They've all been learning experiences that we've taken in our stride, and we always try to do right by the guests and ensure they have an enjoyable stay in our home. As empathetic people, it can really hurt to have a guest not enjoy their stay, especially if something that did not go well was something within your control. We have learned to take those as lessons, do better and not beat ourselves up about it.

DAVE

What I love about operating this home is that we were able to apply nearly four years of STR experience as hosts and augment our systems and processes to make this home a smoothly operating business. We dialled in our tech stack and automations so we could spend less time on mechanical tasks and more time on our personal touch as hospitable hosts. We consulted our cleaning company on furnishings and set up. We applied a usability experience lens to our designing the space so guests found the home both comfortable and functional. Getting this home launched was certainly a labour of love, and it has paid off with favourable reviews. We got to enjoy it ourselves for a week in October 2022, attending the Fryeburg Fair, enjoying freshly baked cookies while bingeing on Disney movies and watching the autumn foliage come into full bloom right before our eyes off the back deck, making all the hard work worth it.

Launching our second STR served as a launch pad for The 5-Star Co-Host, our short-term rental management and consulting company. People from various parts of our network, friends of friends and complete strangers who found us through social media had started reaching out to us and asking questions. Do you recommend a beach house or mountain house for an STR? How much money can this house make? How much work is it really? How do I fund a down payment? I'm having trouble finding a Cape house to buy, can you help? Will you manage this house for me?

KIM

We love helping people and are able to do so through our co-hosting and consulting business, our podcast Hassle Free RE, and just simple one-on-one conversations over the phone or in line at our local coffee shop. We help you analyse, buy, set up, launch and manage your STR through our personal experience and our experience of helping others to date. Our co-hosting properties currently span from Cape Cod to Maine. What keeps us going is our excitement to serve more guests, but also to help more STR owners achieve their goals, whether it's viewing their investment as planting a seed to grow over the next thirty years or renting their house for the next ten and to then upgrade their holiday home to a larger primary home for retirement. We can deeply connect with those goals because we share them too.

ABOUT THE AUTHOR

Dave is a real estate agent, investor, co-founder of The 5-Star Co-Host LLC, and host of the Hassle Free RE podcast. He has hosted many big names from the STR world on his podcast and has served on panels as an STR expert.

In 2019, Dave and his wife, Kim, purchased their first STR, a cosy beach cottage in the desirable neighbourhood of Dennis Port, Cape Cod. Within the first year of owning that cottage, they increased its revenue by 60% from the previous owners and became repeat Airbnb Superhosts. Revenue has now doubled in a few short years while Dave and Kim still use the cottage themselves for two weeks of the peak season.

Dave now helps others analyse, buy and rent out holiday houses on Cape Cod through the co-hosting business he runs with Kim. Before Dave switched to being a real estate professional full time, he worked in healthcare data analytics. He's been able to apply that knowledge to his deal analysis and listing optimisation. Kim works full time at a tech company in Boston and applies her strategy, project management and operations experience from the corporate world to their STR businesses.

Dave and Kim also own and manage mountain houses in Maine and the surrounding states, so they can offer beautiful leaf-peeping weekends in the fall and East Coast ski vacations in the winter. At their core, Dave and Kim love offering amazing, quintessential New England holidays to their guests and light up when they hear how much a guest enjoyed their stay.

Dave and Kim use their Hassle Free RE podcast and YouTube channel to share content and resources to help others recognise their dream of owning a short-term rental. You can reach Dave and Kim and access their content through their Linktree!

Links: https://linktr.ee/Menapace_RealEstate

DIYA LIU

FROM HOUSE-HACKING TO HOST TO HOTELIER

My name is Diya Liu. I own three boutique hotels and a dozen short-term rentals across Texas, Arkansas, North Carolina and New Mexico. My name means "to inspire to travel across the ocean" or "to inspire others who are across the ocean". When I moved to the USA, the woman who stamped my passport said, "WOW! You were destined to move across the ocean!" I like to think that I was destined to travel.

IMMIGRANT BEGINNINGS

I credit my love of hospitality investing to my love of travel, and I credit my love of travel to my childhood. My botanist parents took me on countless adventures to collect plant samples in Northwest China during my younger years. I have fond but faint memories of riding in the back of a rickety bus, getting stuck in the middle of nowhere when said bus broke down, scaling mountains to find rare plant samples and eating wild strawberries that my mom had picked for me out of a hand-sewn kangaroo pocket on my dress.

When I first came to the USA, my parents took me on countless road trips to national parks every time they had a holiday. Half a dozen of us would pile into a car and a single motel room. Mom would pack a crockpot so we could cook ramen on the road to save money – she would somehow make it gourmet ramen with fresh veggies and meats from the local grocer. Mom would also pack her special bologna sandwiches for lunch with lettuce and mayo.[1]

Due to my extremely traditional upbringing, I was encouraged to pursue the classic definition of "success" – good grades, good schools and good jobs. I double majored in chemical engineering and biochemistry at The University of Texas in Austin, I received a full scholarship to go to law school, and I went to work at a prestigious international firm as a patent litigation attorney.

When I started practising law, I loved the mental challenge as well as working with some of the brightest minds in the legal industry. I worked on multimillion-dollar lawsuits and with technical experts from Ivy League schools on cutting edge technology. However, I was unable to travel or have much free time to pursue hobbies. I distinctly remember being uncertain whether I was allowed to go back to Austin for Christmas in my first year working as an associate. Some of my colleagues slept at the offices during busy times to save a precious hour of sleep.

The nine-to-nine grind eventually got to me. On my birthday in July 2017, I vowed to myself that I would find a way to be both location and financially independent. I told everyone that I was moving back to Austin, even though I did not have a job lined up yet. I told everyone I would start investing in real estate, even though I had zero real estate experience, zero connections, zero knowledge. I did eventually find a law firm job in Austin that matched my compensation in New York City and moved back. I bought my first house within a month of starting my new job.

---

1 One of our family friends discovered this amazing concoction on one of these trips. She was an only child, and she did not know how to cook. This recipe was a godsend. She survived on these sandwiches for months after this trip.

I stumbled my way into short-term rental (STR) investing. I have always loved design. Plus, I knew I could beat long-time real estate investors on STRs by being more tech savvy than they were, simply by understanding Airbnb and search engine algorithms. After renting out my rooms on Airbnb for much more than I was earning through longer-term leases, I was hooked.

I closed on my first beach condo in February 2019, despite scepticism from other real estate investors ("I can't fathom this rental making that much money!"). I bought the condo for $115,000 and projected to earn around $32,000 gross revenue my first year. After many weekends of sleeping among construction debris, I was able to push the Airbnb listing live in early March. I remember listing it and getting my first booking eleven minutes later for the first available date. What followed was a frantic scramble to get a dining table and bench before that first check-in forty-eight hours later. Despite the stress, I knew that my idea had been validated – and I was hooked. That rental grossed $41,000 in its first year.

What ensued was a buying spree fuelled by extreme frugality to save every penny I made as a lawyer with a healthy salary. I bought nine STR doors in under two years without any partners or creative financing. I reached over $100,000 of net STR income in less than thirteen months and was able to double that in less than two years. There were a lot of lessons learned in those first ten deals, I could write a full book about them. I will just summarise and say that there were many holiday breaks spent sleeping on a floor mattress or eating microwaved oatmeal in order to finish an STR setup.

All was going well until... COVID-19 hit. Cancellations started rolling in. New Mexico imposed a temporary ban on rentals shorter than thirty days. Despite the initial fear, I realised that this was a golden buying opportunity. I closed on two more STRs during April and May 2020, and these were my best deals to date. The first deal I bought for $94,000 and resold for $250,000 a year later. The second deal I bought for $200,000 and refinanced at an appraised value of $600,500 in July 2022. I was able to pull out over $450,000 of tax-free cash out of the latter deal.

Closing on a deal remotely from Park City... yes I used my laptop to write on!

"I will tell you how to become rich. Close the doors. Be fearful when others are greedy. Be greedy when others are fearful."
– Warren Buffett

I wish I could credit myself for what I did in 2020-2021, but I must give credit where credit is due. In the vein of Mr Buffett's advice, I bought in 2020 when everyone else was fearful of STR investing due to the pandemic, and I resold many of them in 2021 when the mainstream real estate podcasts popularised STR investing and everyone wanted to get in.

Many folks asked me why I was selling in 2021, but I did not want to tell them that it was because I feared a recession was on the horizon.[2] After all, I was not sure there would be a recession. No one can predict a market downturn or when it happens: we can only see warning signs and choose to sell too early or too late. *There is no timing the market.*[3] I probably sold some of my properties way too early, but I have zero regrets: I was able to jump-start my foray into hotel investing in 2021 by offloading some of my STR assets.

I did a variety of other projects in 2021-2022 that should probably

---

2 I did warn my STR Mastermind folks to be more conservative in analysing deals in 2021, especially when I started to see "no doc loans" Facebook advertisements popping up on my feed, and the frothy market due to prices driven up 20-40+% by historically low interest rates.

3 This is not financial advice, but I am personally going to be buying lots of hotels and STRs in 2023. We have created Welcome Capital to pick up many of these assets quickly.

be its own book: wholesaling an STR deal for $100,000 profit (easiest money I made in under twenty hours of work), owner financing STRs for 100% passive income and a flip that probably can count more as a "lesson learned" than a true success. What I learned was that (1) buy and hold real estate was a lot more forgiving than flips, and (2) if I ever were to come across anything that was not neatly in my "buy box", I can still bring value to the seller and the buyer by wholesaling it. For a more detailed explanation of my first ten STR deals and ten lessons learned, please visit workwithdiya.com to get a free PDF of these key takeaways!

FROM STR TO HOTEL INVESTING: THINK BIGGER, DO BIGGER

I have always wanted to get into hotels. I remember so many instances of talking about hotel investing out loud and people's scepticism towards it, including a moment when my date at the time said, "...[you] must think [you] have unlimited money!" in response to my statement that I wanted to get into hotel investing. Another interesting instance was when a syndicator insisted that I "needed" him to get into hotel investing. There was a specific moment of clarity when I decided that I needed to take massive action towards buying hotels: the 2nd of January 2021, I was swimming in Miami Beach and setting my intention for 2021. I decided that I will outsource as much as I can for STR investing to focus on hotel investing.[4]

Thus began my journey of acquiring hotels. I certainly did not have a linear path to success. I also started with a false sense of confidence that I already knew how to analyse or operate a hotel

4 Hotel acquisitions is a full-time job – I constantly tell my Hotel Mastermind folks that they must focus on hotel acquisitions if they want to acquire a hotel. It is not something you can dabble in along with trying your hand at wholesaling, flipping, co-hosting, STR managing and acquiring new STRs. One should focus all or at least a large majority of one's energy in acquiring hotels.

since I knew how to do so for short-term rentals. Reality soon set in that everything was different: analysing (or underwriting) a hotel, financing a hotel, insuring a hotel and operating a hotel. For example, a 600 square foot studio STR is not the same as a 250 square foot hotel room, and the revenue projection data between the two are not interchangeable. Operation expenses for a hotel are very different than those of STRs. Hotel and motel licensing requirements are different from those for STR permits. Lenders that finance hotels are often specialised lenders who only focus on commercial, if not hospitality, assets.

I sought out learning opportunities to improve my knowledge base along the way, but discovered a dearth of learning opportunities for boutique hotel ownership. To learn how to buy and operate a hotel or motel, either one is born into the business or one must attend a fancy hospitality school and obtain a degree for it. I had to learn by piecing together information from a wide range of educational materials as well as from my own mistakes and obstacles in acquiring a hotel. It was due to these reasons that I later created a Hotel Mastermind to make it easier for the next generation of hoteliers, and so I can find future partners to take down hotel deals together.

THE FIRST HOTEL DEAL: SELLER FINANCING A HOTEL

For my first hotel deal, I knew that I wanted a home run. I did not want something that would only pencil out if we became "A+ operators" – I wanted something that would make financial sense even if we were "C- operators". This is a concept that I often emphasise in my Hotel Mastermind: we do not want to assume we will outperform the market. The ideal hotel acquisition should be one where one can increase the valuation of the property without lifting a hammer. Perhaps the hotel owners are tired and only take in-person or phone bookings. Perhaps the hotel owners are only renting the property out part time when they are not on holiday.

Perhaps they do not understand search engine optimisation or online travel agency (OTA, e.g., Airbnb, Vrbo, Booking.com, Hotels.com) optimisation.

An important tangent. I analysed over a hundred deals and was under contract for six hotels (even more non-hotel commercial assets like RV parks and apartments) before finding this deal. A lot of folks come up to me when I speak at real estate conferences to ask how I find a good market. I find this question strange because I do not focus on "good markets" – I focus on good deals. *There are good and bad deals in every market.* Overpaying for an asset in a good market will make the deal a bad one. Conversely, underpaying for an asset in a mediocre market *might* make the deal a more palatable one. In this current market of sky-high interest rates, amazing financing terms will make a mediocre deal an amazing one. If you (the reader) do not take away anything else from my chapter, please take this one paragraph to heart. Bookmark it, recite it, print it out and frame it above your desk. Focusing on markets will make you a lazy analyser. Market is one out of over a dozen factors you must consider in purchasing either an STR or a hotel – do not be reductionistic in your hunt for a good deal!

Going back to our first deal, we found this deal through forging local broker relationships and getting a hint that this seller was looking to sell off market. The owners were a very kind couple who had limited financials on the property because they were older and also owned other assets in the area. While they lovingly took care of this property, they did not optimise the bookings or online presence of the property. I knew that while this project at forty-eight keys[5] was much larger than I'd wanted to tackle in my first deal, I decided to go forth anyway. Finally, I knew that at $750,000 for forty-eight keys, this deal was being sold at well below what the market comparables were for more optimised properties. In other words, this building would be worth more simply if we were to take the existing structure and bring the booking process online.

---

5 "Keys" is a common term in the world of hotels. It simply means number of units or doors.

Everything that could go wrong went wrong in this acquisition process. My initial partners backed out for different reasons, including not believing in this deal's potential. I could not get a lender to finance this deal because of the sellers' lack of financials plus this being our first hotel deal.

Luckily, my lawyer background came in handy. I negotiated seller financing at favourable terms for our team and found a business partner whose skills complemented mine. Another "lesson learned" throughout my acquisitions journey is that the team benefits from folks with a variety of different skillsets. I brought Mike on because his technical background would be useful in bringing the hotel operations into the twenty-first century through technology. I also knew that while my personality might be suitable for negotiations, it is not best for nuanced personnel training or management.

A bank approached us a few months after we purchased the property to offer refinancing early. Despite not having one year of financials, we were happy to take the offer since the interest rates were going up. I did not want to be forced to refinance when the interest rates would be above 8% interest. These were the final numbers:

Original Acquisition: $750,000
Renovation and FF&E:[6] $500,000
Appraised Value: $2,000,000

This deal turned out to be a great home run for all parties involved. The sellers were able to get the full-priced sale they'd wanted despite lacking solid financials on the property. We were able to get our first hotel deal under our belt. Our investors were able to get a bonus equity of $750,000 in the first year, plus additional tax benefits of real estate investing. Our guests are happy to have a renovated option to stay in when they come to visit the beautiful Ozarks.

This was also not an easy win. There were many uncomfortable

6 Furniture, Fixtures and Equipment.

My business partners closing on our third hotel in Blue Ridge Mountains!

moments, such as when Mike and I were living out of a 250 square foot hotel room and doing dishes out of the jacuzzi. There were the worst of times, such as when a roofer literally fell through the ceiling onto my bed while I was living out of the hotel room. I was on a video conference call with my Hotel Mastermind folks when I shouted, "Guys, I have to go. A contractor just fell through the ceiling onto my bed."

What is next? We have only renovated seventeen of the forty-eight rooms. We are combining some of the back building units into larger residences with full kitchens to target the Airbnb/Vrbo crowd. We are also building treehouses and A-frame cabins in the back bonus parcel of land (one acre of forest!) in phase three of the renovations.[7]

---

7 Want to follow along with this and other hotel projects? Sign up to get updates at workwithdiya.com.

THE NEXT BIG DEAL: LOOKING FORWARD

We picked up two more hotels in 2022. We could have easily picked up at least four more hotels, but I wanted to be very conservative in our parameters. Once one has hotel ownership "street cred", it is relatively easy to buy a hotel. However, it is hard to buy a *good* hotel deal. Late 2022 was a weird market where the interest rates skyrocketed, but the sellers were still not adjusting to the market changes by lowering their expected sales price. Despite our very strict parameters, we were able to buy a thirteen-unit beach motel for $371,000 on the Gulf Coast of Texas, walking distance to the beach. We were able to pick up a nineteen-unit hotel (or rather, a series of cabins and cottages) for $1,200,000 with owner financing in the Blue Ridge Mountains of North Carolina. In each of these deals, we were able to bring on cash investors who were interested in getting into hotels but were not ready to undertake their first deal alone.

Looking forward, I anticipate 2023 to be a narrow window of opportunity to buy hotels and STRs at a steep discount with creative strategies. I put together Welcome Capital, a $10million-dollar fund, to buy more hotels and short-term rentals faster. We wanted to take advantage of the current market cycle by buying more deals at a steep discount. As a bonus, we are adding travel perks for our investors so that they can take tax advantaged trips to their investments.

TAKEAWAYS

If you are to take three things away from this chapter, I would suggest the following list (disclaimer: not financial, investment or tax advice):

1. **Buy when everyone else is selling and sell when everyone else is buying.** Ignore the advisers, realtors and gurus who only make a buck when you buy an asset, since they will always tell

you to buy even if the deal is a dud. I told plenty of my students to not pull the trigger on a deal when I felt that the deal was not good enough under the most conservative of assumptions.

2. **Focus.** I find that often newcomers get starry-eyed and want to try every real estate trick in the book. Find one niche and focus on that – if you want to buy hotels, ignore picking up a fifth STR until you have picked up your first hotel. If you want to make it big with STRs, ignore flipping and wholesaling until you have mastered STRs.
3. **There are no good markets – only good deals.** It is extremely easy to be lazy and follow the well-worn path of where others have invested, but I have found that the best deals are not as obvious. In the same vein, do not overpay for any deal.
4. **Find your tribe.** Not everyone will work well with everyone, but no man (or woman) is an island. I have both an STR Mastermind and a Hotel Mastermind specific for our folks to not just learn theories, but also to collaborate with each other in order to tackle bigger projects.

Hopefully my chapter has helped you. If it has, please follow me on Instagram @DiyaESQ or add me on LinkedIn and tag me in a post with your favourite takeaway from this chapter. You can also find all of my social media links as well as get more information about any of my projects at WorkWithDiya.com.

ABOUT THE AUTHOR

Diya is an engineer/attorney turned real estate investor who spends her time travelling the world and buying boutique hotels and short-term rentals. Diya currently owns three hotels and a dozen STRs in TX, NM, AR and NC. She has done over twenty STR and hotel deals using a variety of different strategies: STR-flips, BRRRR (buy, rehab, refinance, rent, repeat), owner financing, wrapped notes, off-market acquisitions and private money. She also owns a 47,000 member Facebook group (Airbnb Professional Hosts),[8] teaches others how to invest in STRs and hotels, speaks on stage at real estate events and is the CEO of Welcome Capital, an STR and hotel fund.

Diya came to the United States at the age of eight, understanding only three words in English (duck, teacher and thank you). Her family initially lived on a graduate student stipend of $1000/month. Without the means to travel in luxury, her parents nevertheless instilled a love for travelling by renting a minivan to drive to national parks, cramming six people into a motel room and making ramen in crockpots.

Diya double majored in chemical engineering and honours biochemistry from The University of Texas in Austin, where she founded a fashion brand and ended up in fashion publications and news outlets such as *E! News*, *Marie Claire*, *Glamour*, *Teen Vogue*, *MTV Style* and more. She attended law school on a full scholarship at Brooklyn Law in NYC, and worked for an international firm, litigating multimillion intellectual property cases on behalf of Fortune 500 companies.

---

8 https://www.facebook.com/groups/AirbnbProfessional

Desiring financial and location freedom, Diya moved back to Austin to start real estate investing while working at a law firm and was able to scale from $0 to $100,000+ in net rental income in less than thirteen months. She quit her job once she reached nine short-term rentals. Today she takes over forty trips a year to find the best markets for investors to invest in. She loves to hike, eat too much food and dance, training over 500 hours a year in Latin ballroom (salsa, bachata, zouk).

Links: https://direct.me/diyaliu

ELA MEZHIBORSKY

I WANTED TO BE A HOSPITABLE HOST, I REALLY DID, BUT LIFE HAD OTHER PLANS

I could start off by telling you about the momentous call we received from Toronto deputy police on Christmas Eve 2018, but let's not get ahead of ourselves. I'll start (almost) at the beginning.

My husband, Anton, and I discovered the world of hosting by chance. We were big fans of the couchsurfing concept and proudly partook in the heartwarming community of hosts and travellers offering free accommodation, exchanging nothing but gratitude, stories, friendships and recipes (having grown up in Israel, Shakshuka was our signature dish to make, highly recommended!).

Travelling was great but we had to make money, and so, back in 2015, with backgrounds in sales, business and entrepreneurship, we set out to run our own digital marketing agency while taking advantage of the freedom it gave us to travel and work remotely, way before COVID-19 made it popular. Now, as much as we loved the couchsurfing generosity, the appeal of renting out our place while we were away, covering rent and maybe even making some extra cash on the side, was quite tempting. We soon realised that our appreciation and passion for memorable travel experiences, combined with a marketing touch, made the perfect recipe for a short-term-rental growth machine. We named it Quickstay.

The next chapter was a thrill as we went from one to one hundred, literally, managing properties left and right, learning the pros and cons of the arbitrage versus management models. We charmed new owners, befriended building managers and condo boards, grew the team, invested in promotion and embraced every automation tool out there to help make our jobs easier and the logistical operation smoother so that we could focus on being nothing less than hospitable hosts. We realised how important the extra touches were – the personalised messages and chocolates on pillows, the comfy sheets, the fluffy towels and all the little touches of luxury that guests would appreciate and not take for granted. Being friendly and courteous, going above and beyond, that was top priority. We were set on building a brand and we had a reputation to maintain. I remember the first time someone wrote in their review "I loved staying at a Quickstay". My heart skipped a beat as I reread it at least twenty times. *At a Quickstay* – if that's not the first step to success, I don't know what is!

We quickly discovered the potential in diversification and made sure our listings were featured across all the main OTAs. We invested in interior design and professional photography, getting better and better at promoting our brand, not only to guests but to inventory holders. We were charming and trustworthy, growing our portfolio and increasing our profits. Guests are happy, owners are happy, everybody wins, right? Not so fast...

With growth came growing pains. Tech and automation helped solve some of the scaling issues we were having (did you say no more copy-and-pasting "Thank you for booking" and "Welcome" messages??? *gasp*). The tools we didn't have, we developed! We joined forces with our good friend, dev wizard and cybersecurity expert, Roy Firestein, who could basically build anything. We added buzzer automation and cleaning scheduling to the mix, daily check-in logs and monthly revenue reports. We were unstoppable!

Our journey to grow a successful company, while never

neglecting the passion of being hospitable hosts, was interrupted by the one factor we least expected – the guests.

The basic concept of being a hospitable host assumes the guest to be a static entity while we do whatever we can to make their stay great, but that's a gross simplification. Any experienced host will tell you that guests are different, to say the least. They have different wants and needs, different ages and ethnicities, different purposes of travel. Guests are human beings and human beings are different. Guests are different in how they appreciate effort, in how they communicate (or don't communicate), and they're very different in how they respond to unexpected problems or inconveniences. With the goal of being a hospitable host, we put emphasis on training our team to communicate amicably, respectfully and effectively. We prioritised resolving problems, going the extra mile and mitigating conflicts as they inevitably occur.

When it comes to different types of guests, there's one more category I need to mention. Sometimes guests differ in whether they tell you the truth about themselves or the intention of their stay; some differ in how they plan to respect (or disrespect) your property, or whether they plan to follow (or ignore) your rules. Some even differ in whether they book under their real identity and whether they have any intention of paying for their stay. It's awful and painful to even think about, but in this beautiful world of hospitality, which I so desperately love, do we acknowledge that there's an ugly side? Dare we speak of bad guests?

When it came to "bad guests", scale and automation had an unexpected downside – we were getting less involved in lengthy conversations and intuition-based "screening" that supposedly helped filter for potential problems. Being so focused on providing the best guest experience, we fell victim to our hospitality getting abused. Local guests were throwing parties, young bookers were being loud and rowdy, and a supposed romantic couple's getaway ended up being a Halloween bash with more than fifty people inside a two-bedroom downtown Toronto condo.

As the list of stories kept growing, so did our strictness. We

Ela and Anton, early QuickStay days (2016), when the first date night away from our new baby, Ari, was none other than a trip to IKEA working to furnish another new property

worked hard to sort out the "bad apples" so that we could focus on what's important, on why we do what we do – the absolute majority of incredible guests, their joy and appreciation, the warm regards and thank you notes, the staggering reviews and the repeat customers – that's why I was in this business!

This was the start of what I now know to be a life-changing journey. I didn't know this at the time, but these early steps set us on a mission to fight the ugly side of hospitality, not just for Quickstay, but for the industry as a whole. But again, I'm jumping ahead, and no, I didn't forget about the Toronto police deputy call, we're almost there, I promise!

Effective guest screening, or what I then thought to be effective guest screening, turned out to be a slippery slope. We started adding strict language to our messages. There were more and more bold sections and capital letters. "No parties, no smoking, no outside guests". Then came the threats of punishment – fines, fees and evictions. As I was reading over these scary messages we'd started sending, I realised we were losing our sense of purpose, turning into bouncers and gatekeepers. Future guests were suddenly guilty until proven innocent. I had a very harsh realisation when I admitted that with this sort of attitude, I wouldn't want to stay at a Quickstay.

We made an attempt to loosen the rules and let the team use judgment, but I hate to say it, it didn't go very well. Some people are more trusting while others are sceptical and suspicious, not to mention that everyone has their own biases and preconceived notions on what constitutes a potentially-problematic reservation.

I tried the route of indisputable rules like "no outside guests", but that resulted in a not-so-tactful refusal by one of our agents to let a middle-aged guest have their daughter over for dinner, leading to a $2500 cancellation.

The last resort was one I really didn't want to use, it was the better-safe-than-sorry approach. I figured that, if all else fails, I'd have to identify the most common factors that led to problems and simply refuse to accept those reservations in the first place. It wasn't long until I had my list of culprits: locals, one-nighters, last-minute reservations and booking.com.

I knew some operators were taking this route. The thought process was simple: since parties are mostly thrown during one-night reservations, we won't accept one-night reservations. It could theoretically work but it didn't sit well with me and there were two reasons why I hated this approach. The first was the financial one: tightening our booking restrictions, simply put, will hurt the bottom line. Better-safe-than-sorry means blindly filtering out legitimate guests just because they fall into a certain group, and this means leaving good money on the table. The second reason was harder to explain, it was my gut that felt wrong refusing to host perfectly good guests that could otherwise become lifelong customers. It was the classic logical fallacy where 'A → B' does not imply 'B → A', meaning that even if we take all problematic reservations (aka "bad guests") and conclude that they mostly fall into one of the four identified groupings, it is wrong to go backwards and assume that a reservation that falls into one of these groupings is bound to be bad. I knew that I would not stand behind this approach in my company, and so, the problem remains.

I was getting angry, helpless and frustrated, fixated on this bump that we'd hit on our road to success. Anton had this assertive and inspirational saying about how we needed to focus on solving problems, rather than causing or dwelling on them. I first brushed it off with an eye roll. "Easier said than done," I shot back. But then he repeated it. Maybe it sounds more poetic in Hebrew, but the direct translation goes along the lines of "don't make problems, solve problems" and so I did.

We were too big for "gut-feeling" screening; totalitarian screening went against our values; and the better-safe-than-sorry approach didn't make sense – I needed a process, a systematic one.

The early version of Autohost was extremely simple. I come from a maths background and was so excited when I got to apply my favourite logic concept of decision trees to this problem we were facing. I'll also admit that I love drawing on whiteboards, especially if colourful markers are involved, so you can imagine how happy this next part made me. I took the marker and wrote my hypothesis on the board:

Not all guests are bad guests.

There was no clapping or gasps of admiration at this mind-blowing revelation I had just shared, my team already knew that. I continued:

The hard part is telling apart the good ones from the bad ones **before** *we let them in, and this is exactly what we're going to do.*

Now I had their attention.

I proceeded to draw a decision tree on the board. It had a few different factors, some obvious, some less so, but they were going to become the criteria with which we would assess the risk level of each booking (the maths geek in me had such a fun day that day!).

I divided risk factors into categories and with a simple algorithm (aka a set of rules) I was able to guide my team on how to systematically sort reservations into four risk groups. For the sake of simplicity, I named the groups Green, Yellow, Orange and Red, to indicate the level of possible concern and severity. We then put together a set of rules and questions that we were going to follow with each guest, depending on which group they fell into. The algorithm was well received by the team, we tested it for a bit, and then gave Roy the go-ahead to automate it. Before we knew it, this magical tool took in a reservation, analysed the factors we identified as possible concerns and spat out the risk category so the agent could proceed with the appropriate level of screening.

Things looked promising! We stopped harassing innocent guests with extra strict rules and threats, and we were able to effectively direct the harsher messages and thorough vetting to those reservations that were bound to be riskier. Of those, some guests agreed to the rules and promised they'd behave (and most of them did), while others chose to accept our offer of no-penalty cancellation, politely acknowledging that this wasn't the right place for their stay given their intentions. I was ecstatic, the revenue kept growing, the team was happy and the cleaners loved us!

I wish I could end the story here, but I can't because we still have that phone call I need to get to. So, everything was going great, we were heading into the Christmas season of 2018, all our properties were booked up and all our guests were screened, what could go wrong?

Around 9pm on Christmas Eve, we received an unexpected call.

"Is this Quickstay? Am I speaking to Anton Zilberberg?"

"Who's asking?"

"This is Detective Sergeant Peters from Toronto Deputy Police. Am I speaking to Anton Zilberberg, owner of Quickstay?"

"Yes, sir, how can I help you?"

"Mr Zilberberg, we have a confirmed sighting of a known gang member, posing with automatic weapons on Instagram from one of your properties. Do we have your permission to raid the place?"
gulp

Needless to say, we gave our permission. If you ask me, Christmas Eve 2018 was the day Autohost was truly born. The next few weeks were intense. We collaborated with the police to discover a Montreal gang that had basically exploited our properties. The screening process, my pride and joy, ended up being our biggest vulnerability. I was devastated, but we're here to solve problems, not to dwell on them, remember?

This launched an in-depth cyber investigation that ended up revealing horror stories that I wouldn't wish on my worst competitors. We discovered that this local gang has been targeting our properties with bookings dating back as early as September of that year. The digital fingerprint we were able to follow identified that reservations made by the same group, all resulted in either chargebacks or suspicious behaviour. A further dive into our recent payment disputes correlated eleven out of fifteen chargebacks to that same group. The reservations, on the surface, were meticulously crafted with impressive and trustworthy-sounding cover stories.

One mystery that got resolved is worth mentioning. It was a nine-day stay in a two-bedroom condo, in a very trendy and vibrant Toronto neighbourhood, and, oddly enough, this one did not result in a chargeback. Full disclosure: it was an Airbnb reservation, so I don't know whether Airbnb then dealt with a stolen card dispute and had to take the hit. Their story was believable, they checked in, they didn't communicate much, and they checked out. The place was mildly trashed, traces of weed were found by the cleaners, and a few random items were stolen. They were clearly not the guests that we thought would be in there but they vanished after check-out, the account was unresponsive, and the damages were manageable, so our focus was to get it ready for the next guests.

The days went on, the incident was behind us and we didn't

2019 – Autohost in the making. Ela, Anton, Roy (and Lianne) working the weekend away to launch a passion project, dreaming to make hospitality safer

think much of it. Kids partying, fake account, the payment went through, we cleaned it up, whatever – I thought that summed it up. The only weird thing was that, at the end of the month, the electricity bill was through the roof (about triple the usual amount) and a quick investigation showed that the spike occurred during the days of this booking.

I won't keep you in suspense and just share that the police investigation we were helping resolve, once all the dots were connected, identified a trafficking ring that rented out multiple properties in that building, ran prostitutes and escorts across the various units, while our unit was the lucky one where they did the laundry 24/7.

I'll save you the details of another story when our team was called in to handle a disturbance complaint, only to discover those same gang members after having been evicted from another property just a few days prior. In this case, police later found stolen jewellery and a hefty amount of fentanyl inside the unit.

We lost over $25,000 that Christmas season; we lost three units under management; and we (temporarily) lost our faith in this industry. Fraud, abuse, criminal activity – that's a whole new level of bad guests I'd thought only happened in the movies.

My mind was blown at how big and common the problem was, and how much money and effort was wasted for lack of effective solutions. Operators, large or small, were helpless. Pseudo screening and holding your fingers crossed is not a way to scale a business, let alone in an industry that's fighting for legitimacy. This is when we took Autohost to a whole new level.

The rest is history, so I'll speed through it: I am now the proud co-founder and president of Autohost – a guest screening, identity verification and fraud prevention platform. We realised that the level of insight and threat intelligence that cybersecurity and automated screening can bring to the hospitality space is enormous. I'm excited to be providing the tools to help keep properties safe, guests happy and the industry flourishing. I'm proud to be advocating for screening practices that are effective, objective and non-discriminatory (because that's a whole other can of worms that I don't even want to get started on). I love that I play a role in ensuring hosts can focus on providing their guests with the best possible experience.

I started out as a hospitable host, but my journey continues by empowering others to be just that.

ABOUT THE AUTHOR

Ela Mezhiborsky is the co-founder and president of Autohost, a guest screening, identity verification and fraud prevention platform for hospitality. She's also the proud mom of two adorable kids, a world explorer, a kite surfer and an avid coffee drinker.

Ela was born in Ukraine, grew up in Israel, and immigrated to Canada with her family at the age of fifteen. After completing her Bachelor of Mathematics from the University of Waterloo and BBA from Wilfrid Laurier, she continued to pursue career growth while never neglecting her passion for travel. Ela started her professional career in the corporate banking industry, as a risk analyst, growing familiar and respectful of the power of the KYC (know your customer) concept. From joining an early-stage start-up to co-founding her own digital marketing agency, she discovered the potential and opportunity in combining all her passions, leading her and her husband to start their own STR management company, Quickstay, which quickly grew to become one of Toronto's leading high-end STR operators. With scale and success came unavoidable problems, exposing Ela and her team to the unfortunate and ugly side of hospitality – problematic guests, fraudulent reservations, parties, chargebacks and criminal activity. That, in fact, is why Autohost was born.

Having experienced the hardships first-hand, Ela strives to empower hospitality operators to employ ethical and effective screening practices, and to recognise the power of automation to help them grow and scale their business. At Autohost, she proudly manages the intersection of clients, product and operations, determined to make the world of hospitality better and safer.

Links: https://linktr.ee/elamezhiborsky

EMILE SAKHEL

REDEFINING THE AMERICAN DREAM

Most people have an image of what the American dream is, and this varies from individual to individual. Some quotes given to me from individuals asked to define it are:

"Having the affordability to do whatever I want, whenever I want, for as long as I want... (with moderation and discipline, of course)."

"Health, being comfortable, knowing you fulfilled your destiny inside your heart, having a true soulmate."

Some desire the bigger house, more money, no debt, paid off vehicle, multiple properties – the list goes on and on. This is a question I ask most people when I meet them, and many aren't sure how to even answer. The origination of this "American dream" was originally illustrated in the best-selling 1931 book *Epic of America* by historian and writer James Truslow Adams. He described it as "that dream of a land in which life should be better and richer and fuller for everyone, with opportunity for each according to ability or achievement."

In this chapter, the evolution of this "American dream" concept in my mind as I lived through various life experiences

Our family enjoying beach time.

has led me to where I am today, feeling grateful, blessed and humbled to have accomplished my "late adolescence goals", which at the time were to have a degree in anaesthesia, a prosperous marriage and beautiful and healthy children. Today, I continue to have deeper desires beyond what were once considered my long-term goals.

Our story kicked off organically as our relationship felt so natural and our perception in life was aligned. I recall a phrase I always told Sarah back in anaesthesia school, as we dated long distance for three years: "Honey, I'm on a train going 60mph, are you willing to hop on and go?" The answer was always, "Yes, my seat belt is on." In 2015, I completed my master's degree in anaesthesia and, shortly after, married my best friend and soulmate. Little did she know, this train after school was going to keep going 60mph. Within a few months of being married, we started to discuss and formulate new future goals for our life. We had a mutual interest in real estate and believed at the time it was one way to establish cash flow. We started looking, and quickly it presented itself, our first real estate mastermind. We joined a national group called Fortune Builders, which was tailored towards full active home rehabs in efforts of building capital to purchase properties and build passive income, which could ultimately result in a foundational family legacy that Sarah and I had envisioned on day one of our marriage! Investing in this programme was quite the chunk of change and a big commitment as we had just begun our life together.

Sarah often said, "I trust you, and will follow your lead." In the first two years of marriage, we realised that with our full-time jobs and the competition in rehabbing, it wasn't coinciding with the time commitments we were capable of providing. We continued to search and seek alternate ways of building our legacy. Somehow, every time we had evening discussions, our conversations always resulted in real estate as the common denominator. We had often talked about legacy building and hustled our way with work, day in and day out, rarely slowing down, and then it happened. The greatest gift of all, our first baby girl. We began to shift our focus back into real estate, the deep desires beginning to intensify. I woke up and began to seek what I had been missing in my life at the time, a coach. It was shortly after I had started looking that my coach arrived. In 2020, we joined a very specific short-term rental mastermind that was catered to building systems and automation for vacation rentals. My coach's philosophies with the "luxury home" niche arena struck close to home when I thought about my upbringing and cultural experiences. A larger home, fully loaded amenities with games, a pool, chef's kitchen and so on... and so it began. I learned the systems, mastered the process, created a product that delivered high level five-star services and launched our first vacation rental in Gulf Shores, Alabama, "Barefoot Bungalow".

The sequential concepts necessary in creating a "system" for me to run on automation was important, particularly since I continue to have my full-time position in anaesthesia. Below are a couple of key fundamentals that have led me to today's success:

1. Continued education/information and applying new knowledge:
   - Daily audiobooks and inspiring books began to shift my mindset. Authors such as Tony Robbins: *Unleash the Power Within*, Mike Michalowicz: *Profit First*, Dan Sullivan: *Who Not How*, Napoleon Hill: *Outwitting the Devil* are among the few that have transformed my mental state and prepared me to take the leap of FAITH.
2. Financial analysis:
   - Utilise third-party platforms such as AirDNA and STR Insights.

- Find homes on the MLS that correlate with your goals and bring excitement to pursue.
- Compare to top properties in the neighbouring area with similar bedroom/occupancy counts. This specific search on a geographical map then helps create a picture of what top performing properties could produce.
- These gross revenue projections, occupancy percentage and average daily rate data (ADR) are then inserted into a cash-on-cash (COC) calculator based on total capital acquisition costs: all out of pocket cost when acquiring the property to 'value adds' towards the property with furnishings/ renovations/amenities and so on.

In 2020, my personal goal COC (cash-on-cash) return was upwards of 40% – the previous property management company on Barefoot Bungalow had made 80k in gross revenue with its pre-purchase condition. Based on the skills created in analysing the home through AirDNA, my projections were 100k gross revenue with value-add design to the home. As we anxiously made our first full price offer, we knew we were just going to take the "leap of faith and learn as we go" mindset. We had the LLC set up shortly after. Our offer was accepted, closing was to be in February, and our goals were to launch prior to the spring break season on the 6th of March! Quickly, we realised we only had weeks to prepare, but wait, we're in Texas and we want to refurnish what was sold as a "turn key" home, find a new clean/maintenance team and learn how to build our listing with new photography, study the marketing strategies, set up the business structure appropriately and learn OwnerRez – a complex software system that would help us grow our portfolio in automation – all in three-to-four weeks with a four and one year old and full-time job? Wowza! Talk about an adrenaline rush!

We rented a sixteen-foot van and drove twelve hours to start our journey. On our way to Gulf Shores, our stressful first experience began. The previous management company had contacted our realtor and said they had guests staying in the property the weekend we were arriving, even though closing had been completed! Here we were, now seven hours away with a rented van full of boxes and furniture, and a second vehicle with our kids/parents following us. Sarah was in the background frantically arguing how we needed the guests to be relocated as we only had a certain amount of time allotted to turn over the home before heading back to Texas and listing to rent. Long story short, we informed the management company we could spend one night in a hotel, but the following morning the guests would need to have checked out and we would be moving in, and so it happened. The initiation of listing/optimisation began for me here:

- Time was created at the end of long twelve-hour workdays to create the listing on Airbnb/Vrbo and the local regional vacation website.
- Creation of organic Facebook ads on buy/sell/trade groups.
- Creation of campaign paid ads through the Meta business suite in Facebook.

In a short six days, our home was completed, set up and listed online. In managing the home, one of the most important factors attributed to the success of our portfolio of homes is positioning our property on page one through three on major online travel agency sites (Airbnb/Vrbo) by:

- Identifying unique amenities.
- Providing a well-furnished and designed home.
- Responsive communication to guest inquiries – an important factor when your property is being compared for travelling clients.
- For those looking to invest in vacation homes, active participation on your listing with title changes, photo arrangements, description alterations, pricing adjustments –a few ongoing changes that need to occur to optimise the listings position.

Fast forwarding to one year later, Barefoot Bungalow became a top ninety-eighth percentile performer in revenue for three-bedroom homes in all of Gulf Shores. Such an enjoyable and rewarding feeling, putting hard work into a home to provide ultimate luxury and comfort that sold itself on the market and became an instant top performing property. We realised we needed to duplicate this process until our personal goals were reached, but how could we acquire the capital to do so? We had an agreement to live on my salary within our means and utilise Sarah's income for investments until our investments could then acquire enough capital themselves to exponentially grow our portfolio.

As we continued to learn and fine tune our process, our strategic pricing tactics, marketing and performance was noted by many colleague investors. I began to be recognised more and more by my peers and fellow mastermind community. People began reaching out to me with curiosity... it began. Family, colleagues and friends would begin to tell me, "Emile, you shine when you talk about the real estate industry, you have so much energy and excitement, it's contagious." Comments were often reported, like, "How are you doing it? What are you doing to generate such high-income returns? How do you have nothing but five-star reviews?" Deep down, along the lines of that deep desire, I had always had the passion to teach, coach, lead, guide and serve. While in most eyes, the time commitments and time devotion in setting up our business model seems always about the money, my journey and mission is to redesign my time for intuitive fulfilment, in turn equating to joy, freedom and feeling alive.

I started asking myself, "Well, what has always been there for me?" and it was a simple answer: my roots. Growing up in the Middle Eastern culture with very traditional and strict religious family members seemed to have moulded me. My parents' involvement with the restaurant industry and catering to serve others in a professional and intricate manner with fancy choices was a natural gift they carried amongst themselves, and it was done with love. Over time, Sarah and I have created big ideas and goals. Mostly, to develop time and financial freedom to allow us to give in more ways than our current jobs. Sarah spends most of her time as a short-term rental specialist realtor in the Texas Hill country/coastal market as well as a luxury custom home builder. I work full time as a CRNA (certified registered nurse anaesthetist) and now manage a portfolio of homes with Host by Mira. One can imagine the hustle that we have recently endured.

This innate ability and natural passion to give to others has led me to this business model of Host by Mira. Being a hospitable host comes with having the ability to establish fast trust with our guests, through photos, concierge service calls, well thought out and designed homes catering, if not to all, most of each family's needs and desires. My goals are to have a family friendly environment in ways that allows all groups to not only feel welcomed into our properties, but greeted with cleanliness, luxury, design and awareness of such little details that were well thought of in efforts for travelling clients to make long-lasting family memories in each of our properties.

The high standards for today, and constantly evolving, is Host by Mira's portfolio, which consists of a total of nine properties, owned and managed. Most of the time delay in business growth has primarily been related to properly constructing specific goals for each property that "fits right" within our portfolio. The quality far exceeds the quantity of homes we desire to have in our company-wide portfolio. The opportunity to have nothing but unique luxuriously designed homes with fully loaded amenities – and be nationally recognised as such – is of primary importance with the brand Host by Mira. The website illustrates easy navigation for future booking clients and investors looking to partner with us with their portfolio of homes. We are now building our team with our in-house designers, back office, social media experts in marketing and increasing our local presence in Destin, Gulf Shores and Texas. Continued efforts are made daily to tweak and refine our concierge business, primarily partnering with local small business owners. Our intentions with the concierge service at Host by Mira is to provide invaluable handcrafted and personal planning for each family's requests and to be nationally recognised as a true five-star service company that cares deeply for every guest and their overall experience at each property. Some services that have become very popular include grocery shopping/stocking prior to your arrival, personalised in-home chef services, spa parties for families or larger groups, golf cart rentals and itinerary assistance with local activities.

While the fruits of our labour in being hospitable hosts is rewarding in many ways, it's hard to forget the one-off guests who scare many folks from managing properties. Our very first guest with the launch of our very first property, after our sweat, blood and tears were poured into it, left our home an utter disaster – from their children hanging on light fixtures breaking them in half, to the worst "brown" bathroom disaster you can imagine spread across the floors and walls of the master – and left us in awe of how this could have been done to a brand-new home. We quickly learned to appreciate and respect the tasks our clean crew had to endure in their daily work. Contrary to the horrific first guest story was a very personable and sweet young couple who had booked our waterfront property in Rockport, TX for their honeymoon. This booking was an opportunity to allow us to offer a service above and beyond what a hotel could, from baking and cooking a fresh assortment of goodies, to setting up a romantic champagne and rose petal display, ultimately welcoming and hosting this couple in a way of instilling lifelong beautiful memories. These moments, this type of hosting, bring the most fulfilment for me and carries the most weight for what Host by Mira's values stand for.

Ninja tip: for us great hosts out there who have this passion for service hospitality to our guests, it is essential to understand and adapt to ever-evolving updates in the industry. Tech companies allow for better home management and automation, providing more opportunity and time to focus on guest communication and personalisation to have continued success on a high level. Some personally recommended tech companies that have worked great for structuring our company include Stripe, AirDNA, STR Insights,

Host by Mira's business name is derived from our daughters' names merged. Its global message is catered towards providing a true hand-crafted luxury experience for all.

Remote Lock, Rankbreeze, OwnerRez, Ring, Schlage, ecobee, YouTube TV and ResortCleaning.

It is my recommendation to those who desire to be in the hospitality industry to start off on the right page, "buying right". Far too often I see everyday folks and investors purchase homes solely on the "desire" to rent and manage, without truly understanding how to analyse specific markets and potential, nor really having any desire for hospitality. Or undervaluing the importance to add value and design to a home. With the ever-increasing supply of vacation homes, it is now more important than ever to invest in homes that have unique characteristics and/or allow for value-add renovation costs to generate healthy revenue streams from a business perspective and lead to an overall positive guest experience.

To date, Host by Mira is becoming more and more recognised on social media platforms as entrepreneurs in various investor groups, acknowledging the level of detail and rigour required to sustain their portfolio of homes at the highest level. Host by Mira, in its short venture of going live, has become a seven-figure income producing business, has consistently proven to deliver the highest five-star service eliciting guest reviews, and it's now publicly being recognised. It's projections of reaching twenty-to-twenty-five vacation homes by the end of 2023-24 will be the breaking point in my bold short-term goals. These fulfilled goals will have provided me the financial freedom to begin delegating more of my time in a precise manner. To give above and beyond, cater to people on a personal and professional level, nurture, care and bring joy to others. For the many millions of people who work for a living, give their time up in ways they can't have back, my message to you is: contact me. When you're granted time off for a vacation away from reality, it is my duty and responsibility, my goal to ensure all efforts are made to provide you with all the comforts of a home you could imagine, moments of joy, relaxation and memories your heart desires. These moments, knowing your vacation is well spent at a Host by Mira property, creating lifelong joyful memories are exactly what brings me true fulfilment. The American dream, to me, is the ability to reach a level of personal financial freedom leading to time freedom, allowing my identity to be truly awakened, steering me in directions to continuously give and bring joy to all those I encounter.

My life motto is: "To live is to love". And with love comes fulfilment.

ABOUT THE AUTHOR

Emile Sakhel is the founder of Host by Mira – a boutique vacation brand that focuses on creating high-touch, luxury experiences for families from spa parties, to grocery stocking, to private chefs. Host by Mira goes above and beyond for their customers to drive home the mantra that "all elements of a vacation get to be a luxury experience". His five-star company focuses on beach markets in Destin, Gulf Shores, and the Texas Hill country and coastal areas. Beyond his work with his properties, Emile also provides consultation services for hosts who want to focus on high-touch experiences for their clients. In his work with hosts, Emile shares his "buy right" methodology and specific STR analysis process that teaches how to become a top property in their markets. In just two years, Emile has maintained consistent five-star reviews on his six-property portfolio and crossed the million-dollar mark in gross revenue.

Emile's commitment to serving people has always been present – whether it be from his Middle Eastern upbringing or his background as a certified registered nurse anaesthesiologist – hospitality and service have always permeated his life. Emile grew up in a household known for their hospitality, amazing food and large family gatherings. Coupled with his transition out of healthcare, he took his knowledge of service, community and hospitality directly into the short-term rental industry and started Host by Mira in 2020 with the intention to uphold the highest level of service possible for families.

Emile is married to Sarah, and is the loving father to daughters, Milania and Clara, whose names inspired the name of his company.

He and his wife, Sarah, are the powerhouse duo behind Host by Mira and are committed to creating unique handcrafted and designed luxury properties that are family friendly and allow for lifelong lasting memories to be made.

Links: https://linktr.ee/hostbymira

FOUAD BAZZI

THE DAD, THE HOST, THE INVESTOR

"...there was no way I was kicking those girls out of a home to be on the streets."

"The absolute truth is that I am a TERRIBLE landlord."

My name is Fouad (Foo-aad) Bazzi, and I am the founder of Crescent Retreats, a portfolio of luxury rentals in Scottsdale and Huntington Beach. Soon, we plan on hosting in Texas, Colorado, Utah, Washington and other states as well. Before I dive further into Crescent Retreats and our story, though, allow me to tell you a secret...

The absolute truth is that I am a TERRIBLE *landlord.* In 2019, I finally accepted that real estate investing would be my channel to generating long-term wealth. However, I also knew that I did not want to bury my passions of customer satisfaction and building brands. So, I did what every sane thirty-seven-year-old with three toddlers would do... I quit my twenty-one-year corporate banking career and bought a handful of single-family long-term rentals (LTRs) and opened a coffee shop with a kids' play place in Dearborn, MI, a suburb of Detroit.

Everything was going fine until a global pandemic came along and punched us in the face. Our landlord for the coffee shop was inflexible and we were on a statewide lockdown, which meant zero revenue coming in for several months. So, we negotiated out of the lease and closed shop. Simultaneously, a tenant of mine at one of our homes had informed me that he and his wife were separating and that they could not afford the rent. This tenant had two toddlers, and there was no way I was kicking those girls out of a home to be on the streets. So, I offered the family six months of free stay until they were able to find somewhere to move to. During that time, I knew this was not the path for me as I would never stronghold a financially struggling tenant to a rental agreement.

Fast forward to mid-2020 and we learned that our one-year-old daughter, Madina, was allergic to tree nuts. To battle those allergies and get her to food-freedom, we enrolled her in a food allergy programme in Long Beach, CA. The programme customised to her bloodwork dictated that we would have to visit every eight to ten weeks for four years. So, twenty-four visits to California from Detroit... and having been a banker, I started to do the maths:

24 visits x $5,000 per trip (airline, rentals, food, etc.) = $120,000 projected cost

Of that $120,000, we estimated $50,000 would be rental costs (because... it's California).

My vision really started to become clear at this point:

Real Estate + Customer Satisfaction (which is Guest Experience in the short-term rental space) + Building a Brand + offsetting $50,000 in expenses = **Buy a home in Huntington Beach, CA, and list it on Airbnb when we didn't need it, but use it when we visit**

CRESCENT RETREATS

When our first son was born, we had a holiday in a hotel when

Madina checking in for one of her quarterly visits to the Food Allergist.

he was four months old. We learned quickly that there was no fun in that! As soon as he was asleep, it was lights out and stay quiet so that we would not wake him up. We vowed moving forward to rent homes on Airbnb or Vrbo when travelling with kids domestically.

When it comes to spending money, I am a pretty frugal individual... most of the time! I do not buy expensive or a lot of clothes, I do not drive an expensive car and I do not buy material items. Where I do like to spend without a budget is on experiences and travel, including short-term rentals. As such, the more short-term rentals we would stay at, I would realise that our expectations were often unmet. Admittedly, much of this is likely my fault. Now that I understand the power of reading listing descriptions since I write them as a host, I probably made many assumptions when booking as a guest. Some assumptions I would make were: if I rent the most expensive house in the area, it must include:

- Amazing coffee;
- High quality, heavy-duty furniture;
- Luxurious, five-star hotel-like bathrooms with glass doors rather than shower curtains;
- Condiments, spice racks and all cookware to be included;
- Towels, napkins, toilet paper and paper towels.

Let's just say, shame on me for not reading and for making so many assumptions.

Of course, all these unmet expectations helped shape my strategy. With one of my goals being to build a brand and eventually achieve a greater than 50% direct booking ratio, I set the approach that our short-term rentals would include all of those items that I expected as a guest when paying top of market rates. Our anticipated spend on furnishing and designing our homes was

Luxury can be inside, outside, or both

budgeted initially at 10% of the purchase price of the home, an expectation that I learned from a legend in the short-term rental space. Luckily, because of some partnerships that we have been able to forge, we have been able to keep our total spend at 6% of the purchase price of the homes, but still furnish with luxury brands and heavy-duty furniture.

Two key items that have brought the most positive feedback via guest reviews and past guest rebookings are the comfort of our mattresses, and the high-end, whole-bean grinder coupled with the high quality coffee we provide.

Another key area of focus for us in differentiating our homes is the focus we put on creating guest stickiness. With all my prior professional experiences being so heavily dependent on relationship building, we are adamant about building relationships with our guests from the second they enquire or book. We do this by ensuring responses to all enquiries immediately, personalised welcome and thank you videos for booking sent via text messages, following them on social media and asking them to follow us back, and a personalised guidebook emailed to them with house access codes, rules, restaurant and attraction recommendations and more!

START WITH THE END IN MIND

"You'd better run this thing like a business."
– My business mentor and real estate coach

Although I am grateful for my years of corporate opportunities and the growth I achieved during my career, I now realise that I am late to the real estate investing game. So, I am moving with purpose and doing it as quickly as I can. I am playing catch up for the years that I missed where I could have begun my investing journey sooner. The verticals that I intend to grow within my scope are:

- STR cash flowing business – Crescent Retreats;
- Asset wealth and accumulation – property acquisition, equity paydown and appreciation;
- Mentorship – TheAirbnbLaunchPad;
- Vertical integration to support STR business and prepare for a potential sale;
  - Acquire cleaning company;
  - Acquire property management company (rather than start my own);
  - Acquire maintenance company or hire a team;
  - Other spinoff companies to help launch peer STRs.

CASH FLOWING BUSINESS AND ACCUMULATING ASSETS

Our end goal is to operate a real estate portfolio worth more than $50,000,000 dollars across multiple regions to provide our guests with every type of holiday that they may look for: beach experiences, ski-in/ski-out experiences, hiking and nature experiences, lake experiences, remote work home bases and more. Leveraging my corporate and entrepreneurial background, I used the following process to define our business:

- Vision;
- Mission statement;
- Core values;
- Branding;
- Financial goals;
- Exit strategy.

This exercise birthed... Crescent Retreats.

Then, to help decide what kind of properties I was going to offer our guests, I became really clear about what kind of homes I wanted to purchase and manage. While some investors focus on having quantity, I am more focused on the overall value of the portfolio. For example, if the goal is to own $50,000,000 in real estate, a quantity investor may acquire five hundred $100,000 properties, whereas I would rather own fifty $1,000,000 properties. Using this ideology led us to the path of *luxury*. To define luxury, for us that meant to model after two of the best hospitality sites in the world: The Ritz Carlton and The Four Seasons. When entering a market, we look at the local Ritz and Four Seasons to identify with their colour schemes, furniture pallets, etc. And there are many reasons we chose to go luxury. Primarily, we wanted to set ourselves up to be recession proof. Again, using the Ritz and Four Seasons, those hospitality giants do not allow recessions to impede on their pricing or standard of travel. So, targeting the same set of clients as they do, we knew that our clientele would be able to afford our prices regardless of economic conditions that were not within our control.

Next, I focused on the data that I found necessary to not only operate a profitable short-term rental business, but also that would help predict appreciation over the years. My primary KPIs (key performance indicators) were census data (I wanted to see population growth expected in a market over the next several years), business investment (money being invested in local start-ups and corporates moving in) and tourism trends. This research led me to Scottsdale/Phoenix, Arizona, and dictates why I like the future markets that I plan to enter.

#HPLT + C – OUR VALUES

Although we began with an initial set of core values, we have evolved in thirteen months and those changed. This is perfectly normal for a business and, as we learned more about our approach to hosting and our guests, we had to pivot to ensure we were tailoring our homes to reconcile what we wanted to share and what our guests wanted to experience.

- **H**ealth – by incorporating exercise via equipment, bikes, swimming pools, beach toys and more, we are able to deliver our passion for health to our guests who are also looking to carry on their routines while on holiday.
- **P**eace – health derives an inner comfort, which in turn leads to an individual's peaceful approach to life.
- **L**ove – health and peace combined make it easy for one to share love in the world, making interactions easy and welcome.
- **T**ravel – experiences, culture, creativity, health, peace and love combine to drive our mission to share travel journeys with our guests.
- **C**offee – because every luxury STR or accommodation should offer the best of the best coffee. We provide a Jura E6 whole-bean grinder at every home and partner with high quality local coffee roasters to provide the best coffee experiences for our guests.

MENTORSHIP

Something I am forever grateful for is the support of my wife. She is my daily inspiration as I watch her grow her law firm. She is my biggest fan in everything that I do. We approach life as a true partnership. As such, our goal was to become debt free, at which point I could leave my employment and become entrepreneurial while relying on her income. As detailed in the intro, a few left turns led me to the STR business. Now that I have the experience needed, coupled with my passion to help people take control of their own path, the plan is to build a community of hosts, starting with a mentorship for beginners called TheAirbnbLaunchPad.

VERTICAL INTEGRATION

My philosophy on starting any business is to begin with the end in mind, which includes the exit strategy. Simply put, build a business so that you can sell it one day. In the event you do not sell, building to do so will push you to grow the business larger than you initially envisioned, and now you get to run that company.

Vertical integration for our business includes the real estate portfolio, the coaching business, owning the cleaning company, etc. In a sale, it is possible to bundle all of this together, or to sell in parts, or keep parts and sell the others. The options are limitless.

EVER GRATEFUL AND ALL IN

I remember being such a proponent for work/life balance when I was in corporate. I preached this to my team. I embedded it with myself. I worked extremely hard and wasted no time while in the office so that I could enjoy my nights and weekends off. Now, as a serial entrepreneur, I understand why corporate trains the individual to value work/life balance. Simply put, people will burnout. Want to know why people burnout? Hint, it is not because they are working too hard. Because I am working more now as an entrepreneur than ever before. Only now, I do not seek or desire balance. In fact, I wish there was more time to put into this empire that I plan to build. The truth is balance is sought after only when passion is lacking. I liked my job. I truly did. But most of the time I was planning my next move. What promotion is next? What is my next role? Will it be with my current company, or will I have to move? But not anymore. Now, I know my path. I know where I am headed, and I have complete control over it. This is my car, and I am driving it. My only issue is... I wish I had more time in the day to continue to drive. Gone are the days where the movie theatre was fun. Now, I have fun underwriting deals and looking for new markets to enter. I am all in.

I am on a mission to scale my real estate portfolio, potentially make an exit, help as many people as possible take control of their own path via investing, grow my mentorship brand (TheAirbnbLaunchPad) and create the best experiences for our guests.

I am grateful for the opportunity to collaborate in this book with some amazing hosts who I enjoy learning from. I am grateful for the opportunity to build my own path. I am ever grateful to you, the reader, for taking the time to learn about my brand and my journey.

The root of my core values and passion is people. I want to pour in and motivate as many people as I can to take control of their own path and find their car to drive. I truly hope that I have left you with the motivation and inspiration to do that.

I am ever grateful. And I am all in!

ABOUT THE AUTHOR

Fouad Bazzi is a former corporate banker turned serial entrepreneur and real estate investor. More importantly, however, Fouad is a father, husband, son and brother. When his daughter, Madina, was one, she was diagnosed with severe tree nut allergies. The programme that was most likely to help Madina overcome these allergies was the Southern California Food and Allergy Institute. Living in Detroit, MI, Fouad knew that the commitment of having to frequent Southern California for several years was not going to be a cheap one. So, having been an Airbnb guest dozens of times, Fouad combined his passion of entrepreneurship, real estate investing and travel to launch Crescent Retreats, a luxury short-term rental brand, and purchase his first holiday rental in Huntington Beach, CA. Through Crescent Retreats, Fouad helps guests set a new standard of travel for themselves via extreme communication and top tier amenities in highly sought-after holiday markets. Fouad's mission is to promote health, peace, love and travel, and he ensures that all Crescent Retreats have an element of each of these four values. All Crescent Retreats also feature an exquisite coffee bar because, well, how can it be a luxury property without a Jura coffee machine!?! Aside from the Huntington Beach Villa, Crescent Retreats also offers five other luxury homes in Scottsdale, AZ, with the intention to grow into other popular holiday markets soon.

As an Airbnb Superhost, Fouad has quickly established credibility with his guests to the tune of thirteen rebookings in less than twelve months. Crescent Retreats has hosted more than sixty bachelorette parties, four engagement parties, multiple real estate mastermind events and many other getaways.

Fouad is also passionate about helping others take control of their own time by way of investing in real estate. To date, he has raised $2m dollars from family, friends and other investors to acquire the Crescent Retreat homes. Fouad also owns @detroit, which mentors others individually and in groups via podcasts and mastermind events. Fouad has appeared on several podcasts including Breakaway Wealth, Uncontested Investing, MAF Podcast and others.

Links: https://linktr.ee/FouBNB

GERAINT JONES (GER)

LLE I ENAID GAEL LLONYDD
(A PLACE FOR THE SOUL TO FIND PEACE)

Very few of us are ready for our journey in hospitality and have formal training.

Most of us either:

- inherit it
- marry into it
- have a lifestyle change
- or need a pension fund

Which one are you?

I live in a fantastic part of North Wales known as the Llŷn Peninsula. Although a very popular tourist destination for people from the Northwest of England, it is relatively unknown to the rest of the world. I realised at a very early age that whatever my chosen journey would be in life, I wanted to spend it at home in a traditional Welsh way. My first language is Welsh and I'm very proud of it.

My journey started when I was about fourteen years old and started a summer job at a local clay target shooting school and, by the age of sixteen, I was spending all my holidays and weekends there. My main role was running the welcome lodge, signing clients in and out, assessing their needs over a cup of tea and generally lots of chat. I suddenly realised that most of our clients were on holiday, had second homes, working very hard during the week just to spend their money at the weekends enjoying themselves. It was at this point I realised hospitality was for me.

After spending time away at college, I returned home and joined the family flooring company, which gave me a very good living for the next twenty-five years and a good grounding in business.

My spare time was spent sailing on a J-35; we raced all over the UK, Ireland and parts of Europe. These years of bonding and teamwork made me who I am today and to appreciate the value of leisure time and hospitality.

My dream was always to give a good customer experience holiday in a traditional Welsh sustainable environment.

Fifteen years into this journey, I partly realised my dream by buying a derelict smallholding called Rhosydd. A house, a set of agricultural buildings and eight acres. We moved into the house, got married and one child later we set up our company 'Rhosydd Bach Holidays' and started on the long process of renovating the cottages. Not sure which was the hardest, dealing with the paperwork and red tape or the build. I took on the task of project managing the work myself with the help of some fantastic local tradesmen. Wow – I learnt so much during that process and two years later we welcomed our very first guests.

I can remember buying my very first laptop, an Acer Aspire at £1400, trying to do budgets, ordering stuff from Screwfix at 2am whilst developing marketing strategies, making adverts and working out tariffs. No Canva, PriceLabs or Mailchimp back then, people were just starting to get used to emails, and social media was merely a distant dream. When people say it's tough today, they really have no idea the hours we put into marketing then, but it worked, maybe better than today. All this was done in evenings and at weekends whilst still running a flooring company.

Germy passion – our cottages

I think the skills I learnt during these fabulous times really made me what I am today and gave me comprehensive knowledge of building and setting up a hospitality business.

My plan was to let Rhosydd Bach to run itself. It was easier back then as laws of supply and demand played into our hands. We are quite remote so our task of marketing and raising awareness was more challenging, and interaction with guests was key to customer retention, which worked very well. Sometimes you need to turn a negative into a positive, which is what we did by selling our remoteness, the peace and tranquillity of the property.

Shoulder months were proving difficult, so I played with hen nights, golfing and activity breaks and it worked well, but my time was being split between this and my main flooring business whilst trying to raise a family. The time came to get some help in as Rhosydd Bach was always supposed to be my pension fund, and not a drain on my time and resources. We signed up with Sykes

Cottages and it gave me time to concentrate on other things.

This worked well at first, with good bookings mainly in the summer. Their commission was killing me but it was less work for me. I realised our prices were static and there was a drop in bookings over the next five years. My direct bookings dropped from 100% to about 20%. I had no way out, so we just carried on.

During the next few years in my journey, a series of events took place that totally changed my life. I lost a very good friend, my closest, and best man at my wedding. Cancer. He had fought it for seven years, during which we still spent time together, got drunk and lived life. One thing I gained from this is that none of us live forever and, whatever your dreams are, you must follow them, live the dream, and don't wait until tomorrow. As someone once told me, 'I really don't want to be the wealthiest man in the graveyard'.

We were busy at work, but struggling to make money, margins were being squeezed and finding staff was a problem. I was bored, and a few years from reaching fifty I'd had enough, so I decided to sell up the flooring company. This was the time for me to take back control of the cottages, follow my dream, run a hospitality business and be a hospitable host.

I was struggling a bit with new marketing trends, systems, and integrations. Although I was very social media savvy, some elements were difficult. A fellow host in the area mentioned this Yorkshire chap who helped people with marketing. I had a look at his websites, made contact and within a day was on the phone with Mark Simpson. I signed up there and then to the Boostly Academy, full price, no extras, a deal on instalments and away I went. Best thing I ever did. Within two months, I had learnt so much and put it into place.

I recognised the value of repeat customers. I started using Mailchimp and added all my past customers in, started with a few newsletters, special offers and each campaign brought in some bookings.

THEN…

Covid hit, turning all our lives upside down for sure. However, I will say this and stand by it, joining Boostly saved us, gave me a community where we could all help each other, taught me to pivot and, when the chips were down, the members in there all bounced off each other.

I now help run the quarterly training bootcamps as well as doing my own daily posts about trends and marketing issues. They have even labelled me 'Mr Motivator' because of my consistent positive attitude to everything in life.

By now we are up to about 60% direct bookings. I do still use Sykes and Airbnb for the other 40% BUT they now work for me. I find it is a fantastic balance for me. I also work part time, on my terms, as a maritime officer for the local council, spending my days chatting to visitors and helping to manage our fantastic coastline.

It has been an interesting journey, with its ups and downs, but it's been an enjoyable one. We are still here, helping others to enjoy the culture, experience, and beauty of the Llŷn.

It was my dream and I have followed it. If you have a dream of being in hospitality or a being a hospitable host then get out there and chase it, chase it hard and maybe one day you will catch up with it and hopefully realise it.

My number one top tip would be: always meet and greet, people love the personal touch, be yourself, be kind and pleasant. Selling yourself is just as important as selling the cottage. This is what has led us to 60% direct bookings. And I would say that 75% of those are repeat customers, and why customers come back and stay with us time and time again, because they like us as well as the property.

ABOUT THE AUTHOR

Geraint is the founder and runs Rhosydd Bach Holidays, a collection of beautiful cottages on the stunning Llŷn Peninsula, North Wales. After spending many years in retail, he decided to start his own business from his smallholding in rural Wales, which in turn allowed him to live, work and raise a family in his community.

He is an avid sailor, having navigated the waters around Britain and Ireland, is a keen walker and is passionate about local history. This has given him the knowledge, contacts and experience to develop his business with a guest-targeted approach. He understands why his guests stay with him and why.

He is positive and passionate about everything in life, as many would agree. He shares his marketing tips and strategies with fellow hosts from around the world, as a valued member of The Boostly Academy. He motivates others to achieve their dreams by setting up their own hospitality businesses.

Links: linktr.ee/rhosyddbach

GLENYSS DE VYLDER

HEART AND SOUL HOSTING

'Does this path have a heart?
If it does, the path is good; if it doesn't, it serves no purpose.
Neither path leads nowhere, but one has a heart and the other does not.'
– Carlos Castaneda

It all started when my husband and I purchased a beachside property. It was a brand-new apartment with amazing views of a best-kept secret beach with a 1950s-esque hamburgers-and-milkshake shop on the corner (Boat Harbour beach in Port Stephens NSW Australia is no longer a best-kept secret! The hamburger shop is gone, too). It was primarily an investment in an area where all the data pointed to strong potential growth, but also a family getaway where we could spend holidays together in this magical seaside location. We had high expectations for rental performance, so we furnished and styled it as a luxury property. We stocked it with quality appliances and amenities and priced it higher than the majority of the holiday rentals in the area. Then we listed it with the local real estate agent, which was the done thing back in the days before iPhones and keep cups. It didn't take us long to realise that the agent was not going to bring in the bookings or revenue to meet our expectations. Instead, they pushed guests to book more traditional and 'reasonably priced' holiday properties. With no bookings taken for that first peak Christmas and January holiday period, I started to look at other options, including engaging a new online start-up.

Stayz was the brainchild of a luxury property owner on the mid-north coast of NSW, who founded it in 2001. He had experienced the same lacklustre results from real estate booking agents and saw the opportunity to help owners make their holiday homes visible online. Excited, I listed our property with Stayz. The first booking came a day later, and we were soon 90% booked for the following three months. I was thrilled! There was so much potential to target and reach our ideal guest, and so many other property owners who could benefit from this. Soon I was being approached by other property owners (and even the local real estate agent!) to manage their properties. They could see my places were succeeding. I was able to showcase our luxury properties to people who would not have found them otherwise. And it gave me the freedom to work from home while raising our kids.

MORE THAN JUST ACCOMMODATION

I always wanted to provide a product and service that fulfils a fantasy, a dream; something I seek and appreciate myself when I look for a holiday. As a guest who has chosen her dream holiday home, when I arrive, I want to open that front door and feel happy that I have made the perfect choice. And when there is something more, something that surprises and delights me, I feel nurtured and know the host cares about the experience their guests will have at their property. A welcome hamper, a chocolate on a pillow, a handwritten note, teas and coffees left out for travellers after a long trip. This is the experience I want all my guests to have – to be delighted in their choice and surprised by something extra. To feel happy that they have found this special place where their fantasy

One Mile Retreat, Boat Harbour NSW – one of our beautiful properties

begins to play out from the moment they open the front door. This is my brand promise. It's more than just accommodation!

BUT I LIVE TOO FAR AWAY!

I realised early that to fulfil that vision of providing more than just accommodation, I needed to develop a team that would support me along with systems and processes to deliver that luxury experience without fail, every time. But I had a problem: I lived hundreds of kilometres away from the properties!

Fridge stopped working? Complaining neighbours? The urge to change the welcome mat or the cushions and throws? Who's going to restock the amenities? Without a managing agent on location, I needed to work out how to ensure that the properties were set up the way I wanted them to be set up, that my guests had everything they needed, and that I could respond quickly to any issues. I needed a team in alignment with my brand promise (to provide a guest-focused luxury experience), a team that could be my ears and eyes on the ground and be highly responsive to anything that needed attention or improvement. This team was the cleaners and tradespeople.

Everything pivots around our cleaners. Their diligence delivers the face of each property and the face of my business. It's our cleaners who ensure that each property is presented in its very best light and is guest-ready every time. They are fastidious about cleaning and are hospitality focused. They take pride in their work and care about the guest experience. The cleaners are key to ensuring that our brand promise is delivered, every time. I work closely with them to make it all work: to attend to any issues, answer any questions, replace anything that needs replacing, improve anything that could be improved and add little touches that enhance the guest experience. They are my 'second in command' and really deserve a much more glamorous title! I just haven't yet come up with one worthy enough...

I also rely on my team of tradespeople to be available 24/7 for any emergency. If a water pipe bursts or the electricity goes down, I can call on one of my trusted team to be there promptly to fix it. Guests want to know that if something 'goes wrong' their holiday is not going to be disrupted – it will be fixed with a minimum of fuss. Having those reliable and committed tradespeople to respond quickly is critical.

One of my biggest challenges early on was my support team turnover, which could happen when least needed or expected. Over the years, one or two of my cleaners have, with little or no notice, just left. One resigned on Christmas Eve, with four check-ins scheduled on the 26th of December (at least I had Christmas Day as a breather!). Thankfully I knew people who went out of their way to find me cleaners who were willing to help last minute. Those local connections are invaluable. This experience allowed me to tighten up my contracts and service level agreements and put the onus on the cleaners to commit to each and every job, give adequate notice and provide alternative options to replace themselves. I also ensure that I have people in the wings who can fill in should the need arise.

THE TECHNOLOGY BEHIND THE PEOPLE

Behind the scenes is the rapid advancement in communication technology. This is why short-term rental properties have become so easily bookable from anywhere in the world. Business is done largely online now, allowing hosts, owners and guests to be a part of this exciting movement. Technology matches guests with properties and experiences that allows us into other peoples' lives and communities and widens our world view.

To operate efficiently as a remote manager, operations are automated and streamlined to provide a smooth flowing service to our guests and owners. The central technology hub of our operations is the property management system (PMS), which enables everything to be managed from the one place:

- Reservations are processed seamlessly.
- Pricing and calendar information flows in real time between the PMS and all booking channels.
- Messaging is automated to ensure guests don't miss any important instructions and information.
- Listing and website content is updated.
- Pricing is adjusted to reflect real-time supply and demand.
- Access codes and check-in instructions are generated.
- Guests' identities are verified.
- Noise levels and numbers of guests in each property are monitored electronically.
- Cleaning efficiency, standards and safety are managed.
- Payments and security deposits are processed.
- Financial and owner reports are generated.

With these systems, procedures and people in place, properties can be managed efficiently and remotely from anywhere in the world.

CHOOSE YOUR BRAND IDENTITY

Rapidly changing developments and opportunities in the industry can be confusing for host businesses to decide what market segment they should focus on. What type of property? One-bedroom units? Three-bedroom family homes? Large multi-family homes? Tiny homes? Unique places? What standard of property – luxury or budget? What type of guest? To stand out, hosts need to establish their brand identity around which segment of the market they want to operate in and develop expertise and reputation in that segment.

Likewise, owners are looking for the right host/manager to differentiate their property and market it in its best light to a specific target market so as to generate and optimise return.

I decided early in the development of my business strategy to focus on managing luxury properties and delivering a luxury experience to guests who appreciate this class of accommodation. My brand appeals to owners who want a higher class of guest and to guests who want to experience that touch of luxury with everything taken care of.

IS BIG BUSINESS TAKING OVER?

Our industry is all about the host, the guest and the community.

Hosting is at the heart of short-term rentals. The industry has evolved from holiday lettings to hosted properties and is now a multifaceted industry with many players, big, small and everything in between. There are multinationals focusing on acquiring properties and expansion. There are dedicated short-term rental property management companies managing properties from two to thousands of properties. Real estate agencies are also expanding into short-term rentals. And there are individual hosts who seek to add to their income and enhance their lives by hosting houses, tiny homes, private rooms, unique homes, farm stays, tents, campervans, hobbit houses and everything else imaginable – down to the original Airbnb concept of an air mattress in the living room!

The industry is at the stage of rapid growth and new entries. Rationalisation is the usual next step. Larger companies are starting to enter and acquire small and medium-sized property management companies. This is a cottage industry evolving to big business. But is the key ingredient lost in the upscale? That is, can large companies provide genuine hosting?

No matter how big these players become, the magic will still need to happen at the level of the host and the guest. As long as people want to explore the world, experience different cultures, meet different people and gain a glimpse into other people's lives, the individual host will always have the best opportunity to meet those needs at the most personal and genuine level.

THE HOST, THE GUEST AND THE COMMUNITY

Individual hosts are the ones who are closest to their own communities and who can create that magical experience for the guest because they are sharing a part of themselves, their lives and their community. The local host brings their community to the outside world and brings the outside world to experience and contribute to their community. They bring people, money and a positive energy to the community through visitors who come to experience and appreciate their surrounds. By supporting local businesses there is a respect for the community and the people who live there. The host can communicate with guests about things of interest – events, local produce, markets, the artisanal bread shop that makes the best walnut-and-olive loaf. You can arrange discounts for local experiences like dolphin watching, theme parks, cooking classes, etc. As a guest, how great to have the door held open to the local community and its different businesses, activities, nature and people! The community will in turn feel good about short-term rentals, which is always a plus when you love welcoming guests to your property and local area and plan to continue doing so.

Responsible hosts run a professional operation – including screening to ensure they are inviting the right guests to stay – and are conscious of their rental's impact on the local community. Such hosts strengthen the industry, which has had a bad rap from neighbourhood noise-dislikers and the media (a few bad stories go a long way). The fact is short-term rental accommodation fulfils diverse needs that other types of accommodation can't fulfil. Fair council regulation should provide clearer guidelines so that short-term rentals can exist harmoniously in the community along with other types of accommodations.

THE HEART AND SOUL OF SHORT-TERM RENTALS: HOSPITABLE HOSTING

As a host, I provide the stage for wonderful memorable experiences with family and friends.

The guest is at the heart of everything I do. The technology, the systems and the people all support the guest – but there are other important aspects to hosting.

I love and appreciate beautifully presented properties. When I walk into these homes, I'm stopping and noticing and feeling. I know that someone has put love, time and consideration into creating the look and feel of the space. That first impression is so critical as it dispels any doubt a guest may have about their choice, especially when fellow guests are happy too.

I am always looking for unique ways to create this special feeling for my guests, to ensure the properties not only meet their expectations, but provide a little delightful surprise. That could be providing a rice cooker for the Asian guests or replacing single-use plastic and chemical-based products with locally produced organic amenities. It might be offering a local's tips for places off the beaten track, or just connecting with guests during their stay. These little thoughtful touches are the magic behind a wonderful guest experience, and many return guests.

Our newest addition – on the Gold Coast

In considering what this chapter would be about, I realised that my story started with an idea to do something better, to cater to a market that was ready and waiting for a luxury home-away-from-home. It started with a decision to explore the internet to see how this could be done. From there, the opportunities to make my properties more widely visible to potential guests opened up through online booking sites and direct marketing.

The happy guest is the key. And there are countless ways to make the guest happy, to delight and surprise them. It is understanding the guests' needs even before they are aware of them themselves. It is being curious and open to little gems you may glean from guests that may be the next thing you introduce. Communication is the sweet point. Listen well: you'll hear what's behind any complaints or politeness... Once, a lady found a mark on one of the bed sheets (after stripping back all the beds on arrival) and declared the place uninhabitable, demanding a full refund. I immediately judged her as unreasonable, but later realised that this incident was a gift that allowed me to improve this aspect of my service. I talked with my cleaners and linen provider and put in place checks to ensure that sheets did not leave the linen provider nor be put on beds unless they had passed these checks. A bit over the top? Not when you could potentially be faced with needing to provide a full refund at the last minute with limited opportunity for a replacement booking.

As hosts, we create the setting for wonderful stories, lasting memories, life transformations, grand epiphanies, world-changing ideas, or the next Nobel Prize-winning novel, simply because we have paid attention to the little details and what our guests want. The experiences our guests have in our properties don't end when the holiday ends. They take their memories with them, post on social media and tell their family and friends. When you do it right, the marketing takes care of itself.

It's about the details. It is the little things that create the total experience, and the little details always have the guest at heart. Choosing the location, the style of furnishings, carefully considering the amenities that your guest may want, the quality of everything, how you'll communicate, the community and local recommendations, pricing for the value your property offers, managing the calendar and monitoring occupancy and tariffs to optimise revenue (local events can have an impact on occupancy and revenue too).

We have digital tools to help us, but the hosting function can't ever be fully automated. Hosting is the human element, the thing that you can't automate. It's the heart of the industry. Hosts take care of the details, supported by some amazing tools that allow us to focus on optimising the guest experience.

Loving the idea of hosting is not enough to be successful in this industry. One also must pay attention to all the little details and the systems and processes that happen behind the scenes. This is what top hosts do to keep their guests coming back and leaving five-star reviews. It makes people's travels memorable, and I like to think it makes the world a better place.

ABOUT THE AUTHOR

Glenyss began her love affair with short-term rentals in 2002 when she and her husband bought a beachfront apartment in a little magical location called Boat Harbour, in Port Stephens, NSW, Australia. After listing the property with a local letting agent, Glenyss soon realised they were not going to receive the returns they wanted. She then discovered a new start up, Stayz, and her journey into short-term rentals began right there.

Leap ahead to 2023 and Glenyss' property management business, *By the Beach Getaways*, has helped many property owners transform their investments into luxury short-stay rentals, hosting over 16,000 guests, earning them thousands of five-star reviews and significantly increasing their rental returns.

Every guest is at the heart of Glenyss' business. She's built it around listening to what the guest wants, including care and attention to the little details that delight and surprise her guests. Behind the scenes are the wonderful people who support her guests and the systems and technologies that support the people.

After twenty years in the industry, Glenyss was thrilled to be awarded the LUXlife Travel & Tourism 2022 Award for 'Best Short-Stay Rental Management Company – Eastern Australia'. The award recognises her industry expertise, dedication to customer service and client satisfaction and going above and beyond.

With nine years straight as an Airbnb Superhost, Glenyss is an Airbnb Superhost Ambassador and Host Community Leader. She loves sharing her vast expertise by mentoring new hosts and supporting existing hosts.

When Glenyss is not helping guests find their perfect stay, she's relaxing with family and friends and taking long walks along the beach.

Links: https://linktr.ee/bythebeachgetaways

HELEN CHRISTOPHER

FROM SUMMER CAMP TO LIFE-CHANGING RENTALS: THE STORY OF BROOKLEDGE

This crazy journey began with "I do!" In 2015, my friends Raymond and Jennie invited my husband Ryan and I to their wedding at Camp Brookledge. This was a summer camp for girls for over seventy years. In 2011, it closed its doors as a summer camp and was privately owned.

At the wedding, Ryan and I were taken away with how beautiful and nostalgic Brookledge was. We loved the old cabins, pavilion with the fireplace, pond and the trees. It was so peaceful, and it was only fifteen minutes from Saratoga Springs (New York). We joked that we would love to live somewhere like this. Never did I think that that would lead me to leaving my teaching career of seventeen years, buying a former girls' summer camp, selling my house and moving our family into a 400 square foot nurse's office. However, that is exactly what happened.

Fast forward to 2020, and I am scrolling through local real estate on my phone. I see that Brookledge is on the market! My brain is asking a million questions. Do we sell our house? What would we do with it? Do I want to live there? The answers always were yes!

We are now living in what most people would consider a

bedroom. The old summer camp had a small nurse's office. It was the only building on site that was insulated and could make it through the cold winter. There was no kitchen, bathroom or even a closet. We had a microwave, small fridge, blow-up mattress and a table. I felt like I was in college all over again. Using the 1970's summer camp bathhouse was not ideal. Ryan owns an auto repair shop and I was teaching second graders, yet we still had to find time to build a new business and a place to live. Winter was coming and we would have to close the bathhouse soon. That meant we would not have running water, a bathroom, shower or any basic amenities.

Helen with Maxine and Lynne after the Styx concert to celebrate the one year anniversary of Brookledge

I did what any person panicking would do, I called my parents. My parents and dear friends Rebecca and Jeff loved this new adventure we were on. They also saw how special Brookledge was. Fortunately, they all came down and helped with the addition to the old nurse's office. The 750 square foot space now had everything my family needed, but we had to answer the question, "What do we do with Brookledge?"

I had a million ideas, but it was an easy decision. We would have short-term rentals and use the pavilion for events. Brookledge would keep the summer camp feel with a nod to the seventies and eighties. We would add glamping tents where the girls had their camp sing-a-longs, renovate the lodge with an indoor treehouse, move the small cabin near the pond atop boulders to overlook the stream and update the pavilions. However, our first rental was a new addition to the property. I wanted to create a log cabin that paid homage to the vintage toys called Lincoln Logs. It is exactly what you picture, brown logs, green metal roof and cute windows. We called the cabin Crook Brook after the stream that runs through the property. This little cabin brought two of my favourite guests into my life.

Maxine and Lynne had rented Crook Brook as a girls' getaway and to attend a Styx concert at SPAC (Saratoga Performing Arts Center). Ryan, myself and friends were sitting around a campfire and I got a call from Maxine. She was having an issue using the keypad to unlock the gate and all you could hear was laughter. Her laugh was contagious, and I knew they were going to be a lot of fun.

That weekend was our one-year anniversary at Brookledge. This was a big deal for us as we now had a place to live, a successful business and I had resigned from my teaching career to work at Brookledge full time. Maxine had reached out to me with a few questions and I asked her if she would mind taking a picture in the morning to celebrate the one year milestone. She said, "Absolutely!" That night, the ladies enjoyed dinner in Saratoga and the concert.

The next morning, we were taking the picture and having fun. I began sharing plans about Brookledge. Maxine and Lynne began sharing how special this weekend was for them. Maxine had lost her husband Paul to complications with Covid that March. He was a drum technician with the band Styx for over twenty years. That weekend, the band and the crew paid tribute to her husband at the concert with custom T-shirts and I knew this was a special moment for Maxine. With tears in her eyes, she told me how much she missed Paul and how special that night was. I was compelled to give Maxine a hug. I didn't know that she had saved a shirt for me. I was touched by her kind gesture.

I didn't realise at that time that Brookledge would also be a special moment for Maxine's friend. Lynne was also experiencing a loss in her life. Her husband Michael had been battling Pick's Disease for the last four years. She shared how hard it was having her husband in her life, but he was really not there. Pick's Disease is a form of dementia in which the brain and nerve cells gradually stop working. In a way, Lynne was also grieving the loss of her husband. This girls' weekend at Brookledge reminded her of the summer camp of her youth. It was a chance to reconnect with nature and disconnect with life's challenges. Maxine and Lynn walked the trails, giggled about the vintage bathhouses and loved being in nature. Spending time with those ladies showed me that saying I do to this crazy adventure was exactly what I needed too.

ABOUT THE AUTHOR

Helen Christopher is a former elementary teacher turned hospitable host and event planner in Upstate New York. In 2021, she bought a former girls' summer camp called Brookledge, which offers guests sixty acres of cabins, glamping tents and event space. As the owner, she helps guests reconnect with nature and disconnect from their hectic lives. Helen has been featured in the Times Union, Ramble and Roam blog, and Connecting Roads. She now lives with her family and two dogs in what was once the nurse's office at Brookledge and enjoys camp life every day.

Links: https://linktr.ee/brookledgeny

CRAIG AND HOLLY WESTAWAY

HIGH-END HOSPITALITY

Like many other hosts, we did not seek out being property managers and never would've thought we'd so much as stay in an Airbnb over a motel, let alone own and run them! We were forced into the short-term rental industry when our real estate agent who specialised in short-term rentals took away our beach house from us.

We have a beautiful five-bedroom home situated in the heart of the Gold Coast, 2km from the beach. We lived only an hour away in Brisbane. Craig was a performance-driven sales executive of twenty-seven years and I was primarily a stay-at-home mum.

We only let the house when we went away, which was always peak season. He told us he would rent it for $1000 per night and he did originally achieve this, but in the process, we lost the use of our home. Between the 30% management fees, the rules, crazy cleaning fees and stripping our home of all its personality and personalisation, this was not how we were expecting it to be. We felt like it was his home, and we were unwanted guests. The final straw was when he rented the property at Christmas for well under the agreed nightly rate. After Craig confronted him with this, his response was that it was in his contract he could do so to get a rental. This was the last rental he ever got with us.

From that moment on, I was tasked with managing the home as a rental, as Craig's high-pressure sales role didn't leave him the time. I managed to triple the return in the first year we took back the reigns and found that I had a real knack for the business, in particular with the guest communications and guest experience.

Seeing these results made Craig super excited and, on the back of this success, convinced me to rent our family home, the one we lived in full time, in Brisbane, as we would often go away for six weeks at a time leaving the place empty and costing us money. I was not keen on the idea; the idea of packing away years' worth of family mementos, belongings, toys and photos each time was daunting. However, I was sold into it by the prospect of more holidays while someone paid to stay and so we listed and welcomed our very first guests for Christmas. My initial response was, "Who would want to stay in Brisbane for Christmas?" After Craig did some research, he thought the price would be $680 per night, and my instant reply was, "No one's going to book there at that price!" The first booking came several days later, a ten-night stay for a family – the CEO of Fortescue metals, one of Australia's biggest mining companies. They were perfect guests and a perfect first stay. We ended up filling thirty-six of the forty days we were away, realising this was a pretty good thing... getting paid to be on holiday as we were earning fifteen times the nightly rate of our cost to stay in Bali at our timeshare.

Craig had always had this bug to be a property developer and, after months of research and searching, we found a property in Auchenflower in Brisbane. His instant response was 'this site is perfect' as it was 350m from The Wesley Hospital and 4km to the city in one of the most sought-after suburbs in Brisbane. Just one catch... or maybe two. The existing run-down house was 'character' listed and thus could not be removed, plus the block was on a steep angle, adding large costs to the build, which backed onto a flood easement. But we love a challenge and so Westcorp Projects was born.

Our family

Two years later, with the sole goal of keeping two for short-term rental and selling two, the four-pack of Park Ave townhouses were completed. Super proud but nearly broken, we styled them on the bones of our arse, under the weight of the huge mortgage we had created and countless budget blowouts from building issues, including legal battles with the architect over crazy design flaws, which had to be rectified to ensure the building would be fire safety compliant.

I was eight months pregnant when Craig called from work one day. He'd had a fallout with his boss of twenty-seven years and parted ways that very day. Needless to say, the stress levels were soaring as we were both without full-time work, were weeks away from welcoming a fourth child, with the two eldest attending expensive private schools, three massive mortgages to pay, as well as trying to maintain a lifestyle we'd become accustomed to. Craig, being the super driven person he is, took it all in his stride and came on board, joining me in the rental game and BnB Booking was born shortly after in 2019.

Back to the townhouses. We'd listed them with a well-known

real estate agency in the area in December 2018. They came to market two months before an election when negative gearing was going to be scrapped by the then opposition who were red-hot favourites to win the election. They didn't sell. We had to pivot and quickly with the bank wanting some income and reduction of debt. We sold one to our self-managed super fund, relieving some debt, and listed all four on Airbnb and other platforms. They were a huge success, earning 300% over long-term rental contracts put forward to us by that same agent. Some things happen for a reason, and we now look back knowing we were meant to keep them as they have been nothing short of amazing and are rented solidly year-round. We are still immensely proud of this project and still love all the fittings and fixtures we – well, I – stressed over selecting at the time.

Now with six super performing properties under our own portfolio, we were catching a lot of attention off the back of our own success stories. Questions were flying left, right and centre, as friends, family and strangers wanted to know what we were doing and how we were earning so much from just Airbnb. It wasn't long until we were asked to take on other people's properties that were underperforming in the long-term market. Time and time again we shot the lights out, with huge returns in comparison to their previous owners' statements. We had very happy owners all round, which meant more word-of-mouth referrals, and here we are today with forty-five amazing properties on our books. Whilst we could've taken an easier route by taking on a 'cookie cutter' approach with units in high-rise buildings, identical and with no need to coordinate any maintenance on amenities, we didn't. What did we do differently? For us, we discovered very quickly that the higher-end luxury homes at over $1000 per night (one of which was over $12000 per night) generated significantly higher returns and were the same effort regarding guest communications as was a $100 per night property. So that's where we chose to stay.

Whilst the homes in this category are certainly more demanding in terms of maintenance and set up, the rewards are much greater also. I really found my niche in the guest communication and guest experience space. Finding out why a guest has booked one of our properties and connecting with them has made all the hard times and bad days worthwhile.

To date, my favourite guest stay was a family who booked a week-long stay at a stunning waterfront home we manage on the Gold Coast. When we accept a reservation, we vet hard, really hard. We ask all sorts of questions to weed out the groups, the troublemakers, the partiers, the youngsters and the liars. After speaking directly to the primary guest who'd booked the property, she explained that her husband was wheelchair bound. Upon hearing this information, I suggested we actually move their stay to a purpose-built accessibility home we managed a few streets away. She agreed to the change and the stay progressed. A few days later, she phoned me in tears and explained that not only was their stay going well, but that in fact it was the first time in over twelve years that her husband had been able to really contribute during a holiday. The menial tasks such as helping with dishes or cooking was normally impossible outside of their own home. In this house, however, the facilities had been designed with this exact intention, with worktops that raise and lower in height, wide walkways and doorways, larger and lower switches and wheelchair accessible bathrooms. The sheer joy and gratitude in her voice was something I will remember forever.

To those not in this industry, it all sounds and looks so very easy (especially when you take off overseas for several weeks at a time, claiming to be still working). To an outsider, it's simple – take the photos, list the property, get bookings, send a lock box code, message a cleaner and cash in. The reality for anyone who has actually done it themselves is very different. If only I could go back and tell myself all the things I know now, I would have saved myself many tears, tantrums and arguments with my annoyingly positive husband. We work very differently but together we make a phenomenal team. Our top tips for anyone either already in the industry or looking to start are: use pricing software, it will pay for itself tenfold. Use a noise monitoring device, such as Minut,

One of the stunning properties we manage

which will ensure you are on to issues before your neighbours can complain. If you're running multiple properties, invest in a property management solution (PMS), such as Uplisting – we love our PMS so much we became seed capital investors in it. The better the fit out and styling, the better the return. Take before and after photos of everything – this will help all round from quality control of cleans to maintenance to guest issues. And pay your cleaners well. They really are amazing people to do what they do, day in and day out. They are the eyes on your property, and without them, the business doesn't work. So, appreciate them, praise them and pay them well.

Learning is earning. You really can never know too much. For us, we continue to enhance our knowledge and skills by always improving and changing things. Read everything you can about short-term rentals. Read other people's listings, their rules, their descriptions, their whingeing on online forums and reviews. Everything that can go wrong, all the crazy encounters hosts have, all the horror stories that every host and guest has. Ask questions and research everything! Reviews from both hosts and guests can tell you a whole lot too. I'd certainly suggest reading between the lines on most of the Airbnb ones, but you'll soon gather a fairly good moral compass from a few thousand reviews. Enrol in courses, in person, online, one-on-one or via Zoom. Some will feel like a complete waste of time, whilst others will be pots of gold, literally. We always go in with the notion that if we learn one good thing, or can fix one pain point, then it's been worthwhile.

Shortly after BnB Booking was born, Craig and I joined a 1200-strong Australia-wide group called BNB Professional where we benefited greatly from all the information shared, the networking relationships we formed, including with 'Million Dollar Host' Julie George and Aaron and Nicole Byerlee, who ran the programme. Being part of a group of like-minded people in a new field, who were encountering many of the same issues we were, not only solidified that what we were doing was a genuine and sustainable business but was reassuring and compelling for us to be the best in this business, in our field. For us, we are scaling fast, and the trajectory is looking great. Our goal of 100 high-end properties by the end of 2023 looks to be on track. Whilst many property managers may have larger portfolios, none have the consistency of high-level properties we have with the retention rate we have. We will be onboarding with Marriott Homes and Villas in January 2023 and are very excited for this collaboration.

To date, we have not lost a single property we have taken on due to poor returns. We have owners who purchase properties solely for us to take on due to the incredible performance we have shown on their current ones. Our whole team are amazing, and we look forward to expanding the BnB Booking family.

ABOUT THE AUTHOR

Holly and Craig Westaway are the co-founders of BnB Booking. They are entrepreneurs in the high-end short-term rental space, having managed properties listed for over $12000 AUD per night. They are multi-award-winning hosts, who most recently won "best luxury home rental company, Australia" and "best luxury boutique holiday accommodation provider, Qld".

They have been published in magazines, spoken at conferences and been featured on podcasts, including Get Paid for Your Pad. They are number one in Australia for gross revenue within the 1200-strong BNB Professional Hosts group. They are ranked in the top 200 API connected hosts in Australia with Airbnb, are part of the exclusively invited companies to list with Marriott Homes and Villas, are preferred partners with both Vrbo and Booking.com, and their properties are listed across ten booking platforms. To date, they have hosted more than 50,000 guests, hosted many top executives, loads of celebrities and sports stars, over four thousand pets and have grossed more than ten million dollars across ten different platforms.

Craig has a strong sales background and joined BnB Booking four years ago, having been number one in his field for over twenty years, and is the numbers man. Holly started hosting in 2014 and is all about guest relations, property set up and taking care of the BnB Booking operations team. To them, it's all about the "one percenters" in every aspect of short-term rentals. Making small improvements daily, for both guests and owners, and ensuring that their high standards along with the guest expectations are always being met. As a company, they're all about returns and protection. Their homeowners see increased returns on their investment properties of more than 300% in comparison to other STR companies and long-term rentals, and they'll happily share the statements to prove it!

Links: https://linktr.ee/bnbbooking

KAREN OCHOA

I THINK I FOUND MY CALLING, AND IT'S CALLED SHORT-TERM RENTALS

I have always loved design and real estate. Even as a child, I loved to explore homes and longed to create my own beautiful space. Growing up in San Francisco was easy for me as I was surrounded by landmarks, beautiful architecture and fascinating people. My mom worked in San Francisco's Pacific Heights neighbourhood, and my sisters and I always visited her and roamed the area. I always felt the energy of the city and loved meeting interesting people.

Fast forward to adulthood, my first "real" job was in real estate, working for a developer in San Francisco and being an executive assistant to a real estate mogul with offices downtown. I felt like I'd really made it. He owned several apartment buildings and a commercial real estate brokerage firm and expanded to developing custom homes in Marin County. I was the gatekeeper to the CEO and was exposed to many interesting people; I got perks like expensive dinners to all the "in" restaurants. I had lots of freedom and flexibility and spent six years in various positions, and learned a lot, reinforcing my love of design and real estate.

By the time I was in my late twenties, I was ready to move out of the city, so I accepted a job in Silicon Valley, as that was where all the exciting work was. Eventually, I moved to Mountain View to be closer to work and so I wasn't spending as much time in the car. I worked for an international real estate firm and worked my way up to VP of project management, starting out as project manager. I expanded into running a fifty-person relocation and furniture project managers group for high-tech Silicon Valley clients like Yahoo, Apple and Stanford University. Then I went on to work at a real estate trust company doing design work and quality control for an upscale mixed-use construction project in Silicon Valley at Santana Row, specifying all finishes and designing amenity spaces for high-end townhouses. It was then that I was reminded of my passion for design. I thrived under high-stress situations and loved creating things. I could visualise a beautiful end result in every project I did and loved it.

I spent my twenties travelling and exploring and loved staying in hotels and experiencing the good life. Growing up, my family did not travel except for the occasional camping trip, and I didn't know what I was missing, but once I got the travel bug, I couldn't stop.

As a teen, I had multiple jobs in customer service and took them seriously. The one thing I did not like was experiencing bad hospitality, whether it be rude customer service or a hotel that was dirty, uncomfortable beds, etc. I became the concierge for the group of friends with whom I travelled constantly, researching places and scoping out the best places to stay. I enjoyed doing it, too, and would strive to take one big trip a year and at least four other smaller trips, happy to spend my money on travel. One of my most memorable trips was spending six weeks in Greece, and all of my best experiences were staying in local homes before Airbnb existed.

I continued to travel through my twenties and part of my thirties until I got married at the age of thirty-four, travelled less frequently, and made a few trips to Maui, NYC and Chicago. I focused on my career and starting a family. Finally, at thirty-nine, after five years of trying to have a baby, surgeries, and multiple IFVs, I had my daughter Olivia who is my heart. I took a big step back from work and consulted on and off as my husband's travel schedule eased. My husband travelled frequently, so my career took a back seat, and I leaned into motherhood, which meant taking on jobs with flexibility as the first requirement and less responsibility for me. This was always hard because I couldn't take on the type of projects I was used to. I'd never thought of myself as a stay-at-home mom, but I loved being able to take my daughter on day trips and couldn't imagine not being home with her. At the same time, I was happy to get the occasional consulting job because I usually had a flexible schedule and did something new. I also never felt like I wanted to be an entrepreneur and was satisfied getting a paycheque, benefits and a higher hourly rate. I was never a risk taker, so owning my own business was not high on my priority list, and I craved security more than anything else.

My husband, then, could not stop talking about real estate and how he longed to own multiple properties and become a landlord who lived off passive income. I always dismissed this, as it didn't appeal to me. In 2017, we moved from Silicon Valley to Southern California for a slower pace of life and to get out of the rat race. I did explore duplexes in Idaho and other lower-cost states, but nothing ever came to fruition. I had not had a full-time job since I worked for Apple in 2017, applied for multiple positions, and was starting to feel despondent.

Fast forward to Covid, I lost six close family members in eighteen months; my mother, sister, mother-in-law, brother-in-law, nephew and uncle. To say I was hopeless and depressed is an understatement, between my grief and inability to attend services for family members, the political climate and being cooped up at home. I didn't see any end in sight. I also had not worked since 2017, and like most of the world, I was confined inside my bubble, binge-watching TV and cooking up a storm!

I could have never imagined how life-changing signing up for STR Secrets Mastermind would be. What I did know was all my previous real estate experience made it a perfect fit for me. I was

Emile Zola Gourmet Kitchen

hooked from day one of the course and very eager to get started with my own properties, as well as a little intimidated about the unknown world I was about to enter, mainly because we were investing our own money into our venture. We started our company, A Travelers Home, Inc., to own and co-host multiple luxury properties in our market. I loved being in a community of like-minded people and learning from others in the industry. Although intimidating at first, I quickly dived in headfirst and tried not to be too frustrated with the difference in how I liked to run the business compared to my partner and felt like we would never get to owning three properties, which was our first goal.

We started by choosing our client avatar: luxury, multiple families who wanted to rest and relax, could afford a holiday, and didn't mind paying more for a more ideal home. Although we live in California, we chose Scottsdale since California is both heavily regulated and expensive. Since we weren't flying at the time, we wanted to be able to drive in seven hours or less or a one-hour plane ride. It took us another four months to secure a property. We bid on twenty and kept losing out to cash buyers and other investors willing to waive the appraisal contingency and take the property as is, but we tried to not lose hope. Finally, in February 2021, we ended up purchasing a property in Phoenix about two miles from Scottsdale, which worked in our favour as it was priced 25% less than a comparable property there and had fewer regulations than Scottsdale.

I always had a vision as a host of providing my guests outstanding customer service, a spotless home, the most comfortable bed they have slept in, a well-stocked kitchen with Nespresso, and a couch they could relax on and fall asleep. Basically, these are all the things I wanted when I stayed at an Airbnb. Imagining myself as the guest made it very easy for me to design. I strived to provide some of the things I loved, hosting and creating a beautiful space for people to enjoy, and it reignited my love of design. It took us several months to get our first property, but we finally got a five-bedroom, three-bath with a massive backyard in Phoenix, AZ. We relied on our realtor, who was a little green, to help us with inspections and repairs. My instinct told me he wasn't a shark like I'd wanted, but I felt we had already invested so much time and energy with him we needed to just roll with the punches. Our showings and inspections were done via FaceTime, which was a little nerve-racking because, since I paid so much attention to detail, there would be things that were missed. Finally, a day before the property closed, my partner took a trip to the property. The house was quickly renovated by a broker/contractor (dangerous combo) who completed the renovation in less than seven weeks. We knew this could be a disaster but were so desperate for a property that we took the chance.

Then came the fun part... we purchased a flip gone wrong, so we spent almost six months getting the property up to our standards, travelling back and forth from California. I was having the time of my life designing and learning about the STR world and couldn't wait to become a Superhost and own multiple properties. We had many bumps entering a hot market and waiting four months for a landscape contractor. He was a nightmare, and we had to fire him three-quarters of the way through the project. The roof collapsed during the monsoon season when we were initially presented with a fraudulent receipt for a new roof upon the purchase of the property, finally having to hire an attorney to get a new roof and our landscape contractor to reimburse us for unfinished work.

We found a local contractor, a team of electricians, a handyman runner and a cleaning company, which made the next property renovation very smooth, resulting in a full gut renovation completed in three months. We now own two properties, and the co-host and I have a new design business, STR Designed, specialising in curating luxury spaces for real estate investors. I visit my properties often, constantly adding unique touches and features. You can absolutely do anything remotely if you want to. There are many tools to help you achieve your goals, and so many people willing to help.

Our first STR helped me identify what I wanted in the second home, which was a more extensive kitchen since we host a more prominent type of family with a backyard that did not need a complete renovation. We purchased our second home a year later, only five blocks from the first, and we chose to do a complete gut renovation. We already had a contractor we trusted, and I was excited to design it and be able to select everything I wasn't able to choose in the first one, which drove me crazy. I chose an oversized island, the floor colour I wanted, and expanded the bathrooms to double their original size, plus my favourite feature, a coffee bar. I absolutely love the way it turned out, and it has helped me go on to design more STRs and reignite my career in design.

I feel like I was meant to be a host, and I love giving my guests a good experience. All my designs are geared towards the guest experience, and I want them to feel like they are staying at a friend's house and are relaxed and can't wait to come back. I know I am in the right business as about 75% of my guests mention how they feel the house was designed well and love how every room and area has a purpose. Being a hospitable host means setting a high standard and raising the bar for others, providing a high level of customer service, including concierge services like a private chef, in-home massages, having charcuterie trays and unique welcome gifts. When guests arrive, they genuinely feel like we appreciate them being at our home and feel special; plus, who doesn't like getting free stuff? I often do things like have a charcuterie board waiting in the fridge so they can have a snack upon arrival, send a gift card to a local pizza place so they don't have to worry about dinner after travelling all day, have a gift waiting if they are celebrating a birthday. This is about making the guest know I care about them, helping set their visit off to the right start. I will also purchase dinner for them or refund them if there are any issues with their stay, such as the pool's heat. Responding to their messages promptly from when their reservation is made is critical and helps set me apart and get five-star reviews.

I have had so many great guests and only one horrible guest, and I really attribute that to choosing my avatar, carefully screening, and possibly luck. Most of my guests come from Canada and the East Coast and are multi-generation and very low-key, with the average age in the mid-thirties with parents and children.

Some of the tips I would give to others entering STR:

1. Decide what market you want to invest in, who is your guest avatar and who you want to host, as this makes all the difference and will dictate the property you choose.
2. Pay attention to the design, as this will set you apart in a competitive market; always try to put yourself in the guest's shoes if you can.
3. You will have good and bad days, but the journey is worth it. There is no such thing as perfect, and it is always a process.
4. Don't be afraid to launch your listing without professional pictures, and don't wait for perfection; fix and improve things along the way and invest in good design and a cleaner.
5. Find a local "on the ground" team of cleaners, handymen, etc., leveraging local Facebook groups and your own network. Don't be afraid to ask questions and solicit advice from your network. Others have been doing this a long time and learned lots of tricks; make sure you employ the latest technology.
6. Always stay at your properties before you launch them and

after to ensure everything works properly so you can catch these things before your guest does.

7. Only use people you trust, or else why bother, as you will spend most of your time second-guessing the work done.
8. Cleaners are essential and the backbone. I am fortunate to work with a company that specialises in STRs, offers full-service cleans, including linens and supplies, and has an online portal with pictures of the home once it's been cleaned.

I have all five-star reviews, and 75% of my guests compliment my design and functionality. Colleagues in the industry advise me to "not sweat the small stuff" and remind me that it's never going to be perfect and always a work in progress, that this is a business and not your own home, so never take things personally. This has been a great piece of advice, and I constantly remind myself to not take things too seriously.

I always try to be a resource for others and mentor and share any knowledge I have about my experience, tools, or tricks of the trade. I love sharing and helping others in my group and industry, and I do not hesitate to help with questions and expertise. I have received invaluable information from others and love to share the knowledge. I have always loved helping and mentoring others and love the STR world, so it's fun for me. I am continuously learning new industry trends and how to pivot and change with the market, the trends and ways to improve my business. Never have I been in such a great industry where everyone works as a team and genuinely wants to help each other, which is a refreshing change.

My partner (former husband) and I have different roles in the business. I am the face to the customer and handle all guest communication, cleaners, handymen, design and other responsibilities. He oversees the marketing and financials and steps in when guests have technical issues with the pool. Having clearly defined roles as partners is critical to success and not wasting time wondering who is doing what. We have made a list of what we are responsible for and check in twice a week to review and collaborate on ways to continue to succeed, which helps us not waste time and to minimise mistakes. For example, he cannot give directions to cleaners, and I cannot provide directions to our pool vendors. This is unconventional and odd to some, but it works well for us. We currently own two homes in Phoenix, one 5/3 and a 4/2, and co-host together.

Personally and professionally, I have grown so much since I started the STR journey and have made many lifelong friends who are always ready to offer support and suggestions. I have had many personal challenges since I started, and I have learned to no longer worry about the little things and that things can be fixed if broken. I am proud of my accomplishments and cannot wait to see what the future holds. Mindset is everything in this business and life, and it's how I've got myself through the most challenging times of my life and helped me succeed. I try to be a role model for my daughter, and she often tells me she is proud of me, which is inspiring. I am excited about the STR world and eager to continue my journey.

Sharon Drive Resort Backyard

ABOUT THE AUTHOR

Karen Ochoa is the founder of A Travelers Home, Inc., specialising in co-hosting, and STR Designed, an interior design firm specialising in creating spaces to help owners maximise their profits. Based in California, she is passionate about transforming short-term rentals into micro-resorts with the feel of being at home. Karen offers full-service interior design and co-host services virtually for owners in the United States and has over fifteen years of commercial and residential real estate design and project management experience.

Before starting her STR business, she provided services to Apple, Yahoo, HP and corporate clients such as Federal Realty Group and PricewaterhouseCoopers. This was when interior design services, creation of standards, space planning, construction and project management were constructed and implemented. With extensive knowledge and experience in customer service and design, she now brings that sense of commercial quality and luxury to STR homeowners and their guests with classic and on-trend design and unparalleled co-hosting services to owners and investors.

Through her STR journey and experience designing her STRs, Karen realised quickly that other owners and operators needed interior designs specific to short-term hospitality, especially as the market grows and becomes more competitive. Her passion is creating curated spaces that give guests a sense of home and luxury. This philosophy of providing the highest level of customer service with a design geared to your locale and target market and meticulous design that guests will rave about. She believes the right design strategy and unparalleled customer service can set your home apart, make your listing stand out from others, and earn a higher return. Her experience and knowledge are best in class, keeping up with the latest technology and trends in the STR market. Her short-term rental strategies for design and co-hosting are focused on improving the guest experience because improved guest experience will maximise returns.

Links: https://linktr.ee/strdesigned

KATIE LEVITT

PASSIONATELY CURIOUS ME

If Walt Disney could create magic in Anaheim that would captivate the world, then I do believe each of us can create magic anywhere. That is a deep belief instilled in me because of my childhood. I grew up in the San Fernando Valley and, at that time in the early nineties, the school system in Los Angeles was subpar. The majority of our neighbourhood ended up at a private school called St Bridget of Sweden, which was filled with the greatest mentors and lessons of life that moulded me into who I am today. What made it special was our small-knit working-class families who truly created a community filled with imagination and hard work because that was the core of our values. It was always with such great love our parents would transform those tired walls of our school into the greatest experiences of our childhood. Of course, most of these rooms were set up with mainly painted cardboard, glitter, draped fabric and repurposed items from our homes, but when paired with dim lighting and music it became a wonderland! The main hall was known to whisk you away on occasions to foreign lands such as an Arabian night, *Wizard of Oz*, or even a *Journey Under the Sea* to name a few of the spectacular handcrafted experiences.

The haunted hallway on Halloween and the autumn festival were my favourites. The dark and spooky hallway was filled with familiar faces who would playfully scare the living daylights out of us, and we would scream in laughter. After all, we knew every ghoul, ghost and witch in the place, and they were known to break character. I remember exiting the hallway with our side-splitting, could barely breathe laughter, nodding to my friends, and running all the way around to do it again.

The autumn festival was the best of all. Not only was our playground transformed into a fully-fledged carnival, but hello, we got to step out of our plaid dress uniforms and into a free dress. Oddly enough, I remember outfit planning to be twinning with my friend. We went matching in our St Bridget's T-shirts. Sure, we missed the point, but the carnival was a taste of sweet independence being able to go on rides by ourselves, being given five Bridget bucks, a roll of tickets, and an hour before we had to check in with our parents. We were practically the teenagers we'd heard of in our books.

Those years taught me to do the little details with great love, which will create a feeling for those who experience it. This is a practice I bring to all areas of my life, and I believe is one of the strongest assets that I bring to hosting.

A PEEK BEHIND THE CURTAIN

After a long, successful career in cosmetology, I dreamed of changing my career path to something with more variety in its creativity. For as long as I can remember, nothing excites me more than seeing how it happens or being behind the scenes where everything gets created. On New Year's Eve, 2011, my resolution to myself was to go to bed early, wake up refreshed and create the life I have been dreaming of for years. I wasn't sure what this meant yet, but I was determined to follow my curiosity down different paths to discover what was right for me. In a passing conversation

Fall Festival 1990

with a long-time client who was in the live entertainment industry, I remember asking him, "If you ever need an intern for an event, please think of me, I would appreciate the opportunity." Less than a week later, I found myself in Miami working my first event. I was blown away by every detail that went into it behind the scenes to make it happen.

Over the next few months, I continued to work events, while simultaneously balancing my clients' hair appointments. Life got exciting travelling around the country, learning so much about events. In the midst of it all, something happened that I would have never expected. Spoiler alert... there was a romance brewing in the background.

During an insanely humid summer evening in New York City, my boyfriend's – now my husband's – company, Wide Angle Group, shut down Times Square to produce that summer's blockbuster movie premiere. Did you know you could rent out Times Square? I certainly had no idea and, since Ian and I had just started dating a month before, I was thoroughly impressed! I was standing with Ian in the back of house, behind the red carpet. The event should have been wrapping up soon, and everything had been running smoothly. Suddenly, one of the electricians from the crew came over and told Ian something quietly. Ian immediately looked at me.

"Kate, you need to move away from this area right now... the generator is going to blow!"

Panicked, I quickly moved as far back as possible, pressing

myself against an 'I LOVE NYC' souvenir shop window. Suddenly, the power cut and Ian turned back to make eye contact with me with the biggest smile. By this point, I had been crying my eyes out, terrified about what was going to happen. He now also looked panicked and came rushing over, saying, "What's wrong?"

Standing there quietly wiping away my streaming tears, in my work polo, of course (which is one of my most notable red carpet looks), I looked up at Ian. "You said the generator was going to blow, thank God it didn't!"

Ian laughed with relief, hugged me, and miraculously, while remaining calm, explained to me what had happened. It had in fact blown! The generator had run out of fuel at the perfect time, exactly when the host signed off on the live broadcast. It ended up looking like it was intentional and planned perfectly!

I went from sheer terror to sheer relief because nothing blew up! Who knew 'the generator is going to blow' meant that it was simply going to lose power, not blow up Times Square? The event was a success.

This is the best example of how Ian balances me. When I panic, he is the soundboard with so much experience in life and events that he makes me feel safe and invincible when we work together. I focus on the little details, and he sees the bigger picture. This dynamic has been key to our success. We tied the knot on the Amalfi Coast in 2013. I am luckier than most because on that day I got to marry into a family of three. I started my vows on our wedding day to his children Madison and Samuel. At the time, they were twelve and ten. On the 14th of August 2013, our partnership became official with two little ones in tow.

IT'S THE THOUGHT THAT COUNTS

Our hosting journey was originally set to start in January 2015 after purchasing the property during the previous summer. After we got married, Ian and I made the decision that it was more important that I stay at home with the kids to give them stability as Ian's event schedule takes him all over the world on a regular basis. Collectively, Ian and I found it possible to buy an investment property to become a holiday home and STR. After looking all over southern California, we found our dream in practically our own backyard, just thirty minutes from home, but it felt like a world away. We closed on a five-acre property.

The Santa Monica Mountains are known to be home to the mystic Topanga Canyon, a Mecca that is rich in its history, for its beauty, drawing in hippies, outlaws and artists since the 1950s. Our five-acre property lies here. Our goal was not to make the house look like a typical home, but a high-end villa at a hotel, planning each area to be its own escape. After spending the holidays there, we both agreed that we'd succeeded because neither of us wanted to leave, let alone share it with the world. Friends, family and friends of the family came quite often to stay... so really, we just did a four-year soft opening. It wasn't very profitable, but it taught me a lot about hosting guests. It taught me how important it is that each stay should be uniquely tailored to the occasion. This varied from anniversaries, birthdays and honeymoons. However, people also came to stay and make amends with a diagnosis or broken hearts. Our place once had to become a safe place for a multigenerational family to seek out peace when gathering to spend the final moments with their mom. No matter what the reason may be for staying, one thing remained true: everyone voiced how peaceful it was and how they had felt renewed. This was and still is something so special to me.

* * *

The beginning of daylight started to dance between the slats of the shutters and into the room. I'd been up since 4am. Our youngest, then almost three, woke me up so I could snuggle him in his bed, and he was back off to dreamland. Usually, I drifted back to sleep too... but this particular morning, my brain was wide awake since before 5.30am because I had been working on something. I was quietly giggling, still in our son's bed, when I heard shuffling of feet and looked up to find my husband standing in the doorway.

"Is everything all right in here?"

My phone chimed again. I giggled more and gave him a coy smile. A few days earlier, we had been on a road trip with our three kids in Montana. Sharing a glass of wine, Ian and I were alone sitting around the firepit. I'd decided to revisit the idea. Finally, what was in my head broke the silence.

"It's interesting..." I started, hoping to draw him in. "I don't think I've seen all of us smile this much or be this relaxed since the start of the pandemic."

Ian added, bringing to life the brisk night's fireplace conversation, "I agree, it's been an amazing adventure; I don't think we would have taken this trip with the kids at their ages if it wasn't for flights being grounded and the Reed's offering us their Airbnb."

"That's kind of where I'm going with this. Before you say no, hear me out." His hand gestured for me to go on. "There's so much sadness in the world right now, look at what a gift this trip for us has been just getting out of our own space, it feels freeing. Not everyone is fortunate enough to be able to travel far or have another home they can break up the monotony with. I think it's time we put Topanga on Airbnb."

What seemed like an hour of silence to me was finally broken. I was already feeling the rejection coming from him. "I don't know, Kate."

"I don't know either. I do know people are suffering mentally and emotionally, and the parks and beaches are closed. There is nowhere for people to go to escape. Think of everyone who has stayed there in the past, and how they were able to feel their stress melt away or reconnect with the ones they love. The night after the riots I talked to my grandma and asked her what is the difference between today with the pandemic and the Great Depression? What she said keeps playing in my mind."

"What did she say?"

"She said that during the depression we had community and purpose. That yes, they were hard times, but people could lean on each other. She said that President Roosevelt knew that people just sitting around wasn't good for individual households and society, so he enacted a multitude of programmes to help our country. There were camps put together for young men to work and give them something to do. She was a young child at the time but remembers how the adults talked often about how important it was. Ian, I think she's right. I know how hard you have worked to make sure we keep our core employees on. I'm proud of you for figuring it out. We are living in a moment of history that our children will talk about to their children and even their children's children. They are looking to us. I want them to remember how we showed up. Not just for them, but for who we are in the world. I want to teach them, that we show up when others go home. That we open our home to strangers to keep the people we love working because, I know as well as you do, we need to be proactive in spreading happiness."

By the time I've got this far in laying out my inner thoughts, I'm choked up by my conviction and tears were filling my dream-shot eyes. To me, I'd just delivered the speech of a lifetime. In a way, I felt like I was channelling my inner Roosevelt. Through the flickers of the firepit, I could see there was no standing ovation... just Ian staring off into the distance. He finally spoke up. "I'll think about it, let's discuss it when we get home."

I thought to myself, "So, you're telling me there is a chance?"

* * *

My phone chimed again. I giggled. Ian was still standing in the doorway, wondering what was going on.

"So, that chiming noise... It's potential bookings."

Ian's face changed from half asleep to wide awake. I saw him gain a sense of urgency.

"I need to get my laptop and see this."

Within the first ten minutes live on Airbnb, we had three

potential bookings. Luckily, only one of them booked, because I had no idea what I was doing before I submitted it. Cleaning fees? $25.00 seems fair. Charity host for free? Why not? Ian logged in and we fixed everything super quickly. But then and there our hosting journey began. I'll never forget that moment snuggling with my son. I was trying to talk myself into going back to sleep instead of pressing submit. But something inside me kept me from dozing off. As cliché as it is, they always tell you to 'trust your gut'. I knew that this was my inner conscious finding the courage to submit and put our house live and available for the world. I knew I had to do it before my mind could talk me out of it. The moment I hit the button, my heart fluttered with sheer terror and excitement. It was at this moment that I woke my heart up to my purpose and passion in ways I could have never dreamed.

* * *

They say the only difference between anxiety and excitement is your willingness to let go of fear. The quote "Can't wait!" by Bart Scott is one I tell myself often when I feel fear creep in. This happened a lot during those days before we welcomed our first official guest. There were exactly six days to set up. We got the band back together and went to work after months apart; as I'm sure you know, nothing can feel better in life than being reunited. There was a buzz in the air. The day finally came. The 2nd of July 2020. We welcomed our first guests, a family of three. Two days later, we received our first review, and I was hooked! The journey from that day to today has been such a learning experience. We have hosted thousands of people, twelve weddings, bought two more properties, and have had our house trashed from an illegal Instagram-promoted party.

Most notably, my original intention has remained constant. For the past two and a half years since we opened our doors, we have been able to give work to people from all parts of our lives. Old family friends, childhood friends from my days at Bridget's, hairstylists I used to work with, both our older children, neighbours and my

Family fun

mom to name a few. They have all been a part of our operation at one point or another, which makes it fun. Some are just passing through and I think it's so great that we can enjoy the moment and make new memories. Others stick around and I am deeply grateful to have them be a part of the team. This goes further than the team, though. They all become a part of our story.

If you want my two cents?

If you have this book in your hand, I hope you realise it's so much more than just a book. No matter where you are in your hosting journey, there are so many resources in this book. It is filled with like-minded hosts, who are knowledgeable. Some have training/systems they can share with you. Some will teach you how to invest or scale. Personally, I can offer you a friendship and listening ear. If you have a question that I don't know the answer to, we can figure it out together. The most important thing is to know that if you haven't found your community yet, I promise you it's somewhere in this book. I encourage you, no, dare you to pick at least one of these amazing hosts to reach out to. If you do it, let me know because it will make me smile! Whatever road you choose, FIND YOUR COMMUNITY! I found mine from the Thanks for Visiting podcast and class, it changed my income, it changed my mindset and it led me to this book today.

"There is a story behind every booking."

A wise man penned these words, and they were like a mirror looking into my soul. This was something I lived by before I came across Mark Simpson's quote. He somehow managed to tuck such meaning into something I would explain in long, drawn-out sentences. If every host made this quote their mantra, our industry would be unstoppable. Know this. Whatever your guest tells you is something, no matter how small it is, or if it's in passing... they want to be seen, heard and recognised. We all do!

"Keep your corner of the world clean." – Lynn Fernandez

This quote was told to me by my mom. It's a quote from my childhood friend's mom. Lynn is one of the most elegant people I have ever met in my life. Maybe it's why those words mean so much to me. I was probably about ten years old when my mom said these words to me for the first time. It became a goal for me immediately. We don't need to change the whole world; we just have to be great in what we do with our corner of it. This will have a massive impact on those around you. I think the opportunity to host is a wonderful platform to spread good into everyday life.

ABOUT THE AUTHOR

Arguably one of the greatest decisions in her life went down on the 1st of July 2020. Katie Levitt and her husband Ian decided to turn Levinaia, their private estate, into a holiday rental. Since that day, Katie hasn't looked back, only forward to a future of what beauty and adventure she can share with the world. To Katie, Levinaia was an endless art project she'd work on with her husband. They had referred to it as a love letter to their children, but now for all their guests as well. Before Katie had the epiphany to share Levinaia with her guests, she was a stay-at-home mom. While occupied with raising her kids, Katie dreamt of a passion project that could only be achieved at its best once her youngest started school. When reflecting on this chapter of her life, she finds that through years of seeking out a purpose she discovered many passions, but nothing compelled her to share them with the world. So, when did Katie have this realisation? When figuring out how to serve her community in a time of need is how she found her purpose that conclusively developed into her passion. Since then, Katie and Ian have welcomed thousands of guests, acquired two more properties in their favourite regions of California, and hope to forever show guests luxury comforts in the magical jaw-dropping locations that Levinaia has to offer.

Links: https://linktr.ee/Katielevitt

KIM FITZPATRICK

THE ACCIDENTAL DISRUPTOR

I **honestly didn't mean for all this to happen.** I was just trying to pay for my kids' after school activities.

I started out on this journey as a single mom, newly divorced, trying to make ends meet as a PE teacher fleeing an abusive relationship. I had nothing but food stamps, government assistance and hand-me-down furniture when I left. Thanks to the government, I got an apartment and a new start for my two young boys and me. It was so hard to make ends meet for a family of three on a teacher's salary. I was always trying to figure out ways to stretch the budget and earn more income. Renting a room in my apartment on Airbnb was at the forefront of my mind for a solution, but it wasn't permissible under my rental contract. If you know me, you also know my lack of any sense of direction, so that didn't lend well to Uber! Nor can a single mom with littles afford the day care to be away from home any extra hours.

What to do, what to do?

In a series of continued challenging life events, cancer took my dad at the age of sixty-two, followed by my mom three years later. Within months of her passing, my grandmother, favourite uncle and family dog passed too. I was super alone, super stressed and super exhausted trying to be both parents and grandparents to my kids. I was frustrated, sad and lonely. Add to that, I broke my foot on the last day of the school year and couldn't walk, bear weight, or drive my kids anywhere for an entire summer. Gah. No chance for extra income. No chance for changing my financial situation. No chance for fun. Just alone with my thoughts and stresses.

Until...

I decided to take my first of many bold moves to improve my kids' life circumstances. I used the money my parents left me when they passed away to put a down payment on a home. I gave my kids a choice in where we could live. I said to them, you can have a bigger inside of the house (square footage in adult terms), a bigger yard to play in, or you can stay in your same school boundaries. I couldn't afford three, or even two of the things on the list. They wanted less chaos and upheaval in their lives and chose to stay in their school district boundaries and keep close to their friends. From there, I looked for a suitable home. I found a great little 1,400 sq ft home for us in a nice neighbourhood, near their friends and near a huge park connected to a college campus, which far exceeded any lawn we could dream of. Three bedrooms meant that the primary suite was for guests, the bigger second bedroom was for the boys to share and the little third bedroom was all mine. The boys and I shared the hall bathroom, while guests got their own private bathroom within their bedroom.

The guests didn't have a separate entrance, so that meant we got to see them, chat with them and share life with them. I got started in the true OG way of Airbnb. We had an extra room and an air mattress. Yes, you read that right. Air mattress. Not a fancy bed with extra charging ports on the nightstand and a coffee bar with all the accoutrements. Just a bare bones place to rest their head at a safe and welcoming home. Luckily, this type of listing appealed to young people taking a semester of study at the nearby college, so I got several mid-term renters, with a few one or two-nighters sprinkled in between. I made more money than I thought was possible from something like this! Cleaning was done by me,

It all started so I could give my boys a better life!

and a breeze because it wasn't too often. It was great to start to be able to cover expenses and keep my kids in sports and activities after school.

We got to know our guests and to really learn their experiences. I was having a great time, and as with everything I do, working to improve what I offered my guests. That summer, I went garage sale shopping, looking for a garden hose, a shovel and whatever else useful. I had $32 in my pocket. Amazingly, I happened upon an almost brand new, perfectly good high-quality mattress from a family whose mom came to live with them but only stayed several weeks before being moved to a home. They were asking a hundred dollars. Sheepishly, I offered $32, only because it was everything I had. I was so appreciative to them for giving me such a tremendous deal. I kept thinking, "This thirty-two-dollar mattress is going to pay for itself in three nights." I was in heaven. I remember feeling like a "real" host now!

That mattress was everything. It created a real income stream where I could now make strides in hosting beyond just extra money for my kids' activities. I searched social media to see how I could host better, offer more and really do the best with what I had to give a five-star experience to my guests. I found mentors online, I researched and listened in Facebook groups, I absorbed like a sponge! And I hustled. I listed my couch in the living room on Airbnb as well. Eventually, I found a sleeper sofa at a great Black Friday price, and increased the cost per night in that space too. My kids and I developed funny lingo. They would ask, "Do we have couch people tonight?" – meaning 'are we eating dinner as a picnic in mom's room or at the table like a "normal" family?'

Yes, it was a full house sometimes, yes it could get a little crowded. And yes, my family and friends all tried to deter my efforts and caution me. They feared for my safety. They thought I'd have people stealing from me or worse. But I was there welcoming guests into my home. I saw, made eye contact, and had conversations with each of them. I knew more clearly what I was doing.

Of course, it was inconvenient at times, and sometimes I'd get nervous about guests. But here's the thing all the naysayers missed. They missed having a conversation with the amazing, elderly Japanese couple who were in town visiting their daughter at college. They missed witnessing the traditional Japanese breakfast with miso soup and a dozen tiny bowls set out for breakfast and the fact that my guests unknowingly offered my kids an educational and cultural experience on a Tuesday morning before school. They missed the French-Canadian college student having conversations and laughing with my boys while trying to improve his English for school. They missed the distance runner who was in town training at the Nike world campus. They missed getting to share life with a professional athlete for several months during Covid. They missed the eighteen-year-old student away from his home state, who wanted a bit of a mom figure to help him navigate life away from home for the first time, who, a year after leaving us, came back and left very generous Christmas gifts on the porch. His biggest gift to me was the card that said he'd graduated with his family counselling degree and was constantly impressed with how well

I parented my kids. So super sweet to hear that kind of feedback. Also a bit awkward because he was there when days with my kids (and I) were less than ideal for guests to experience!

The naysayers missed the young Korean couple who shared stories and meals with us, and who I took to play basketball with me so he could play with the Americans, a life goal of his. They missed learning about the Korean way of celebrating the New Year, and the customs I still participate in because of them. They missed getting invited to a boxing class with my guest and being able to experience something new and fun that I didn't know about, right under my nose in town.

Ultimately, the naysayers miss so much in life. They are not in the arena with us. They are not who we need as our advisers and mentors. We miss so many opportunities in life when we listen to them.

I believe this hosting journey is filled with fabulous opportunities and experiences. Whether we host in our homes, or across the country, adventure awaits us as hosts. And so do resources, even more than naysayers, if we are willing to reach out to them. This book is just one small piece of evidence showing us that we are surrounded by like-minded folks, striving to create great experiences for our guests and other hosts. I believe humans, and our ability to reach out and connect with them, is our greatest resource. Fostering interactions in ways that bring us together, to help us all gain positive experiences in life is the role I have chosen to live. But I digress from my story.

Guests are amazing, beautiful people who give to me and my family as much or more as I give to them. They, by their nature, display cultural experiences that get shared with my kids, tell interesting stories, give important information back to me as a host and about my spaces. I appreciate hearing both their feedback and their praise. I strive to stay at the forefront of hosting, to stay current and relevant, to keep providing amazing experiences and, in turn, give my children something I could never give to them as a struggling teacher.

I found freedom to follow my own passions as well

Let's skip to the "where is she now" part. This one room and my pull-out sleeper sofa created enough extra income that I eventually purchased a condo very nearby. I pretended as I managed that the condo was across the country, as a way to mentally practise remote hosting. Due to the way it was laid out, I was able to turn that one-bedroom condo into a two-bedroom by (cosmetically) converting the large dining room into a bedroom. It was able to generate income beyond predictions using that strategy. I used funds from that property to purchase a cabin in the Smoky Mountains of Tennessee, which I themed after Dolly Parton (after not seeing any other cabins themed after her in her hometown and near Dollywood. Pirates, yes. Tropical themes, yes. Dolly, no. Weird!). That little cabin created enough income for me to be able to partner on a waterfront beach place in Destin, Florida. My partner and I then bought a beautiful long-range-view cabin in Blue Ridge, Georgia that same year. We have since parted ways and I kept the Destin, Florida condo. I've now sold my Tennessee "Dolly cabin" property for two and a half times what I bought it for in two and a half years. By using a 1031 exchange, I'm now the new owner of a place in Montana that overlooks Flathead Lake, close to a ski resort and a mountain bike park. It's amazing what can be accomplished when you just keep striving.

I quit my teaching job two school years ago in my early forties to fully pursue this lifestyle of travel, adventures and so much quality time with my boys, I can actually call it quantity time too.

In addition to hosting my own properties, I'm active in helping other owners get their properties up and running by being at their location when they can't be, to get them all the boxes open, set up and operational in a much faster timeline than they can do on their own. With more than a dozen set up experiences under my belt, I have an efficiency I can guarantee, a work ethic that rivals anyone, a huge network and knowledge of STR resources that go beyond unboxing, and the ability to mount an army when needed to get things done. It's a fun burst of intensity to get other owners' properties photographed and guest ready in a week. I absolutely love helping hosts grow as much as I love giving my guests great experiences with their loved ones.

This is my OG Airbnb dream path, and this is lil' ol' me rockin' it.

I'd never put my guests on an air mattress anymore. My kids have their own rooms now and are almost grown and out on their own. We don't share our time at home with guests anymore either. I still rent out the primary suite in my home to guests, but as a whole home listing, and we lock off the kids' rooms when they are with their dad and I'm out travelling the world. I check-out of my own house like a guest, and I let my housekeeper clean behind me to make everything perfect for them. My mortgage is covered many more months than it's not, and by the end of the year, I live for free, thanks to my guests, even though I reside here with my kids half the time. I'm well past the days of talking to my kids about the "couch people". For me, and my limited cash flow and savings when getting started, these were all necessary steps in the learning process, the discovery process, and the transition from employee to self-employed freedom. I accidentally disrupted my life as a struggling teacher and mom with no time or energy left for her kids at the end of the day. I disrupted the rat race to create a successful, entrepreneurial business and can now share time and activities with my kids, and can show them the world, or just see it myself. I disrupted the stress and naysayers to find freedom, gratitude and a tribe of positive friends across the globe on a similar path. I owe so much to this journey and the people who have taken it with me.

It's with great passion that I strive to give and to continue to grow, so that I can lift other hosts up as well!

ABOUT THE AUTHOR

Kim Fitzpatrick is a former teacher, single mom to two teenage boys, and the founder of Full Send Life (FSL), a short-term rental (STR) simplifying and consulting company. She helps STR investors/owners solve the stress of billions of decisions and actions while simplifying processes so that owners can productively work ON the high-level needs of their business, instead of grinding IN their business. FSL believes in the principle of leaving people better than you find them. Whether guests or an investor/owner, FSL strives to help destress, simplify and create amazing experiences, both in business, travel and life. Kim has been featured in podcasts, articles and YouTube videos, and is an inspirational leader for STR investors/owners. Additionally, those looking to quit "the W2" and pursue a lifestyle of freedom outside of the nine-to-five look to her social media as an inspirational guide for what life can be like on the "other side". She's hosted more than 1900 guest stays, and to date has set up eleven properties for herself and clients. Additionally, Kim has been a Superhost for twenty-two consecutive cycles. She is a board member for host2host.org, a trade association by hosts, for hosts, as well as an integral part of several masterminds. Kim travels extensively, works remotely and, even though it's hard to keep track of where she is, she calls Portland, Oregon home... at least until her amazing boys fly the nest.

Links: https://linktr.ee/Kim.fitz

LAURA WEGNER, THE SUITE LIFE™ WHISTLER

HOW THE THEME OF GENEROSITY LEADS TO DISCOVERING A NEW FRIEND AND A NICHE SUCCESS

Do you think they're criminals? What if they trash our suite or take advantage of us? *Wham,* a massive hot-flash and a double-dose of doubt flooded over me. As if on cue, Masha – a single mum from Kyiv, Ukraine – and her two teenage daughters pulled up in front of our home.

Inviting this family into our rental suite meant ignoring our standard business operating procedure – and that unsettled me. Welcoming unvetted guests? Yeah, right. Allowing three people in a two-person space? Hard pass. Offering one year rent-free? Sputter-choke-blue-face! You get the picture.

Thankfully, my fierce logic and deep optimism re-engaged before our guests got out of the vehicle. This isn't business – it's a heart-stance: making a difference, being generous, extending hospitality and helping create possibilities for this refugee family that may not exist apart from us.

I closed the gap between us and welcomed this family with words and a warm embrace.

But hugs are an inadequate counterbalance for war-born fear and turmoil. This family desperately needed peace, safety and stability. Masha compared fleeing Ukraine and escaping to Canada to *jumping off a mountain.*

I wondered if there was a mountain on earth high enough to qualify for that kind of extreme parental freefall? My musings evaporated as she offered, "...And you jumped off the mountain too!" I took a moment to think on that. I smiled and offered, "We jumped together."

Masha and I deeply connected through shared goals, personality similarities and faith-based common ground. She often says, "You're the perfect person [Host] for me," acknowledging how in sync we are. The more she shared her heart, the more I recognised similarities in the way Masha and I approached and navigated life.

We understood one another immediately; as one courageous navigator to another.

Throughout my adult life, being an optimist, a courageous navigator, a possibility creator and a person with a generous spirit has come naturally to me. As a highly intuitive teacher with a master's in applied linguistics, I often see others' greatest strengths, talents and abilities before they do... and I see potential where others see roadblocks.

I honed these skills and attitudes as an educator of underprivileged kids. Assessing patterns and evaluating my students' potential became one of my greatest super-powers. As it turns out, my business venture benefited from these skills as much as my students had.

Identifying the right investment property is all about evaluating potential. That's how we successfully navigated our first property purchase in Whistler: synthesising data; teasing out patterns; extrapolating potential; *and* partnering with an elite real estate agent (Dani O'Neill, a member of John Ryan's team). Prior to partnering with Dani, more than one agent suggested:

"If you buy a property in Whistler... don't expect to cash flow."

Especially with only 10-20% down. Dani had a different opinion. It would be challenging... but not impossible. With her help, Oz and I crunched the numbers and decided not to let others' perception of possibility hijack ours.

ABOUT LAURA AND THE BIZ

My name is Laura Wegner and I'm the founder of The Suite Life™ Whistler, in Canada. I uploaded our first holiday rental property in January 2020. Two years later, I signed up for Eric Moeller's and Jasper Ribbers' Legends X Program: an intensive training course for hosts looking to build a scalable short-term rental business. During this course, I gained the knowledge and the tools necessary to expand my business exponentially. As my knowledge base grew, so did my vision.

The Suite Life™ has a two-fold purpose: 1) offering boutique ski-in/ski-out holiday rental spaces on the slopes of Blackcomb Mountain, and 2) operating an Airbnb management company that supports and educates investors who want to build their portfolio through maximising their ski-in/ski-out property's revenue potential in Whistler.

If you own a Whistler ski-in/ski-out property (or you'd like to own a ski-in/ski-out property here) I believe I can help maximise your return. Out of 1000+ one-bedroom listings, my property has been identified as the fourth most profitable in Whistler according to AirDNA (and yes, the income they've posted is spot on).

Read on as I reveal how the theme of thoughtful generosity led me to discover a niche success in Whistler, Canada... and how this core value motivated and inspired our family to give back by hosting a refugee family in one of our suites!

THOUGHTFUL GENEROSITY: A CORE VALUE AND A HEART STANCE

I believe in being kind, generous, thankful, faithful and giving

The Suite Life™ Whistler is a true ski-in ski-out property located on the slopes of Blackcomb Mountain in beautiful British Columbia, Canada. Our complex features the largest heated pool in the benchlands plus three hot tubs! What's not to love?

back: welcome to my core values. These attitudes are foundational to the company I'm building – and the life I live.

On the business side of things, core values communicate who the company is, what we stand for, and what we're striving toward. These values are not only the soul of the company, but they're my heart stance – and they have the capacity to have a powerful impact on our guests' lives.

I'd like to introduce you to a core value that's transformed my business life *and* my personal life simultaneously.

I call this value thoughtful generosity.
(Is that a thing? I'm a linguist. I made it a thing :)

Hospitable hosts tend to tune into this naturally. The *thoughtful* component represents the well-thought-out plan to enhance a guest's stay. Thoughtful generosity is an attitude that recognises guests have different needs then implements a plan to help the team anticipate and meet those needs on a case-by-case basis:

> **We extend *thoughtful generosity* and gracious hosting to our guests to help them feel at home.** We fill our suites with many thoughtful extras. These special touches

> say, "Welcome. We're so glad you're here. Enjoy!" We believe that anticipating and meeting guests' needs is an exceptional way to build our brand and customer loyalty. We know that going the extra mile isn't just a saying, it's a commitment... and we're all in!

I anticipated that being a generous host in Whistler would set me apart from other holiday rentals; and that it would enhance and elevate our guests' stay; but I'd never imagined generosity would catapult me to the most profitable one-bedroom category in a crazy competitive market like Whistler!

The theme of generosity has also had an impact on my personal life this year. I used to think helping others required being flush with cash... when it only requires being flush with compassion. We offered one of our rental suites to a Ukrainian refugee family to bless them. And, as it turns out, the blessing was reciprocal. Generosity sent me a precious new friendship and introduced me to a new language and culture as well. As a linguist, that qualifies as Christmas!

I feel blessed... and thankful!

Maybe you're reading about my journey today and you're not feeling particularly blessed or thankful as you reflect on the circumstances of your life. You've suffered loss... doubted yourself... or just can't seem to catch a break. Maybe you've even had to start a new career or business that requires significant retooling like I have. I get it. I've been there.

Stepping out into something new is uncomfortable... it's risky. Ask Masha and I... it feels like jumping off a mountain.

But building something from scratch isn't just risky. it's crazy difficult: whether you're an immigrant building a new life in a foreign country or an entrepreneur building a business from the ground up, the attitudes and principles that spearhead success overlap.

1. Work hard and educate yourself.
2. Encourage yourself and others along the way and persevere!
3. Navigate courageously and have a little faith.

In my intro, when I explained how Masha (my most memorable guest) and I deeply connected through shared goals and attitudes, these three points are the goals and attitudes I was referring to.

WORK HARD AND EDUCATE YOURSELF

"The best investment by far is anything that develops yourself..." says Warren Buffet, CEO of Berkshire Hathaway. He unpacks this educational strategy further by adding two additional pieces of advice: 1) be the best in your field, and 2) learn to communicate better (in writing and orally). Why? Because when you communicate better, "...you increase your value by 50%."

When I shifted my focus from hosting my own holiday rentals to managing other people's, one thing was clear, I needed to educate myself... immediately. I researched the options and signed up for the Legends X Program.

I was starting at ground zero and needed a plan.

As an efficiency person, I wasn't interested in reinventing the wheel. I was looking for 'a company in a box' without even knowing if such a thing existed. Legends promised to deliver what I needed most: a company playbook, protocol for hiring team members, a method for automating systems, advice on coordinating a tech stack, how to market the company and seamlessly onboard properties. And they delivered! Best. Decision. Ever. 2022.

For Masha, upping her game in Canada meant focusing on the communication component of Warren's advice. In Kyiv, she was known as a competent, articulate and accomplished real estate lawyer – an expert in her field. Here, her competency is linked to her level of English proficiency (both written and oral).

Her conversational English is strong, but during a recent job interview at a law firm, she was told it wasn't strong enough. I was sitting in the hallway. I heard the assessment. My heart sank.

We exited the law office and walked in silence down the stairs towards the foyer of the building. As we left the building, I confessed, "I heard the whole interview." There was no delicate way to ask an awkward question, so I blurted out, "Are you disappointed? Do you want to talk about what's on your mind?" We opened the doors and entered the car.

Her hands were shaking with emotion as I handed her a tissue and then grabbed one for myself. There was a very short moment of tears, followed by sheer resolve and a declaration: "They said I need to improve my English, so I will improve it!" Done.

Masha didn't make excuses; she made progress. She researched her options and signed up for an ESL class immediately. Since her first class was weeks away, and she didn't want to lose momentum, I asked her if she'd like to try using language learning software. She said she would, so we gifted her with one. You've got this, Masha!

ENCOURAGE YOURSELF AND OTHERS ALONG THE WAY AND PERSEVERE

I love to hear about a person's journey: what they've learned; how far they've come; and where they're headed next. It fascinates me. And I'm genuinely excited, inspired and uplifted when I hear about success. It fills me with so much joy that you'd think it was *my* accomplishment!

Although I'm enthusiastic about celebrating other people's wins, I was reluctant to celebrate my own. Generous with others – not so generous with myself. Maybe you can relate.

Six months ago, I shifted my perspective. Instead of focusing on the tonnes of things I still had to learn in this business, I started focusing on how much I've achieved and how far I'd come.

One perspective weighs in on deficit;
the other weighs in on ground gained (and celebrating wins)!

Be kind to yourself. Encourage yourself and others along the way. Freely celebrate your wins and surround yourself with people who celebrate your accomplishments with the same joy and exuberance that you do. You deserve it! You deserve it! You deserve it!

Masha also had a major shift in perspective this past year with deficits and wins. Except hers involved uber perseverance, courage and some major white knuckling. She wanted to learn to drive, but there was a problem: she had a phobia of driving. A twelve-year phobia!

Masha and a wayward Ukrainian mailbox had a bit of a run-in. She was pregnant. The accident was traumatic. She never drove again. But somewhere between phobia and Canada, she decided that driving would be a win. And I promised to teach her.

Masha never really felt *ready* to drive, but she showed up, gripped the wheel and stepped on the gas anyway. I understood. I was well acquainted with the *start before you're ready* scenario, and the negative thoughts and nerves that accompanied it.

During our first driving lesson, I noticed Masha doing something unusual. She was trying to drive with her toe on the brake and her heel on the accelerator... simultaneously. Turns out her previous driving instructor was more intent on yelling at her than instructing her. With my encouragement and over forty lessons, she's done a 180. And she's an excellent driver.

Her daughters and family in Ukraine are stunned she's driving.
Masha and I are ecstatic!

How did she transition from phobia to proficiency? From ground zero to excellence? She stopped saying she had a phobia (I suggested that and she took it to heart :); she had support and encouragement; she shifted her thinking to see driving as a win; and she uber persevered!

NAVIGATE COURAGEOUSLY AND HAVE A LITTLE FAITH

Being a courageous navigator requires bravely planning or directing a route or course without being deterred by danger or pain. Sounds a lot like building a business, but more aptly defines fleeing war-torn Ukraine in search of safety.

When you find yourself in treacherous, uncharted territory, take courage... and have a little faith.

During the pandemic, my gourmet coffee service that thrived for over a decade died. It happened quickly... and it was deeply painful. Bye-bye income. Bye-bye stability. Hello future!

The only income-generating potential I had was renting out a Whistler condo we'd purchased and freshened up a few months prior. I was new to the holiday rental industry and had no reputation and no traction with the online travel agencies... and occupancy rates were nil.

A barrage of defeating and unproductive thoughts overwhelmed me. The odds were already stacked against me *prior* to the pandemic. Everything's changed. What if I can't do this? What if I can't cover costs... let alone cash flow? I think I'm in trouble.

As the onslaught of negativity dissipated, a deep optimism and dogged determination rushed back in: What if I *can* do this? What if I knock it out of the park? It's time to have a little faith! That's the moment the trajectory of my thinking, my attitude and my future moved closer to success.

That was the day I stopped asking myself, "What if I fail?" And began asking myself, "What if I succeed?"

Asking, "What if I succeed?" is the hallmark of a courageous navigator. Masha and her girls are three of the most courageous navigators I know. Can you imagine upending your life at a moment's notice? The mental and physical toll of their journey was

Laura showing her Ukrainian Guest Masha how easy it is to leave her twelve-year driving phobia in the dust!

no doubt staggering. Masha describes how each day was punctuated by prayer, the kindness and generosity of strangers, and the sheer will to survive and move forward – even in the face of danger.

The train station in Kyiv was a mob scene. Three train cars for four thousand evacuees. Nerves frayed. Tensions rose. Gunshots rang out. And panic ensued. A small child and the train engineer lay dead from a ricochet bullet. Would Masha or one of her girls be next?

They made it on the same train to Poland, but were separated. With travellers packed in like sardines, Masha navigated her way to the girls by tip-toe-perching along the windowsill that spanned the length of the car, "...like Spider-man." A week and several trains later, they arrived in the Netherlands exhausted.

Within twenty-four hours, they had to find cost-effective (preferably free) accommodation. They prayed. LinkedIn Netherlands posted a list of hosts willing to take in Ukrainian refugees.

The first option that popped up listed seven criteria: the Ukrainian must be a single mum, an accountant or lawyer by trade, with teens (two teens max, girls only), no pets, must speak English and have a personal recommendation from a local. Their family fit the description perfectly... and it was free! Answered prayer and grateful hearts!

GENEROSITY OPENS HEARTS AND DOORS

Generosity is one of my core values. It's the foundation of my company, and it permeates everything I do. People respond to generosity. Most recognise it, value it and are willing to extend it. If this describes you, thank you, you hold a special place in my heart.

I knew generosity opened hearts, but I'd never experienced it opening doors. The fact that you're reading about my journey here is evidence of that. I'm deeply grateful to Jodie and Julie for inviting me to be a part of this amazing project!

If you're at the beginning of your hosting journey, I'd encourage you to: 1) work hard and educate yourself, 2) encourage yourself and others along the way and persevere, and 3) navigate courageously and have a little faith.

At every stage in your journey be kind to yourself. Encourage yourself and others along the way. Freely celebrate your wins and surround yourself with people who celebrate your accomplishments with the same joy and exuberance that you do. You deserve it!

* * *

Last Random Thought: I strive to be a hospitable host. And when I'm travelling, I like to be a gracious guest. If you're dying to know the crazy-shocking-but-generous culinary delicacy my most memorable hosts offered me in Papua New Guinea... it's sago grubs! I like mine well done. Tastes like bacon. Hospitable hosts really *do* have the best tips :)

ABOUT THE AUTHOR

Laura Wegner is the founder of The Suite Life™ located in Whistler, Canada. She's a businesswoman, an investor, a persuader (PI), an encourager of hopes and dreams and a majority shareholder in four successful companies (one with a gross revenue of $1.5million).

The Suite Life™ offers modern, one-bedroom, designer-inspired spaces, boasting both style and comfort. These premium ski-in/ski-out properties are especially suited for couples looking to unwind, decompress or blaze their own trail in one of the most vibrant and visually stunning places on earth. Out of 1000+ listings, Laura's one-bedroom property has been identified as the fourth most profitable in Whistler according to AirDNA.

The Suite Life's™ purpose is two-fold: 1) offering boutique spaces and 2) as an Airbnb management company that supports and educates investors who want to build their portfolio through maximising their ski-in/ski-out property's revenue potential in Whistler.

Although Laura only entered the hospitality business in 2020, her family and friends will tell you that the 'gift of hospitality' has lived in her forever. That coupled with her generous heart and knack for anticipating and exceeding needs has led to her business success.

Many of Laura's property reviews reflect her true host nature, such as:

1. A great communicator – typical of an elementary school teacher.
2. Spotlessness – a reflection of her obsessive desire for cleanliness.
3. Including thoughtful extras – evidence of her drive to anticipate and exceed needs.

4. Being generous – a heart stance Laura highly values and liberally extends to others.

Beyond The Suite Life™ Whistler, Laura devotes time to her passion for teaching, applied linguistics, mountain biking, skiing, volunteering at her local church and reminiscing about her wildest travel adventures.

Links: linktr.ee/thesuitelifewhistler

LESLIE ANNE MORRIS

WHAT TRUE PASSIVE INCOME LOOKS LIKE WHEN INVESTING IN SHORT-TERM RENTALS

What does "passive income" look like to you? Growing up, I got a taste of passive income by playing the classic board game Monopoly with my family. There was no better feeling than when somebody landed on my property and had to pay me rent. I still remember the thrill of buying all the properties in a coloured group and then building houses to increase the rent and eventually upgrading to hotels. I wanted to earn the most money in the most efficient way, and real estate was my path to getting there. Looking back, I guess I was getting a glimpse of my future career as a hospitable host and full-time real estate investor in short-term rentals. No wonder I loved playing Monopoly so much! However, it would be decades later that I would realise my dream... quite by accident.

BUILDING A DREAM

Banking was a natural career choice for me. Did I mention I was always the banker when I played Monopoly? What I loved about commercial banking was working with my clients and building profitable strategies to move forward. I spent over twenty years in a satisfying banking career working with high-profile clients like SpaceX. However, while banking helped finance my travel to forty-five different countries, something was missing. I didn't mind working hard and putting in long hours for my clients. However, I wanted much more than a standard salary.

One day, while reviewing a report, I saw the CEO's $16million annual compensation. Something instantly unlocked inside of me. Why couldn't I have that too? At the time, I was a senior vice president at the bank. I knew climbing that corporate ladder would take more than perseverance and patience. I needed to arm myself with the best arsenal. I knew that would require an MBA from a reputable college, so I immediately enrolled and was accepted into graduate school at the University of Southern California. While earning my MBA, I soon grew restless and no longer wanted to work for somebody else. I wanted unlimited earning potential but wasn't sure how I could achieve that with a simple side hustle. That's when I realised my extensive travels brought me a hidden gem: a true love for real estate.

I've always had an affinity for cabins. I've stayed in cabins all over the world, including Alaska, Iceland and Finland. Cabins bring me a vibe of a cosy private relaxing retreat, no matter the geographical location. They universally provide a perfect getaway from the hustle and bustle of everyday life. So, it was time to purchase my own cabin. In 2019, I researched Airbnb's top five markets to invest in. They highly recommended the Smoky Mountains because of its location and low square footage cost. And I was immediately sold on the idea. What's not to love when I discovered that Dolly Parton and my beloved whiskey and moonshine are from Eastern Tennessee? That's when I pulled the trigger and purchased my first cabin in Tennessee's Smoky Mountains. My initial dream was to buy one property and have the flexibility to have holidays there and rent it out between visits. However, I didn't realise how profitable an investment in short-term rentals would be. I couldn't stop at one cabin. Soon, I was robbing my retirement to build up my real estate portfolio and making plans to buy more cabins. So, I began building my dream one cabin at a time until I eventually moved to Tennessee in 2020. I never imagined this "cabin infatuation" would become so lucrative and allow me to quit my over twenty-year banking career. But that's exactly what happened. Focusing solely on real estate investing has allowed me to grow my portfolio to $7million in just three years. And I'm not stopping any time soon.

The truth is we all have the power to write our own story, become wealthy through passive income and live our best life. And short-term rentals can be your ticket to getting there! As I was building my dream, people were continually asking me the same questions about how I achieved it, and could they do it too? That's when I decided to write a playbook full of tips and tricks for doing so. I am in the process of writing that book now.

A SHORT-TERM RENTAL PLAYBOOK

Right from the beginning, I knew I wanted my rental cabins to be unique from others in the marketplace. As a whiskey and moonshine connoisseur, I named one of my cabins Whiskey Whispers Lodge. No detail was overlooked. If prospective guests love whiskey, they'll want to check out this property. Not only do I want my cabins or properties to look different, I want them to *feel* different. I want my guests to get to and from the property safely, be happy and feel like they're being catered to. I don't view myself as someone just selling them a roof over their heads for a few nights, I am in the business of selling them time to create memories.

To achieve those coveted five-star reviews, I consider each of my properties to be its own functioning mini-hotel. The day-to-day business operations of a short-term rental are exactly that of a hotel, with one caveat – virtually everything is procured in advance electronically. There is no face-to-face contact. Prior to check-in, you secure credit cards, have guests sign rental agreements and collect security deposits. Automatic door locks allow guests to

Leslie and Josh at
Whiskey Whispers Lodge

check-in without any physical assistance. As guests check-out, you begin to prepare the property for the next guest. You want it to be a smooth, seamless process.

I aim to provide a concierge-style experience for each guest. A good (in-person) concierge greets their guests with a friendly, caring and patient attitude. You can do the same virtually, but it takes some work. When I bought that first cabin, I wanted to be that perfect concierge, but soon realised, even with the help of technology, it was extremely difficult to do when I lived across the country. And it was causing me many sleepless nights as I had no foolproof playbook to rely upon.

You too may think you could be the perfect concierge, but what happens when you have a full-time career and suddenly you are fielding phone calls day and night because one of your guests can't find the remote or the laundry detergent? I don't know about you, but I have no desire to be a concierge my whole life. I'd rather have a concierge waiting on me! I got into short-term rentals because of the promise of passive income. However, this income sure didn't appear very passive to me as I was fielding these inconvenient phone calls from guests. I needed a local team that would be at my guests' beck and call, just like their favourite concierge would. Building that team didn't happen overnight. I needed to create a great playbook to communicate strategy to my team and show them how to execute the plays. There's good reason why I'm often referred to as "that strategy lady" in the real estate field!

Once you have a property management team in place, it enhances your ability to be hands off. The result? Sweet peace of mind. As an investor, you can acquire properties out-of-state if you've set up the appropriate relationships with a well-vetted property manager who can do the marketing, accept bookings, vet clients and create an award-winning team to maintain your property as you live and work elsewhere. All the while knowing that if you wanted to have a holiday at your asset yourself, you could. Not only does that feel good while you are generating a profit, it puts you in control. But keep in mind that profit needs to be passive in order to scale properly.

TIME IS MONEY

I've seen a lot of people try to cut corners when it comes to investing in short-term rentals because they want to make the most money they can. Often, they believe that self-managing might be a great way to avoid giving away a percentage of their profit. Unfortunately, property management isn't something you learn in a day or two. While you are busy learning the ins and outs of property management, you might be leaving valuable money on the table. And most importantly, the task takes precious time away from what you really want to do. Benjamin Franklin once said long ago, "Lost time is never found again." In my own life, I've recognised that time is money. We all are given just twenty-four hours in a day. No matter how rich you are, you can't buy more time. However, you can spend your time more wisely. Some people want to spend more time with their loved ones and not be tied to a nine-to-five job. Others have big dreams that they want to achieve that require a lot of both time and money that they don't currently have.

Investing in real estate in a passive way allows you more precious time and money to realise some of those dreams. It's time to fulfil your own dream, not somebody else's version of your dream. I am not afraid to dream big. I never have been. My ultimate bold goal is to empower 1,000 women to become millionaires through real estate. That's $1billion in net worth that didn't exist before. I would never share this lofty goal if I didn't believe I could do it. As a motivational speaker and frequent podcast guest, I travel throughout the United States sharing secrets on how to create true passive income through real estate to audiences who want to do this, but don't know where to start.

Surprisingly, many people don't quite get that by managing your own short-term rental, you are trading the hot commodity of precious time to become a hospitable host. Allow me to let you in on a little secret – hospitable hosts aren't created overnight.

WHAT GOES INTO BEING A HOSPITABLE HOST?

There are some essential ingredients to being a top-notch hospitable host. For starters, there's a team of people behind the face of that hospitable host that needs to be managed. There are the cleaners, vendors that do speciality work, a maintenance crew and a team that does revenue management, social media, sales and customer service.

I formed my own property management company, Josh's Cabins, after learning firsthand what it takes to be an exceptional hospitable host. I am often asked why my female-owned business is named after a male. Let me explain. Josh is my ex-husband. We met when we were in our early twenties and got married in the sunny Maldives on the Indian Ocean. With a thirst to see the world, we invested all our money into travel. While I wish I had this money today so I could invest in my expanding real estate portfolio, I realise that if we hadn't travelled so much, we might not care so much about hospitality. An unexpected perk from travelling the world was we became lodging connoisseurs.

Josh always played the role of the hospitable host when we purchased new cabins when we were married. It came naturally to him. While I was underwriting and buying the property, he was the one communicating with the guests to ensure they would have a great experience and return for years to come. As a businesswoman, branding was top of my mind when I chose the name Josh's Cabins. Not only is it a unique and memorable name, but it is highly Googleable and puts a face and name to our brand. Most of our reviews specifically make reference to Josh, even if our guests have never met him. The guests don't need to know that these are Leslie's cabins, and there is an entire team of women (besides Josh) that I've hired to take care of the properties.

By forming my own property management company and purchasing properties specifically in the Smoky Mountains, it saves me time, money and unnecessary headaches. Those headaches can come at inconvenient times. At one of my properties, we had some guests who didn't speak English as their first language. At 2am on a weekday, they called Josh about a strange sound in the cabin. In broken English, they made reference to it sounding like it was a countdown to a bomb getting ready to explode. And they didn't know where the sound was coming from. They looked in every drawer and every cabinet to no avail. They were anxious because it sounded like it was picking up speed and beeping faster and faster.

With years as an experienced Airbnb Superhost, Josh immediately went out to the property to investigate. It turns out it was the water alarm. When there is a leak, the water tank alarm starts to emit a sound like a smoke detector battery that is dying but even more annoying. Josh was able to fix the problem right away, and we got another five-star rating. That's the kind of service your guests expect when you are a hospitable host.

Can you imagine getting that kind of phone call in the middle of the night? What if you are in another state or another country? What would you do? What would your plan look like? Would you call one of your vendors to go and check it out? But can you be sure they would answer the phone at 2am? Wouldn't you rather have somebody else, like your property management company, just handle it? Chances are, you would never even know there was a problem unless it was a costly repair. It certainly wouldn't be reflected in your online reviews because the problem was handled so fast.

Leslie at Emerald View Retreat

When you run your properties like a concierge service, guests can relax, knowing you are there when they need you. We've got team members on call in the area to make sure any issues are promptly taken care of and ensure that the guest is happy and satisfied. Not only that, Josh's Cabins has created jobs for others in the local area. It's a win, win!

FOLLOW ME ON THE ROAD TO FINANCIAL FREEDOM

As the real estate market continues to fluctuate and interest rates do the same, it's easy to question whether now is the right time to invest in short-term real estate. Sometimes it feels that hindsight is twenty-twenty. While you might be kicking yourself because you didn't take advantage of some investment opportunities in the past, it's never too late. The best time to buy real estate is NOW. Most investors, including me, wish we would have started much earlier. But you can't go back in time. It all starts with that first property. But you need to take some action to make it happen. Take Dolly Parton's advice, "You'll never do a whole lot unless you're brave enough to try."

There are plenty of excuses and roadblocks to not getting started, particularly for women. Did you know that only 31% of real estate investors are women? That's BS! When I heard this statistic, I knew I needed to do something about it. Sure, I would continue to expand my real estate portfolio. But I have the power to do much more. I could boost that statistic by empowering 1,000 women to become millionaires through real estate investments. And better yet, I could show them how to do it by revealing my playbook. My track record is proof I can do it. Starting with just one property, in three short years, I have built my portfolio to ten properties.

One of the wealthiest entrepreneurs in history, Andrew Carnegie, once said long ago, "Ninety percent of all millionaires become so through owning real estate. More money has been made in real estate than in all industrial investments combined." That statement still holds true today and is the key to building wealth – even and especially when it comes to inflation. Historically, real estate has proven to be a stable investment during inflation. Better yet, a recent *Forbes* article pointed out the strongest inflation protection investments are property types with short-duration leases or rents. Yes, short-term rentals! I've always firmly believed the road to financial freedom is paved with real estate investments.

Before signing off, I'd like to leave you with something I believe wholeheartedly. It's my philosophy on life. I believe all things are possible in this moment, at this time, if you have the power to believe in yourself. My wish for you is that you don't hold back. Dream big. What I've learned from investing in the Smoky Mountains will surely help me as I continue to diversify my real estate portfolio and branch out into other areas. I just learned my neighbour, Dolly Parton, made it onto the 2022 *Forbes* list of the 100 Most Powerful Women. That's not surprising to me whatsoever. She's not afraid to dream and play big. Same here! I love this quote from Dolly, "When they say, 'Less is more', I say, 'That's BS. More is more'." And I want more! Not just for me, but for others who want to pave their way to financial freedom through short-term real estate rentals. Reach out to me if you want to join me on this journey. Just one caution: it's addictive! As I finished writing this, I just bought my eleventh short-term rental cabin. And oh, by the way, I am building number twelve!

ABOUT THE AUTHOR

Leslie Anne Morris began her Smoky Mountain investing journey while earning her MBA at the University of Southern California and working in Los Angeles as a commercial banker. For over twenty years, Leslie helped high-profile clients like SpaceX and closed a $50million private equity deal. She applies the same underwriting strategy to building her growing real estate portfolio. And today, she is sharing her playbook to motivate others to do the same while creating truly passive income in short-term rentals.

From the minute she closed on her first investment cabin in 2019, she knew she had made the right choice. The cash flow allowed her to rapidly scale her portfolio to double digits and a value of $7million in less than three years. Besides that, Leslie fell in love with Tennessee and moved there in 2020. She quickly founded two sister companies; a property acquisition company, Invest in the Smoky Mountains, and Josh's Cabins Management, a full-service property management company. Her one-stop shop allows out-of-state investors an opportunity to create passive income by offering concierge-style service to guests without the hassle of self-management.

She travels extensively throughout the United States as a highly sought-after motivational speaker focusing on the incredibly lucrative short-term rental asset class. Recognising the lack of female real estate investors, Leslie has made it her mission to be a driving force to empower women to begin real estate investing. She aims to empower 1,000 women to become millionaires by investing in short-term rentals. She has been featured on ABC, NBC, Fox and CBS networks. In addition, she is a popular guest on highly rated real estate podcasts and most recently was highlighted by the Tennessee Department of Tourism Board.

Links: linktr.ee/leslieannemorris

LOUISE AND CHRIS DANIELS

UNIQUE SPACES TO CREATE SPECIAL MEMORIES – A JOURNEY INTO THE UNKNOWN

We bought a school that had a train, not that we knew it at the time. 'Potential', 'project' and 'fundamentally sound' were the agents' terms, a view loosely shared by the surveyor after thirty pages describing the boundary hedges and excusing himself from any responsibility. The walls ran wet, it rained in the bedrooms and the windows were on the verge of falling out. One room had not been opened for fifty years! We saw the potential in the old school, substantial and stately, having educated children for 300 years from a time when Charles II was king, America was being colonised and the Great Plague and the Fire of London were recent memories.

We were proud owners of a Grade II listed pile of ancient bricks!

Five years later, it was transformed; a phoenix rising from the ashes via the planning system and with help from builders – some excellent, some not – but with most of the work done by us. We were proud owners of a seven-bedroom house, with a thirty-foot dining room in the old school hall. It really was too big for our family of four, and so started our journey into the short-term letting industry, not that it really existed as an industry at the time.

There has been property to let for centuries; indeed, the world's most published book has Jesus' birthplace as a barn conversion offering short-term rental accommodation attached to an inn! The major growth occurred when we were all given holidays of twenty days a year plus bank holidays and travelled to the coast to stay. The clue was in the name, 'self-catering', and some recall how this meant taking your own bedding, collecting firewood for stoves and cleaning it on leaving, as cleaners were not included – very different to today's expectation of hotel standards!

But we didn't consider we were part of an industry. In the early noughties, the majority of bookings were still through travel agents and, whilst reading a brochure, Chris discovered you could hire a large house. The company had introduced a website enabling him to see that, although there weren't many, they were well booked! We contacted the company to see if they were interested in our house. Their initial response was disinterest, despite telling them about Robin Hood, Sherwood Forest, the Ducal Estates, Lincoln and the cathedral and how the Mayflower Pilgrims originated from our villages, until they discovered we had seven bedrooms! As large homes were in demand, they decided to despatch a lady from the Yorkshire region to see us.

She arrived late – it was a long way – a very prim and proper lady, telling us we were not in a hot spot, but they wanted larger houses, and we would do well. She had a chart to prove it! She gave us a four-star rating and said to get five stars we would need to add lining to our curtains and more wallpaper. She was putting us in the East Midlands region so she wouldn't need to come again, took a couple of photos and left.

And so, we got our first advert, 2.5 x 1.5" with two tiny coloured photos in the Midlands section of a vast catalogue highlighting Birmingham, the Black Country Museum and Shakespeare's birthplace in Stratford, a mere three hours away from us by car. Tucked away in a sea of two-bed cottages, barn conversions and spare rooms, our advert looked so small and insignificant. All our hopes and a large financial risk were pinned on its success.

Chris had had enough of working for others, the routine daily grind delivering high tech projects to stress-inducing timescales and taking risks beyond his pay grade. So, he set up his own company to develop software and websites. The idea was to downsize. We had enlisted an agent to sell the house who promised gold, a pot at the end of the rainbow, and outlined his not insignificant fees to attract a buyer. But we really didn't want to sell, we loved the house, and so the idea of others having parties, family reunions and friends sharing the love we had for our house appealed. On discovering that we could split the mortgage and buy another house to live in was a possibility, and we went for it.

* * *

In the days before IKEA online, you drove to the store, piled the trolley high, shoved the boxes in the boot and drove home. Only we needed to furnish an entire house for eighteen people, a cavernous warehouse of empty rooms. So, one evening, we ended up pushing eight trolleys full of mattresses, bedding, chairs, tables and everything needed around the store, fighting off the assistants who earmarked them as abandoned trollies and finally snarling up the checkouts. To add to the complexity, IKEA delivery was 'subbed out' to another company who offered all the efficiency of a hot butter knife. They claimed there was too much, then agreed to take it, itemising, cataloguing and numbering everything late into the evening.

The next day, an unmarked lorry arrived. The vans they had weren't big enough, so they must have got this lorry from a mate as it was truly gruesome, battered and hammered like the remnants of a space rocket after several re-entries. Whilst unloading, they proceeded to transfer grease from the van on their shoes and spread it liberally over carpets, furniture and any other surface that merited the new style of decoration – as if we didn't have enough to do in mass construction of furniture piles, we had a clean-up operation the size of the Exxon Valdez!

It was thrilling to receive our first booking but also terrifying; it

Diamond House, Notts

was getting more real. The first booking was Christmas, then New Year, so we had the deadlines, but the new house wasn't ready. A wet autumn and a mass of security fencing was hampering progress on site, deadlines came and went, until in early December the completion was done.

We sorted our personal items and packed up our valued possessions, some went into attics and sheds whilst the rest was bundled into the car for the drive down the hill to the new house. In a short time, we amassed enough to live on, although the sofas had not arrived, and we camped out on deckchairs and picnic tables for that first Christmas.

Our mad rush to get ready ran to the wire. When our first guests were welcomed through the back door, we were still discovering drawers to be emptied and carrying things out through the front! But finally, they were in, just ten weeks after we thought it would be a good idea.

* * *

Chris wrote the code for the Diamond House website and joined the local tourist association, got himself involved, made some friends, and wrote some more websites. Eventually, he cracked a route to the top slot on Google, enabling an increase in direct bookings, and the house was becoming more popular. We ditched the agency who charged through the nose yet still would not give us bigger advertising space. We were, I suppose, pioneers of the Book Direct movement! At this point, everything was completed by hand via telephone calls and some emails. Cheques had to be taken down to the bank weekly, bookings monitored on our own calendars and prices fluctuated depending on who answered the phone! Yet the bookings kept coming, people wanted to stay with us to explore Nottinghamshire and we have had many returning families through the years!

Chris cleaned the house, mowed the lawns and maintained the gardens, managed the website, and took the bookings in between taking the children to school, piano, violin, dance, basketball (Rebecca played for South Yorkshire with fixtures all over the county) and ballet (Edward was at Elmhurst in Birmingham, a round journey of five hours), whilst I taught full time, ran our home and did all the laundry. As our business grew, laundry became a bigger issue; we used a laundrette providing service washes until, unfortunately, the business closed overnight. So, we did it ourselves, bought a second drier and our lives were festooned with bedding for several years until eventually we found a commercial laundry and now take pride that if it's good enough for Center Parcs, it's good enough for us.

* * *

We are also the custodian of another property that's more a stately home than a house. We don't really remember how we came to own it. More an act from above when Chris met the Lord – not the real one, of course, but Lord Naal, whose wife was the seller. The house was a Prebendal House for Southwell Minster, steeped in history. It is beautiful, a classical Georgian country house, perfectly proportioned with an air of opulence befitting Downton Abbey. It was three years after we opened Diamond House, and this had the potential to become our next holiday property. We took photos of some of the rooms and advertised it. We took our first booking for eight weeks' time, even before we owned it; the real Lord was on our side and wanted to secure a future for this great house.

The mortgage was possible, but the survey failed. The young surveyor – more used to three-bed terraced properties in Sheffield – trashed the house and everything about it. The final salvo was her opinion that a holiday home wasn't viable, we 'weren't in a tourist hot spot'. We argued our case, pointed out the mistakes in the report, such as getting the age of the property wrong by 200 years, and that we already had a business nearby and had taken bookings for the house already, and amazingly, they agreed. All we needed now was funding to upgrade the house, buy fixtures, fittings and open. We met the bank manager who liked our story and was 'by our side', even if his bank wasn't. He gave us credit cards with jumbo budgets but no cash. It was 'all he could do'. So, we took them and spent more on furniture, bathrooms and cutlery. We had a bathroom fitter, we decorated all the rooms, laid new carpets, and even had the cleaner's children making IKEA furniture on the lawn!

Somehow, we were ready on time. It wasn't perfect, it's an old house, so perfection is a goal, a dream, an impossibility. The walls are crooked, floors spooned and ceilings suffer from wattle fatigue, but it's joyous, relaxed and loves people. Treat it badly, it fights back and sometimes it just all goes wrong for guests, but that's rare.

* * *

We had been "on call" every weekend for over eighteen years before the pandemic struck, ready to jump to action and solve any problem that was imaginable, from bees swarming, rats in the garden, guests setting off fireworks the size of which wouldn't have been out of place in the Normandy landings, as well as the more mundane heating, plumbing and lighting glitches. Over the years, we had honed our response systems, and even whilst holidaying

Dunham House, Notts

on the beaches of Spain had replaced a fridge, repaired a grill and sorted other problems to the delight of our guests. But, for the first time since we opened, we had no guests, just the costs associated with running the houses, which was scary.

We all remember the rule changes, some legal, others simply guidance, but backed by insurance companies' rules, an operating nightmare.

It was too hard to adapt both houses to the sea of regulatory Covid guidance and we were rather liking the slower pace of life the first lockdown afforded, so we decided to sell our larger property, Dunham House, and plan our retirement. I've always maintained that your biggest asset is also your biggest liability – your house, your car, or even Boris Johnson for the Conservative party – so we put it on the market.

We focused our attention on Diamond House. Our daughter reminded us that all we had was time in lockdown. Both children came back home during this time, and we all upgraded, repaired, redecorated and reorganised everything from the booking systems, cleaning processes, guest information, even a new drive, new roof, new doors and playframe. We were so busy! Rarely in business can you stop running and take time to thoroughly assess the business and make such radical changes.

By Christmas 2021, Diamond House was again fully open, demand was good, and we were reaping the rewards of all our work. However, Dunham House still had not sold. We had received a lot of interest from all sorts of people absolutely loving the house with loads of ideas of how to use the space, but nothing had come through, so here we were with an empty house. So, we advertised Christmas and New Year 2021, and they booked in three hours! But the heating had been off for eighteen months and failed to start, several radiators had sprung leaks, many of the toilets, cisterns and basins needed attention and roof repairs beckoned. Somehow, we opened and made it through the Christmas period, after which we stayed shut for a further three months whilst we got all our new processes in place, redecorated and recarpeted most of the house and tackled two years of growth in the garden.

The house responded well. It loves having guests as much as we do and it was clearly meant to be. Not that if someone decided to make us an offer we wouldn't consider it, but the house wants to welcome guests who appreciate staying in a unique property akin to a National Trust house.

* * *

The pandemic has served to reinforce the importance of family and friends. Over twenty years, we have provided over 150,000 bed nights and seen a rapid growth in our market as the benefits of a private retreat with catering options, no inflated bar bills, and the comfort of safely putting children to bed was realised. But, for Chris, it was a property business. Guests could book online, the website gave directions to the house and a key box let them in. With the focus on the property, he was value driven, cutting costs and providing the lowest prices he could. We were good value, but something was missing.

We realised clearly for the first time how privileged we were to be able to provide a service that was so loved by our clients and how important it was to be that hospitable host to provide the stay they wanted. At one stage, we offered a catered meal to our groups and we enjoyed being part of their evening with a couple of particularly memorable groups. One hen party explained they had enlisted the services of a butler to help us serve the food for the evening, if it was okay. It sounded fine to us and so we were a little taken aback when confronted by a 'butler in the buff', entirely naked save for his small serving pinny. He was a genuinely nice guy earning a few quid to supplement his student grant and did an excellent job of buttling.

The second was a party celebrating Grandma's sixtieth. All the participants dressed up for their 'murder mystery' evening arranged around dinner, and we were met by a rather impressive bishop complete with full robes. The guests started to assemble in their finest, gowns and uniforms before Grandma appeared as a star turn as Nel Gwyn, complete with a large fake bust with everything hanging out. Our son was only twelve and was in shock at such a sight, disturbed that all the other guests seemed to take it in their stride.

We have become more aware of the importance of hosting; it's what sets you apart from the competition. Chris had always considered this a property investment, when in fact it is two businesses in one. Since the pandemic, we have transformed how we run the business, as well as improving the property, considered our ideal guest and worked hard to do everything we can to enable them to have the best stay. I have created welcoming interiors, which are colourful yet respect the period features we are proud of. This is especially true when welcoming families to our homes. We try hard to create not just a home from home but an exceptional place that they will remember and love. Last summer, for the first time, we were invited by our guests staying at the house to a barbecue to celebrate the Platinum Jubilee. As we sat in the garden chatting, watching a family playing games and enjoying themselves, it was an honour to realise our hard work was enabling people to create such unique and special memories.

The upshot has been more bookings and increased turnover, more to reinvest in the property, more direct bookings with increased returners and profits.

And the train? By the time we bought the house, the full-sized steam train and tender had been removed. The previous owner had bought it scrap for £7,000 some thirty years previously, then following a £750,000 renovation programme, it now runs on the North Norfolk railway. If you want to know more about it, or to stay in one of Nottinghamshire's earliest schools, you'll just have to visit!

Our top ten tips to success: do your research, identify your ideal guest, design everything around them from your advertising to the toaster you choose, identify a good team around you, ensure the property is spotlessly clean, use software for everything you can, read up on all the tax rules, get a good accountant and buy a 'pink booklet' (in England) with details of all the regulations, then go for it! It is an adventure we are so glad we have been involved in and one that will continue to bring joy to those who stay with us.

Chris and I are proud to be hospitable hosts, it is much more fun and we look forward to welcoming you to Nottinghamshire.

ABOUT THE AUTHOR

Country house parties are no longer the domain of the rich and famous. In 2003, Louise and Chris Daniels founded the Big Country House Ltd. Together with their children, Rebecca and Edward, their purpose has been to provide unique spaces for guests to create special memories. They have hosted family parties, unforgettable birthday weekends, reunions of college friends and many more, including gamers, musicians, vicars, crafters, all in the magnificent setting of an English country house.

Louise, a primary school teacher with over thirty years of experience and being given an OFSTED Outstanding Teacher Award, is a real people person who loves to host. She engages with social media platforms and carries out PR, runs the booking platform and wrestles with the payment gateway! As well as supporting Chris in their hospitality business, she also runs a thriving papercraft studio with regular classes, Zoom calls and many creative activities.

Chris has a degree in electrical engineering and after a twenty-year career in a variety of global projects, designing submarine cable networks, CCTV systems and manufacturing CAD equipment, rose to senior management yet aspired to run his own business. He has used his numerous DIY skills to renovate then manage their homes. He manages the properties, built and runs the websites and handles the back office. He is also regularly called in to answer those 'little' queries from our guests.

In 2015, Chris became aware that the local council was closing the Tourist Information Centre. Retford is not a hotspot for tourism. With the help of volunteers, they opened Retford Hub with a community shop, art gallery, Pilgrim Museum, studios, workshops and a café, which they ran for six years, whilst continuing to host guests from around the world. They handed over the baton of the Hub in 2021 and now enjoy the freedoms of travel in their tiny caravan, whilst still running a thriving hospitality business, using modern technology to work more remotely!

Links: https://linktr.ee/louiseandchrisdaniels

MELANIE KRIEL

ABUNDANT REWARD FROM INVESTING MY HEART IN AFRICA

Always a high-heeled city slicker at heart, I grew into a well-educated go-getter, forging my own successful career path. Goal orientated and driven, I knew exactly how to steer my life toward exponential achievement in the corporate world.

Fast forward: girl meets farmer, buys her first pair of sensible shoes... and then marries him.

Contrary to the astonished anticipation of my family, I slipped into farm life like Cinderella's foot into the proverbial glass slipper. Living the farming community culture of warmly welcoming visiting family and friends staying over became my second nature. It was evident that hosting was inextricably knitted into the very fibre of my DNA.

I was home and hands-on throughout my children's lives. This privilege I don't take lightly, for it was on the farm that I helped them to find and strengthen their wings. When it came time for my son and daughter to fly towards their tertiary education goals, the notorious 'empty nest' syndrome spurred me on to doing something new. My heart was craving a fresh challenge that would keep me focused, enthusiastic *and* make financial sense.

We had already sold the family beach house and instead acquired a two-bedroom investment apartment on the North Coast for which an agent handled the letting process on our behalf. The ocean's serene setting intersecting with luxurious charm in an upmarket precinct was a fantastic offering. My exquisite abode ticked countless boxes for holidaymakers yearning to unwind on the magnificent beaches of the warm Indian Ocean in the quaint village of Shakas Rock.

With my African heart that beats to the rhythm of the earth, reducing our carbon footprint and living sustainably are paramount in my endeavour to create a superior level of plushness, confirming the uncompromised comfort of my guests remains my main priority.

During a visit to my daughter in Stellenbosch where she was studying, I stayed in a charming little Airbnb. After lengthy conversations with the owner, my soul felt stirred and inspired by her suggestion that I take control of our own letting process.

Fast forward (again): 2017 hailed the inception of my hosting business, Beachfront Apartments in Shakas Rock. The concept of Airbnb was still very new in Kwa-Zulu Natal, South Africa. It certainly challenged the traditional way of doing things. This was the perfect opportunity for me to get to know and understand my clientele, their needs and their desires. I ensured that I stayed ahead of the trends by lavishing my guests with the experience they didn't even know they were craving. Already a master at delivering on promises, here I crafted my artisanal recipe for exceeding expectations abundantly.

It wasn't long until friends and friends of friends commissioned me to Airbnb their rentals too. Recognising that it was a buyers' market at that time, purchasing a second property in the same building made perfect business sense.

I now had two magnificently appointed offerings boasting the sought-after allure of the ocean, splendidly fitted and styled according to my ethos. Glass doors open onto an expansive balcony

Melanie Kriel, CEO of Beachfront Apartments and Co-Founder of Short Term Rental Made Easy

with panoramic lookout points to ensure that, even while indoors, guests remain integrated with the awe-inspiring surroundings. My business was growing, and so was I.

Next, my website was born, which enabled me to harness the exponential benefits of direct bookings.

Then I faced an enviable problem: I had more booking requests than I could fulfil. Committed to remaining helpful to guests I was unable to accommodate, the 'Awesome Hosts Referral Group' was formed whereby hosts could share referrals for a small commission. This ever-growing concept has been an outstanding networking platform, and our synergistic group currently collaborates with fifty-five hosts/owners and 450 properties.

They say: "Africa is not for sissies." *They're* right! Covid and its concomitant lockdown erupted a downward spiral; the treacherous Natal riots and looting added to it, and later the natural disaster of the floods nearly took us down. Numerous setbacks were hitting thick and fast and seemed insurmountable. With the goal of being a beacon of hope in a tornado, I ran regular online meetings doing my utmost to maintain my hosts' motivation and encourage them to remain level-headed while thinking outside the box.

Researching host archetypes piqued my interest and has become a strong driving force. With so much focus being on the guest avatar, the host and their hosting style had been completely overlooked. As I delved into the depths of this rabbit hole, I realised that there are ideal hosts and ideal guests, and they are naturally attracted to each other (or repelled, of course) depending on their uniqueness. I learnt the tricks around how to authentically attract the clientele you prefer to host instead of accepting any booking simply to fill beds. I could anticipate behaviours and get inside my guests' heads while leaving a magical mark on their hearts.

As others started picking my brain to glean from my success, I realised how much I enjoyed imparting my knowledge for the benefit of their growth. Unpacking hidden gems to kick-start a host's business or revolutionise an existing model toward increased profitability became a superb outlet for me.

And so (fast forward some more), I launched Short-Term Rental Made Easy (STR_ME), an online course that I present together with a business coach. This comprehensive course unpacks the nitty-gritty of our dynamic industry. As a significant tool for the framework of hosting, it expounds on the unobvious and highlights the intricate detail that keeps guests returning. STRE_ME is profoundly compelling, and I would be delighted if you would join me on a journey to ignite the growth you want to enjoy while travelling yours.

ABOUT THE AUTHOR

Melanie Kriel, CEO of Beachfront Apartments established in 2017 in Shakas Rock, South Africa, and co-founder of online course Short-Term Rental Made Easy, is renowned as a gracious host par excellence.

An eco-luxe spin on bespoke self-catering getaways on the beach ensures Melanie's guests leave with indelible memories encapsulated in a consummately tranquil environment that keeps them returning for more seaside magic.

As a member of the iLembe District Tourism Forum, founder of the Awesome Host Referral network and collaborator with local businesses, Melanie is highly esteemed in her community. This impassioned eco-warrior relishes life with her husband, two children, four dogs and two cats on their farm in the Midlands.

Links: https://linktr.ee/beachfrontapartments

SCAN ME

MICHAEL ELEFANTE

THE FAST PATH TO FINANCIAL FREEDOM: HOW TO MAXIMISE PROFITABILITY BY PROVIDING AN ELEVATED CUSTOMER EXPERIENCE

If you are reading this, you may recognise my name or recall watching my videos on social media platforms such as TikTok, Instagram and YouTube. I have garnered over one million followers on social media, producing educational content about investing in and managing short-term rentals. My journey started in December 2019, when my wife Jill and I listed our first rental on Airbnb. Our goal was to supplement our income and work towards attaining financial freedom within ten years. Our ten-year goal happened within the first twelve months with just three properties. At the time of writing this chapter (December 2022), I own and operate six short-term rentals that produce between $80,000-100,000 per month in revenue. Many are quick to point a finger and speculate that this is sheer dumb luck. Maybe you are as well... But I'm here to tell you otherwise.

Anyone can get started in this industry and list properties on sites such as Airbnb and Vrbo, but few are willing to do what it takes to perform at this level. It takes countless hours of research, creativity and execution to craft such an undeniably desirable experience to reach an occupancy and average daily rate to produce six figures per month with only six properties. Finding and setting up properties is only half the battle. Providing unparalleled hospitality is where most hosts fall short. In order to remain relevant and prosper long term in this industry, it is critical that you provide a consistent and positive experience for all guests. Over the past three years, I have accumulated over 500 five-star reviews. My name is Michael Elefante, and this is my story of what I believe it takes to be a *Hospitable Host*.

There are three crucial aspects to being successful in the short-term rental industry. Research, design and management. Let's start with the most critical: research.

Doing adequate market research will help narrow down what market to invest in, what postcode to invest in and, most importantly, what types of design or amenities travellers desire the most in that specific market. Having a deep understanding of who your customer avatar is, before making the investment into property or design, is critical. Who will be renting your property? Will it be families with children? Groups of friends celebrating special occasions such as a hen or stag party? Business travellers? Once you have decided what your customer avatar looks like, you need to decide what type of design, amenities, sleeping arrangement and features you need to provide.

When first considering a new market, I always start on a site called AirDNA. It provides trending data for short-term rental markets around the world. It gives you a bird's-eye view of historical trends in a given market for things such as rental supply, occupancy rates, average daily rates and top performing properties. The top performing properties section is very useful. I'm not necessarily trying to compete with the high-end, luxury type properties that typically appear here. What I am doing, however, is noticing trends or similarities between these top performers. Where they are located, what design trends they have, what amenities they provide guests, etc. This helps me craft the vision for what type of property I want to invest in and how I want to design it. Doing the appropriate market research will help you maximise the return on your investment and provide an unparalleled guest experience.

Design is something that most hosts, including myself, struggle with. While designing a short-term rental property is not easy, it should not be overlooked. Spending the extra time, effort and money to design a unique space is critical to marketing, booking conversion and guest experience. Marketing short-term rentals on sites such as Airbnb is no different than posting content on social media. Thanks to technological advancement, smartphones and social media, our attention spans as humans have shrunk. You have about two to five seconds to capture someone's attention before they lose interest and continue scrolling. We are all guilty of it! Think of TikTok, for example. For every one video you watch in its entirety, you likely scroll past five to ten videos, deciding if you want to watch the entire clip within the first two seconds. A prospective guest scrolling to find the perfect short-term rental on Airbnb is no different. There are hundreds, if not thousands, of listings in each market. You have one photo, a title and about two seconds to capture someone's interest. If a guest does click on your listing, you now have a splash page with five photos, title and description for them to review. These five photos must showcase the top five moments or experiences at your property.

Do not overlook the opportunity to create an Instagrammable moment at your property. People will book a property for the opportunity to take one photo to post on social media and show their followers where they are staying. We live in a digital world, and it is critical to give your guests the opportunity to take photos and create lifelong memories. An Instagrammable moment can be an interactive mural painted on a wall, greenery wall with a lighted sign, a themed games room, an outdoor entertainment space with a fire pit, hot tub or grill with string lights hanging up, etc. The list goes on. The point I'm getting at is that you should aim to create such powerful moments, paired with professional photography, in order to tell the story of your property as someone scrolls through the photos. You want them to envision themselves having a great

Michael and Jill hiked over 400 miles in 2021 while travelling in a camper van

time there with friends or family and creating those memories with each photo they scroll past. This will not only increase your impression and click through rate on your listing, increase booking conversion and boost revenue, but it will elevate guests' experience and increase the quantity of quality reviews you receive. All these things will help you rank higher in Airbnb and Vrbo search results, which will lead to... more impressions, more clicks and more bookings. This is what I refer to as the Airbnb perpetual life cycle. It's the gift that keeps on giving. It all starts with in-depth market research, thoughtful design and, of course, what we will talk about next, phenomenal management.

It's not difficult to manage short-term rental properties... But it is easy to do a subpar job, which will cost you both your time and money long term. What separates good hosts from great hosts is the ability to set up a flawless system and provide unparalleled hospitality. Running short-term rentals is not a passive source of income, although you can automate much of the day-to-day management to make it mostly passive. There are three main aspects to short-term rental management: guest communication, cleaning and maintenance, and revenue management.

Guest communication tends to be the most time-consuming aspect of management. It is critical that you use a property management software that can automate as much of the guest communication as possible. You can create message templates and schedule automated triggers to when those messages are sent. This can include reservation confirmation, check-in instructions, house rules, day after check-in follow up, check-out instructions and review requests. By automating these messages and including information about the property and level setting expectations, you can eliminate much of the unnecessary guest questions. If a guest has all of their questions answered before they think to ask them, they will have a more seamless experience from check-in to check-out. And they are much more likely to leave you a five-star review.

I have found that telling a guest I left them a five-star review and requesting a five-star review in return if they had a great experience drastically increases the quantity of five-star reviews I receive. This is critical to the long-term performance of your property on OTAs such as Airbnb.

Another great way to elevate guest experience and eliminate unnecessary guest communication is to provide a digital guidebook. I have personally used Hostfully digital guidebooks for my properties in the past and highly recommend them. There are many advantages here, but there are two key benefits I want to share with you. Number one, the digital guidebooks are web-based and the person that booked the reservation can easily share the link with everyone in their group. This will eliminate confusion and complication if certain members of the group arrive at the property before the person who made the reservation. Everyone has all the relevant details and information regarding their stay. Number two, the guests' experience will be more seamless with a digital guidebook. You can relay all the relevant information about the property, how to use certain amenities and even recommend tours and activities locally. Having a digital guidebook can eliminate a lot of unnecessary guest communication.

Cleaning and maintenance is one of the most difficult things to monitor if you manage and operate short-term rentals from afar. You will live and die by your cleaners. Nothing causes more headaches and bad reviews than an unclean property. Establishing great communication and expectations with your cleaners is absolutely critical. Your cleaners need to let you know when something is broken or a guest leaves a mess at your property. You do not want your guests letting you know that things are broken or do not work properly. Guests are not shy to ask for a refund or leave a bad review if there are cleaning or maintenance issues.

Calling, emailing or texting your cleaners your schedule is a thing of the past. I encourage you to leverage a turnover and cleaning management software such as Turnover BNB or Resort Cleaning. You will be able to seamlessly sync your calendars between your property management software or the OTAs you list your properties on with these tools. Your cleaners will get notifications when bookings are confirmed or cancelled. This will eliminate late or missed cleans and eliminate much of the day-to-day communication that takes place between you and your cleaners. If your cleaners do an outstanding job consistently, I recommend tipping them or giving them a raise. You will be their favourite client and they will be motivated to continue to do a great job with your property.

The quicker you address maintenance issues for a guest the better. Most guests are reasonable and understand that certain issues cannot be addressed immediately within the hour. However, what is important to guests is that you are responsive, and you let them know you are working towards a resolution as fast as possible. The quicker you can address issues as they arise during a guest's stay, the better experience they will have and the better chance you have of obtaining another five-star review.

The last piece to the management puzzle is revenue management. One of the most difficult parts of becoming a top producing short-term rental investor is learning how to maximise occupancy and revenue through an effective pricing strategy. For me, it is non-negotiable: you must use dynamic pricing software. Dynamic pricing software will save you countless hours per week and help you boost occupancy and daily rates. The best dynamic pricing software allows you to leverage both your own specific customisations and their data and machine learning to automatically change your pricing every day of the year. This will do two things. One, it will make sure you are not leaving any money on the table during the days with the highest demand. There are many reasons a specific day could have a higher demand than the next, but it is way too much to keep up with on your own, especially if you do not live in the market in which you operate. When demand is higher, it will raise your prices for you. Number two, a dynamic pricing software will lower your prices when demand is low. This will help you capture bookings where ordinarily you may have been priced too high. Setting appropriate prices is how you will not just stay in business, but will help you thrive long term.

The short-term rental industry is getting increasingly competitive and only hospitable hosts will survive. The relationship between supply and demand in a free market has its way of working out over time. There are times when demand is high and supply is low, where everyone seems to be making loads of money. There are, conversely, times where supply is high and demand is low, where 80% struggle and 20% thrive. The supply and demand relationship with short-term rentals will vary by market but is not that different to any other industry. As this industry continues to become more competitive, it is important to understand not just how to survive, but how to thrive. It all comes down to becoming a hospitable host. Those who do the research, invest in the right properties, design them to curate amazing experiences for guests, and master operations and management will thrive. I should know... Not only are most of my properties top performers in each respective market, but I have taught over 900 people how to successfully invest in and manage short-term rentals.

We welcomed our first child into the world in 2022.

In 2021, I founded a coaching and mentorship programme called BNB Investor Academy. The foundation of this programme is built on helping others achieve financial freedom through short-term rentals. Investing in and managing short-term rentals has been life-changing for me and my family. Building a programme that helps others replicate what I have done is incredibly rewarding. I take great pride in being a thought leader in this industry. One of the rewarding things about investing in real estate, creating content, building coaching programmes and helping others succeed is the lifelong relationships that have been formed. Several of the many amazing relationships I have developed are with people who are also featured in this book. Although I consider myself a thought leader and an educator in this space, I also know I still have so much to learn.

I'd like to leave you with a motto my wife Jill and I live by. The motto is "why not us?" This motto gives us confidence in all areas of life and business. For a long time, I was so nervous to make an investment into real estate. I was not only scared to fail but scared to succeed. There was a turning point in our lives in 2019, when we finally gave ourselves permission to take risks and be successful. This motto led to so many other things in our lives. We wanted to quit our jobs and spend our time travelling. This helped fuel our decisions to invest in short-term rental properties, with the goal of becoming financially free at a young age. In the spring of 2021, this dream became a reality. We quit our jobs and travelled around the USA for a year in a camper van. On the back window of the van, we had a homemade bumper sticker that read: Why Not Us?

I encourage you to adopt this motto in your own life. After all, if I, or anyone else for that matter, can be successful, why not you?

Thank you for taking the time to read about my story and what I believe it takes to be a hospitable host.

ABOUT THE AUTHOR

Michael Elefante is a real estate investor and social media entrepreneur. He has garnered over one million combined followers on social media and has been featured in *Business Insider* and dozens of podcasts. Michael is the founder of BNB Investor Academy (https://www.bnbinvestoracademy.com/), a coaching programme that has helped over 900 people find, invest in, design and manage short-term rentals successfully. BNB Investor Academy includes lifetime access to a video course, a private Facebook mastermind group with hundreds of members and six months access to a calendar filled with dozens of coaching calls each month.

Michael is also the co-founder of the following companies: Home Team Vacation Rentals, a property management company built to streamline high passive income investments for homeowners. Home Team currently manages properties across the United States, with the majority of properties currently located in the southeast. Somerled Designs, a design studio geared towards helping short-term rental investors amplify guest experience and maximise their revenue and ROI by conducting in-depth market research analysis and executing flawless design. STRhub, an online marketplace and hub of resources that helps simplify investing for short-term rental investors.

Michael became financially free in his twenties and found his true passion in helping others achieve financial freedom through short-term rental investments. He has garnered over 500 five-star reviews on Airbnb in less than three years, with an average property review rating of 4.92 stars. Michael prides himself on selling 'the experience' to travellers, by providing unique stays with thoughtful design and amenities. He lives in South Carolina with his wife Jill, daughter Kennedy and their two German Shorthaired Pointers, Peyton and Maple. The Elefante family loves to travel and spend time outdoors.

Links: https://stan.store/melefante6

MIKE SJOGREN

FOUR INVESTING RULES I USED TO RETIRE MYSELF, MY WIFE AND MY MOM WITH STRS (IN LESS THAN EIGHTEEN MONTHS)

I wish I could say my wife Krysten and I got into this because we loved hospitality or that we had a passion for creating amazing experiences for guests. We didn't. In fact, we had never stayed in a short-term rental before we got into all this. For all we knew, Airbnb was some Silicon Valley tech company that was somehow tied into real estate.

Yet here we are, five years later, 100 rentals across five states, three boutique hotels, 30k+ podcast downloads/month (Short Term Rental Secrets), 500+ active mastermind members, founders of one of the top STR interior design firms in the US (On Design Interiors), host of the world's largest host-driven STR conference (STR Wealth Con) along with my good friend and fellow HH author Bill Faeth.

So, if you're reading this and you're brand new with no experience whatsoever, good, you're in the right place.

More importantly, after this chapter, you'll be equipped to replicate these results and the results of all these HH authors in less time, with fewer mistakes and less headaches.

I'll give you the story of why we got into this industry then share my four rules to building a wildly profitable STR business without giving yourself another job.

Growing up in a loving, middle-class home, I learned how to work hard. My parents always had my back and instilled a belief that I could achieve anything if I wanted it badly enough and worked hard enough. So, I followed the advice I got from my parents and teachers:

1. Go to school.
2. Get good grades.
3. Get a "good" job with a "good" company.
4. Save 10% of your income in a 401(k).
5. Work for forty years and one day you'll retire a millionaire.

So that's what I did. I went to school, got good grades, got a good and "safe" job as a certified public accountant (C.P.A.), saved 10% of my income in a 401(k), married my beautiful wife, got a house in the suburbs and a couple of cars in the driveway. From the outside looking in, everything was great. I may have hated my job, but I was comfortable. It paid well, I was good at it, and everyone around me said I was on the path to success (whatever that meant).

Then everything changed a couple of weeks after our son was born. It was a beautiful summer morning and we were all excited for our newborn photoshoot. We had a few cute outfits laid out, the diaper bag was packed and ready to go, but when I picked him up out of his crib, his lips were a little blue and his skin was very pale. A quick call to his doctor confirmed we needed to take him over to the local hospital and have his vitals checked.

Okay, no need to panic, just take him over to Beverly Hospital and have him checked out. No problem. We got him in the car and gave the photographer a call to reschedule our photoshoot. After apologising several times for the last-minute cancellation, we hung up the phone and turned around to check on our little guy. "Caiden, you doing okay back there, buddy? Caiden..." Krysten unbuckled her seatbelt to reach back and give him a little shake to wake him up. "Caiden... Wake up... Caiden... Caiden!"

Krysten grabbed the phone back and started dialling. "9-1-1, what's your emergency?"

"We're on our way to the hospital, our son's lips are blue, and we can't wake him up, please send an ambulance to meet us!"

The next seven minutes were the longest of my entire life. Driving at nearly double the legal speed limit in a Jeep down a major highway to meet an ambulance while screaming and shaking our baby boy to wake up will be imprinted in my mind forever.

Fortunately, the medics were able to revive our son almost immediately after we met the ambulance, and we kicked off the next eighteen-month chapter of our lives at the world-famous Boston Children's Hospital.

While we were extremely fortunate to live near one of the best paediatric hospitals in the world, Caiden's condition was extremely rare. After the crazy ambulance rendezvous, he was admitted for extended observation and testing. Every day was a new test; cat scans, X-rays, MRIs, G.I. tests; I even had to hold the poor guy down for a spinal tap. It was the worst few weeks of our lives, and I would not wish that experience on my worst enemy.

But the absolute worst part came one morning when the doctors came in to give us their daily updates and the realisation came over me that we'd been there for three weeks straight, I was out of holiday allowance, I was out of sick days, I had a mountain of hospital bills piling up and I was going to have to leave my wife and my baby boy in this place and go back to a cubicle to trade time for money. It was the lowest I have ever felt in my life. At a time when my family needed me there the most, I couldn't be there because I'd put us in a position where I needed to trade time for money.

After I explained this reality to Krysten, I looked her straight in the eyes and made her a promise, "I don't know how I'm going to do it, but I'm going to find a way to build us a business that gives us the income we want without ever trading time for money again."

I knew rental properties were going to be the vehicle and, after I met a gentleman named Marcos in a business mastermind group that introduced me to STRs, I planted my flag and made a promise to

Enjoying some quality family time outside our very first STR in the White Mountains of New Hampshire

Krysten and myself that I would get us to $15,000/month in income and have a portfolio of properties that required no more than two hours/week of our time. Those were my marching orders and, within fifteen months of starting this business, I was able to retire myself, my wife and my mom through short-term rentals. More importantly, our son was able to outgrow his rare lung condition and is now a happy and healthy six-year-old boy.

So, how do you build a similar freedom story for yourself? Before I break down the four rules you will need to master to build a highly profitable and scalable short-term rental business, your first action item is to get extremely clear on your goal. Be specific. "Financial freedom" is not specific. "I want to travel" is not specific. How much do you need to make to be financially free? Where do you want to travel? How long do you want to stay there? Here are a few examples to get your mind going:

- I will profit $10,000/month in rental income from STRs and I will work no more than four hours/week by the 31st of December 20XX.
- I will profit $10,000/month in rental income from STRs and I will spend two weeks in the Mediterranean by the 31st of December 20XX.
- I will get to $10,000/month in rental income from STRs and retire my mom by the 31st of December 20XX.

Take some time and really get clear on what you want from this business. I see too many people start and scale this business only to realise eighteen months in that all they really needed was three or four nice short-term rental properties to make an extra $10,000/month and spend their time home-schooling their children or road-tripping across the United States. Instead, they now have twenty-five mediocre properties that they're running and netting the same as three or four luxury properties could have, and spending ten times more time in the business than they ever wanted when they got started. Do NOT become that person.

RULE #1 – KNOW YOUR NUMBERS

The first rule for investing in real estate: you make your money when you buy. In other words, know your numbers. Leveraging tools like STR Insights and AirDNA are a non-negotiable when starting or scaling your STR business. A quick rule of thumb that I use to narrow down my search: the property needs to generate annual revenue equal to or greater than 20% of my all-in costs. As an example:

Property acquisition price:	$500,000
Closing costs:	$10,000
Furnishing and decor:	$40,000
Total acquisition cost	$550,000

Therefore, the projected annual revenue (based on AirDNA comparable properties) must be greater than or equal to 20% of the total acquisition cost, which in this case equals $110,000.

Once the deal passes this quick test, I will run it through a deeper analysis in my STR Secrets Deal Analyzer. If you want a free copy of this and a bunch of free video trainings on how I analyse markets and properties go to www.STRsecrets.com/HHresources

RULE #2 – PROFESSIONAL DESIGN IS NOT OPTIONAL

I have been saying this for years. Professional design is not optional. This is an absolute must and quite frankly it is the BEST money you'll spend on your business. If you listen to the STR Secrets Podcast, then you have heard me say this constantly over the last few years. I would rather see you purchase a smaller property and have a larger budget for design than buy the bigger house and have no budget for design.

When analysing a property in a new market, I'll go on AirDNA and STR Insights and search for the top producing properties in that market. I'll review the top five-to-ten listings and specifically look for what makes the listing stand out and also what people are mentioning in the reviews. Is it the location, the amenities, the unique design? What makes these properties perform better than all the others? Then, we'll compare that to the property we're acquiring and write out the ways we could outperform the competition. What design elements would make this property stand out? What amenities can we offer? Then we meet with Krysten's team to review our notes, create the design mood boards and create a unique property that stands out in search results.

If you're interested in our free STR design templates or would like to get in touch with our design team head over to www.ondesigninteriors.co.

RULE # 3 – THINK LIKE A CEO

There are two very different approaches you can take to profiting with short-term rentals. You can build a side hustle, or you can build a business. There is no right or wrong way but there is a very real distinction. The key difference between a side hustle and a business is that a side hustle requires you to trade time for money. A business is built to produce income through processes, systems and people.

If you are looking to build a business, then I want you to ask yourself a simple question anytime that you are working in your business: "How can I automate or document this in such a way that I never have to do this job again?"

Start with the automation. Getting your technology stack set up and integrated will automate 90% of the operations in your business. The central hub for all your technology is your property management system (PMS), so choose wisely.

Choose a PMS that:

1. Integrates all your properties' calendars.
2. Distributes your properties across all your preferred online travel agencies (OTAs).
3. Can automatically send messages to guests.
4. Can automatically schedule tasks (such as cleanings).
5. Integrates your locks to automatically generate and send guests their access codes.
6. Integrates with your dynamic pricing tool.
7. Has an open application programming interface (API) that integrates with additional software in the future as your business scales.

Once you've automated as much as you can, now it's time to figure out where your time is going in the business. The most effective way to discover where your time is going in the business is by conducting a two-week time study. I've personally done this dozens of times and hundreds of our mastermind students can attest to the value of this study. To conduct this study, all you need to do is pause every fifteen minutes and write out what you are doing. This does not just include work items; write down EVERYTHING you do every fifteen minutes for two weeks. If time is our most valuable asset, then we need to know exactly where all yours is going. So, every fifteen minutes, write down what you are doing, then at the end of the two weeks you will identify all the tasks that are taking the most amount of your time. Those are the tasks that we want to delegate first. But before we can delegate them, we need to document them in a standard operating procedure (SOP). The next time you need to complete that task, you're going to record yourself doing it using software called Loom. Then, you're going to document it step by step in a Google Doc with screenshots. Make it so detailed that a six-year-old could follow along and get the job done.

Once you've done that, it's time to move on to Rule #4.

If you want a printable time-study and SOP templates and a video training on this, head over to www.STRsecrets.com/HHresources.

RULE #4 – BECOME THE CHAMPIONSHIP COACH

Becoming financially free through short-term rentals is absolutely possible, as you've heard from countless authors in this book. However, in order to become truly free, you must have complete time freedom and the ONLY way to achieve this is by building a great team and becoming a championship coach.

Championship coaches do three things exceptionally well:

1. Write the playbook.
2. Recruit A-players with clearly defined roles and responsibilities.
3. Create a winning culture that creates alignment and gets the most out of each player.

We discussed creating your playbook in Rule #3. One SOP that you MUST add to your playbook is your Employee Onboarding Checklist. One of the biggest mistakes I made early on and that I see so many hosts making is they realise they need help, so they go out and hire a virtual assistant. Then the person shows up on the first day and the host has no plan for them. "Hey, you're going to shadow me for the next seven days then you'll be off and running." Imagine being in their shoes for one second. You just accepted a job, you're all excited, and on the first day you receive no formal training, there's no real plan, your manager is running around like a chicken with their head cut off and you're supposed to help them fix everything. It doesn't exactly give you the warm and fuzzies that you made a wise choice to join this company.

Now on the other hand, imagine showing up on the first day to a scheduled Zoom meeting where your new boss introduces you to all the other team members (including cleaners, contractors and any other guest support staff), reviews the company's mission, vision and

Caiden got to help cut the ribbon at the grand opening of our first boutique hotel in 2020

values, then opens a Google Sheet that has been shared with you outlining your onboarding plan for the next two weeks, including a review of your role and responsibilities, a checklist of items and trainings for you to complete, contact information for every member on the team, a number of regular tasks that you will shadow your boss on at predetermined times each day, scheduled review meetings throughout the first couple of months and then what your regular team meeting cadence looks like. This is a completely different vibe and shows your new team member that you've got your act together and they joined a team that is going places.

So, take the time to build your onboarding checklist and your SOP playbook.

"A-players" will demand this because they only want to work with other A-players. Also, A-players want to know how they will be measured. In your job description, throughout onboarding and on each team meeting, make sure to spell out what results they are responsible for and will be measured against. As an example, all our guest support staff are required to respond to all guest inquiries within ten minutes or less. We track this and review this key performance indicator (KPI) every week in our staff meetings. This transparency creates massive accountability and a mutual respect across all our team members because everyone can see that they are all pulling their weight.

This ties into our core values and the culture that we built. We have a high level of transparency in our company, both personally and professionally. At the start of our weekly staff meeting, each team member shares a personal win and a professional win. I have found that by making the time to understand each team member's personal goals and by doing what I can as a leader to put them in a position to hit those goals, it creates a bond and loyalty that is unmatched. In addition, by tying their responsibilities and compensation into the company's performance, it creates alignment so that when the company wins, the entire team wins. Everyone on the team sees all our KPIs each week, including our revenue and when our targets are hit, and the team gets a monthly bonus. We also cover the cost for our oversees team to have two team retreats per year at a resort of their choosing and are encouraged to bring their entire family. These little perks go a long way in becoming a championship coach and getting the most out of your team.

If you follow these four rules of investing, it will fast track your success and allow you to become a highly profitable, financially independent, hospitable host.

I wish you nothing but success and, if I can ever be a resource for you, please reach out.

ABOUT THE AUTHOR

Michael is the host of the Short Term Rental Secrets Podcast and founder of the Short Term Rental Secrets Mastermind, a mentorship and mastermind programme that helps investors launch, automate and scale their short-term rental portfolios. Michael is also the co-founder of the industry's largest host-driven conference, The STR Wealth Conference.

Michael and his wife Krysten founded a national short-term rental investment and management company in 2017, as a vehicle to build passive income so they could stop trading away time from family for a paycheque.

That vision came to fruition within fifteen months, when their short-term rental portfolio replaced their income and Krysten and Michael both left their corporate jobs.

They are based out of Boston, MA, and currently have a portfolio of 100 short-term rental units across five states, including three boutique hotels on Boston's north shore.

Links: https://linktr.ee/mikesjogren

MONIKA SCHMIDT

FROM SINGLE MUM TO SUCCESSFUL HOST

Hi! **I'm Monika.** I love being active – preferably outdoors – I'm adventurous, quirky, savvy and always give things a go! I have a full-time job and I founded my side hustle Hotel Your Home in 2021. I am also a single mum to my three now teenage sons.

Thankfully, becoming a single mum in 2007 allowed one of my core survival skills to kick into overdrive – I have always been savvy and found a way to make things work! I made a pact to myself that my boys wouldn't suffer, nor miss out on the life I'd envisioned we'd have as a 'family' due to financial strains that many single parents face, one I was faced with all those years ago.

When my eldest son started school and the first fortnight of school holidays came around, I looked into the option of staying at an Airbnb, a little trip away to celebrate his first term at school. Back then, there weren't many options available within my budget and within driving distance (easy to cart kids, bikes, scooters, boogie boards and our dog!), but thankfully I found one down the South Coast and sent a request to book!

After the three-hour road trip winding down the Clyde River Mountain, I was able to park the car, pop our dog and my lads into a secure yard with some snacks and a footy while I went inside and made myself a cup of tea to recover from the long drive with way too many 'are we there yet's and 'he is looking at me's, or 'Mum, the dog farted's.

It was so cute that they'd run into the Airbnb and 'shotgun' a bed, it really did feel like a home away from home (but a holiday location!). Another perk – other than bringing our dog and not having to pay for a kennel or find someone to come and house-sit (as, let's face it, that was not an option as it meant they'd potentially use my air conditioning and utilities, and I could NOT afford that!) – was the kitchen. I could bring food and snacks from home and find the local grocery store to buy fresh milk and other essentials to prepare sandwiches, dinners and even the four-packs of their favourite ice creams, saving us a fair bit of money by not eating out.

We would later wander down to a local café, by the beach, which had been recommended by the host with the bikes/scooter and our dog, and just like that, we felt like locals!

HOW I GOT INTO BEING A HOST

I remember being at one of the Airbnbs I'd booked that was in a suburb where you benefited from having a car to get to the local places of interest. It was neat and homely, not dissimilar to our home, and I thought, "I wonder if 'my' home would go okay on Airbnb!?"

Once home and school was back, I tided my home, placed some decorative pillows on the beds (after retrieving them from the night before's pillow cubby turned pillow war), took some photos, logged onto Airbnb.com and started to create my listing. Moments later, I'd listed my place – a four-bedroom kid-friendly home in a normal middle-class area in Canberra (eek). Before I knew it, the dates I'd made available on the calendar were booked!

Before long, every second weekend that my boys would go to their dad's, I would make those nights available and stay at my dad's house (thanks, Dad!).

Me and my lads

I ended up 'making' money after I'd paid for our next mini break away... It was a no-brainer!

HOW I STARTED MY BUSINESS

I was now also co-hosting my sister's place in Canberra as her and her husband had moved interstate a few years before. The rental market was low at the time, they'd moved and were struggling to find good (if any) tenants to rent their three-bedroom, one-bathroom suburban home longer term. The option of selling very quickly was on the cards. I posed the idea: if I furnished their home and listed it on Airbnb, would they give it a go for three to six months? They said yes! Four years later, it's still going strong as a "**comfortable, quiet, family and pet-friendly home**" in a quiet suburb of Canberra!

In late 2019, I'd signed up to have a granny flat built in my large backyard that was no longer used for playing with trucks, jumping on the trampoline or having water fights. My sons were now too old to allow guests into their teenage-smelling and styled bedrooms while at their dad's, and seeing the profits to be made, I wanted to have an Airbnb of my own! Canberra Granny Flat Builders and Fixed Price Extensions (CGFB) worked with me to come up with a design that faced the sun with large windows to see the sky (my home is facing the opposite direction, gets pretty chilly in winter and very hot in summer). In the planning stage, they asked what my intention for the granny flat was. When I told them it was to list on Airbnb, they then told me that they had a number of granny flats they'd built for other customers that they used as display homes for potential customers. These were vacant and not being utilised, so they asked if I'd consider managing them on Airbnb, ensuring that once a month on a Sunday was blocked to allow it to be a display home to be opened to the general public. I, of course, said yes! It was great, the granny flats were all very well designed, styled and furnished, had all utilities and CGFB were paying homeowners a weekly rental figure to have them as display homes. Airbnbing them made CGFB a small profitable return while still having access to them on days they wanted to show potential customers through their regular display homes – win-win.

2020, the Covid-19 global pandemic. Stuck (I'm supposed to say 'safe') at home – but honestly, who was 'safe' with three almost teenage sons? No school, no social catchups, no sports/training sessions, no gym – safe for whom?! My outlet became watching Netflix – too many hours of Netflix. CGFB and my sister's Airbnbs lost so many bookings due to the pandemic, it was all going belly up. Then it turned and, as people positive with Covid needing to isolate from loved ones and hotels were having issues with it spreading via the air conditioning, Airbnb became a great solution and were now being booked in two-week periods. It took a load off the cleaners and deep cleans were becoming the norm – it was a huge win for the Airbnbs I was managing! In December 2020, Hotel Your Home was founded.

CLEANING TEAMS THAT SUPPORT ME AND HOW I SUPPORT THE ENVIRONMENT

Working my day job in the office means I am unavailable during changeover hours, so I needed a cleaner. I asked around and found a highly recommended lady doing residential cleans – another single mumma with three boys! After a chat and explaining what Airbnb was about and what I needed, she was on board! Teagan (TSC Cleaning) started looking after the Airbnb I was hosting and now has a team of staff that support her to support me.

We supply our properties with sustainable products to reduce waste. Covid forced us into having tighter cleaning and sanitising regimes, which is a plus for both guests and homeowners. By having sustainable products, we reduce waste to landfill by using refillable products such as Zero.com, Who Gives a Crap and washable microfibre dishcloths that are sanitised with the washing/laundry.

HOW HOTEL YOUR HOME HELPS OUR COMMUNITY

I used to have a sense of unease that Airbnbs (short-term rentals) were taking away the usual rental homes from locals. However, when I sat and thought about it, I knew I was creating a job for Teagan and, in turn, she was creating jobs for others that needed work during school hours. My sons often grab a mower and do the lawns of Airbnbs I manage, they ride their bikes to ones that are close by and bring the wheelie bins in and out for bin collection days. For properties that aren't within rideable distance, I task local kids with the 'bin management' and they get paid each week. So, in short, my business Hotel Your Home and STRs are helping many in our community. STRs are also bringing revenue into our communities, which I love, as I am big on supporting local.

I love that I can literally do this job from anywhere!

WHAT I DO NOW

Hotel Your Home helps homeowners who want to dabble in the shared services world – when people have an idea and the courage to give it a try. I'm here to provide my experience and expertise. I'll sit down and have a cuppa with homeowners/investors, show them other listings similar to theirs, provide statistics using AirDNA and provide the level of courage and ease to allow them to move past the imposter syndrome and 'it's too hard' to take a chance, all while sticking to the facts.

Whether it's an investment property that is going to be a full-time dedicated Airbnb, or homeowners who are travelling for a few months (because we can), we're here to help:

- Set up the listing.
- Suggest furniture and bedding configurations.
- Photograph the listing.
- Marketing.
- Guest communication – including local and up-to-date

activities, must-see places, local markets and walks, cafes to try and places to wine and dine.
- Organising the cleaning and guest changeovers.
- Linen hire and laundering.
- Providing bin management.
- Reporting any maintenance and damages to the Hotel Your Home office to start the Air Cover claims process.
- Gardening services.
- Maintenance repairs service.
- Vendor management and inspections.

WHAT DO I WISH I COULD HAVE KNOWN?

- Scheduled messaging is not only a lifesaver but keeps guests informed from when they click 'book' right through to when they depart.
- Local tips support the community and give guests that sense of belonging – the one I had with my three boys all those years ago.
- Hidden gems around the area give guests that real community feel.
- Having a spare lockbox on site means no late-night trips to take spare keys when 'lost, left or locked'.
- User manuals in a folder reduce guests' questions.
- A clear house guide with local advice, Wi-Fi details and my logo left onsite is handy.
- Being pet friendly where possible.

MY JOURNEY

If nothing changes, nothing changes.

As I have had a less than smooth life, I want to show that if I can do this and if I can back myself that YOU can too. We are amazing and, with self-belief and grit, you can do whatever you WANT!

ABOUT THE AUTHOR

"Playing the hand you're dealt – with positivity, determination AND a smile."

Founder of Hotel Your Home, single mum Monika hosts multiple properties in Australia's capital, Canberra. Helping and inspiring others to help themselves is something she strives for.

In 2007, Monika faced the stark reality of no longer having a double income to provide the 'traditional' lifestyle that she had hoped for her three very active and boisterous boys. The prospect of this really got her thinking.

You'll now find Monika helping others host and manage their properties on Airbnb. Most of her listings are family and pet-friendly properties that, unlike hotels, provide space, flexibility and freedom to ensure her guests enjoy that 'home away from home' feeling. The same feeling Monika enjoyed all those years ago with her lads.

Today, Monika strives to support others to gain the financial independence that she was so determined to achieve years earlier. Most of the team she employs to clean the properties are also single mums. To provide an additional source of income, the cleaners are also encouraged to hygienically launder the linen at their home, which affords them a more family-friendly work-life balance.

Links: https://linktr.ee/HotelYourHome

NATALIE PALMER

HEALING THROUGH HOSTING

2ND MARCH 2022, 11:00PM

At that moment, they realised how much blood I had lost, and that my baby was without oxygen. I was rushed in for an emergency c-section, and as the anaesthesiologist put me under, the last thing I heard was, "If anyone in this room is religious, now is the time to pray."

Darkness.

* * *

Let's back up, shall we? How did we get here? In order to know that, I first need to tell you about myself, and how this ties into me being a hospitable host.

I was born and raised in Southern California, to parents who emigrated from Poland. They were college sweethearts, and in 1981 my dad moved to Long Beach. My mom had one semester of university left, so she stayed back temporarily. In those few months, the communist government enacted martial law, and the borders closed to anyone coming in or out.

They wrote letters back and forth for *years*, not knowing if things would ever change. If you know your Cold War history, you know that thanks to President Reagan and Pope John Paul II (who is from my mom's hometown of Krakow and actually confirmed her into the Catholic church) things did change. In 1984, three years later, my mom was able to make the move to California and was reunited with my dad.

This was by no means the end of their struggles. They had left behind all their family and friends, bringing nothing with them but their ambition, work ethic and hope for something better. I guess, for them, this wasn't anything out of the norm. You see, my family came from a long line of things being taken and families being separated. During WWII, my paternal grandfather was taken to a labour camp as a teenager by the nazis (he did manage to escape), while my maternal grandmother's childhood home and land was seized by the communist regime, and she, her siblings and my great grandmother – a single mom while her husband was at war – became homeless in an instant.

My dad began taking classes at CSULB, while my mom started cleaning houses. She would have the news on all day while cleaning so she could learn English. Soon enough, they had secured steady jobs and we're saving to buy their first home. In 1993, I entered the picture, and in 1997, my younger sister followed.

My parents lived the definition of the American dream. My dad's career sent him all around the world and my mom became a programme manager for an aerospace company. They worked constantly. I was always so envious of the girls in class whose moms were on the PTA or could volunteer to chaperone school field trips. I hated when my dad was gone for so long or my mom worked late, but... this is how it's supposed to be, right? My parents left everyone behind to move here. *Growing up means you have to be ready to be apart from those you love most.*

When the recession hit, my dad lost his job. I could sense my parents were stressed, but I was secretly happy. My dad threw himself into so many passions and hobbies, the biggest one being skiing. He loved it so much, he decided to become a ski instructor in

Big Bear. The following winter season, I joined him as a children's ski instructor. In 2011, after years of driving up every winter weekend, my parents purchased a short-sale condo in Big Bear.

By 2017, I was half in half out as a freelance social media manager. This was also after working as a wedding coordinator, a rock-climbing instructor, website designer, you name it. Nothing stuck, and I was realising that the one thing I feared most to be true was probably true: *Growing up means you have to be ready to be apart from those you love most.*

In one final attempt to pursue something more creative and fulfilling, I had an idea to list the Big Bear condo on Airbnb for one week between Christmas and New Year. It's the busiest week of the entire year in Big Bear, and I figured that must mean we could get a few hundred bucks, right?

First, I had to convince my parents. I'd take care of everything. They weren't crazy about the idea of welcoming complete strangers, but once they agreed, it was a family affair.

My dad started tackling those pesky repairs we'd put off for years, while my mom and I cleared out our snow gear and personal items. We deep cleaned every inch, working for days to make every detail perfect. I loved it. And I loved that we were all doing it *together*.

On the 22nd of December, we were ready. I published the Airbnb listing and, forty-five minutes later, we had our first booking. Five nights at $2,500 total!

Now that was fun. "Mom... dad...?" I started asking. "What if we opened up just a few more dates into the new year? It was so much effort getting everything ready, we may as well rent it out a bit longer."

They said yes, and we were off to the races.

For the next three months, we were rented out 100% (now I know that means we were priced too low, but hey, you gotta start somewhere).

We drove four-to-five hours round trips with snow chains every few days, making the home perfect for every back-to-back check-in.

Violet hanging out in the pack 'n' play at seven months while we renovated the newest property

My mom and I were the cleaning team, my dad was our handyman and the reviews were five stars.

By the time the ski season ended, we were hooked. My parents reinvested the profits into a condo three doors down. While renovating the new unit, neighbours approached me to manage their places. They saw how often we were booked and figured I must be doing something right. Just like that, I was managing four places. In the next couple of years, I'd doubled that to eight. I had to outsource the cleaning and handyman but was able to manage everything remotely. For the first time in my life, I truly loved what I was doing.

I loved hosting so much that on the weekend of the 29th of February 2020, my wedding day, I refused to block off the calendar. I still wanted to host!

We had our first daughter Violet in December. A few hours after she was born, I received an email from MTV interested in filming a project in one of our properties. I was still in a hospital gown, Violet latched onto me, filling out Docusigns on my phone to get the filming contracts signed.

I had officially done it. I had built a lifestyle for myself that checked off all those boxes I could only dream of; I was passionate about hosting, good at hosting, making money from hosting and I was able to work from anywhere while hosting. Even in a hospital bed while holding my newborn.

In April 2021, my husband and I purchased our own investment property in that same condo complex. After years of managing for other owners, this was a dream come true. It was a total fixer upper, and I couldn't wait to do the renovation ourselves. My whole family was back in Big Bear, this time with Violet in the pack 'n' play in the middle of our construction zone. It was exhausting, and having an infant didn't make it any easier, but I loved every minute of it. There were days when everything went wrong, became more expensive, or fell behind schedule. We drove each other absolutely crazy, but we were together.

I became pregnant again when Violet was just six months old. We were still mid-renovation, but this pregnancy was rough. I had to leave the project behind, but my parents oversaw the last three months to the finish line. I thought the pregnancy was difficult, but nothing would prepare me for the delivery.

2ND MARCH 2022, 9:30PM

I was sitting at the dining table, thirty-seven weeks pregnant, my fifteen-month-old asleep in her room and Eric on his way home. I felt one single contraction, and suddenly a gush of liquid was streaming down my legs, completely soaking the dining chair and leaving a puddle on the floor. *There goes my water breaking...* or so I thought. I looked down to see... blood? Lots of blood. Like *a lot* of blood. *Oh my God, I've never seen this much blood in my life. And damn, these were my favourite pyjamas. I'd better get this stain out before we leave for the hospital.* (Can you tell that I'm a host who takes pride in her unmatched stain removal skills?)

I headed to the sink to work on this stain and grabbed some rags to soak the blood out of the dining chair seat cushion. I was dialling the hospital and simultaneously checking Eric's location... he was ten minutes away. The nurse who answered told me some blood must have mixed in with the amniotic fluid and to make my way over whenever I can. I thought there would be more panic, but thought *I guess we're good?* Eric arrived, his parents followed shortly after to watch Violet, and we were off.

All I had to do was sit in the passenger seat and time my

contractions. It was the worst pain I've ever felt in my life. I was getting dizzier and dizzier. I felt a constant flow of blood, really wishing we had taken the car with black upholstery instead of the beige. I was passing out. Something was seriously wrong. *Eric, can you drive any faster?*

We arrived. Eric sprinted for a wheelchair. We got to the front desk. I was literally collapsing out of the wheelchair onto the waiting room floor. The receptionist told us to sit down and relax while she called for a room to be prepped.

Eric looked at her, back at me, and back at her again, as if to say, "Are you not seeing what I'm seeing?" She seemed to get the hint and made a half-hearted attempt at getting us into a room faster. I was eventually wheeled in, unable to hold myself upright, and was as white as this piece of paper you're reading right now. Eric was told to go back to the waiting room and "hang tight while we get a doctor to check her out".

He became adamant that we needed a doctor NOW, while the receptionist repeated some line about how "birth is always stressful for first-timers!" *B*tch... it's not our first time.*

Finally, a doctor.

I was blacking out and have no memory of getting undressed and being put onto the hospital bed, but I snapped back at the next thing I heard. I felt a burst of fluid, as the doctor pulled her hand out of me and announced to the team that had poured into the room, "Her water never broke, I just punctured it now. The placenta ruptured."

My water never broke? So that gush that happened over an hour ago was... just pure blood? No amniotic fluid at all? Okay, so I'm going to die right now.

At that moment, they realised how much blood I had lost, and that my baby was without oxygen. I was rushed in for an emergency c-section, and as the anaesthesiologist put me under, the last thing I heard was, "If anyone in this room is religious, now is the time to pray."

Darkness.

* * *

When I awoke, Eric was next to me, sobbing.

"What happened? Where's the baby? What did we have?!" We were waiting to find out the gender at birth.

"It's a girl, she was born at 11:05pm, but when they pulled her out, she wasn't breathing."

Oh my God, oh my God... this can't be real. This isn't happening.

"They resuscitated her, but..."

But???? But what?? Oh my God.

"Her levels are low. They don't know how long she was without oxygen. She's in the NICU."

A doctor entered and explained that I'd had a complete placental abruption. That one contraction I felt at 9:30pm was my placenta detaching from the uterus. Baby was born over an hour and a half later, so who knows how long she had been without oxygen. She would be transferred to another hospital with more advanced equipment for her needs, while I would stay behind to get three blood transfusions over the next few days.

This couldn't be happening. Everything I had done in the last four years was to build a life where my family could stay together. I had created something that let us all work together, that let me stay home as a mom. Now, having not even met my daughter yet, they were taking her away from me. How stupid was I to think I could create my own success or be a good host? My own womb wasn't even hospitable!

I had finally started believing that there was a path in life that didn't mean having to be away from those you love so often. This was shattering all of that.

I begged for them to let me see her before the transfer. Hours later, they finally agreed, and brought her to my room in some giant acrylic box with dozens of wires hooked on her. My c-section incision was still raw. I could barely sit up to see her but managed one little foot tickle before she was rolled away.

Finally, after the longest four days of my life, I was discharged.

We drove straight to the other hospital, and I held baby Scarlett for the first time. After one full week in the NICU, we brought her home.

Every single nurse and doctor told us that mine and Scarlett's recovery was unexplainable. Based on my blood loss, an emergency c-section should've been fatal. Based on how long Scarlett is suspected to have been without oxygen, she should have serious neurological delays. But we're both here, and she is absolutely thriving.

* * *

Before Scarlett's birth, I had finally figured it all out. Because of hosting, I was doing something I loved, making an income from it, and doing it all from home so that I didn't have to be doomed to the same fate all the generations before me were. I could live out the dream and didn't have to lose out on time with my family. Right?

Wrong. Despite everything I had been working towards – all so I could be with my family – Scarlett's entrance into the world was marked with her being immediately taken from us.

I was still hosting as I was healing, never blocking off a single calendar date. It was a good distraction from the trauma, but so much of the hosting business had been automated. I needed a bigger distraction.

Six weeks after Scarlett's birth date, I decided to start a podcast to share my hosting knowledge and experience. I would record episodes in my dimly lit room, in the dark hours after the girls were asleep.

The reviews started rolling in, and listeners were loving it. Women from all over were telling me how motivated they were to start hosting too. They, too, had been searching for something that they were passionate about, good at, could make money from and that would allow them to work from anywhere.

In my darkest days, hosting was there for me. Whether it was a five-star review from a guest or a podcast listener. Whether it was a thank you text from our cleaner about how grateful they were to

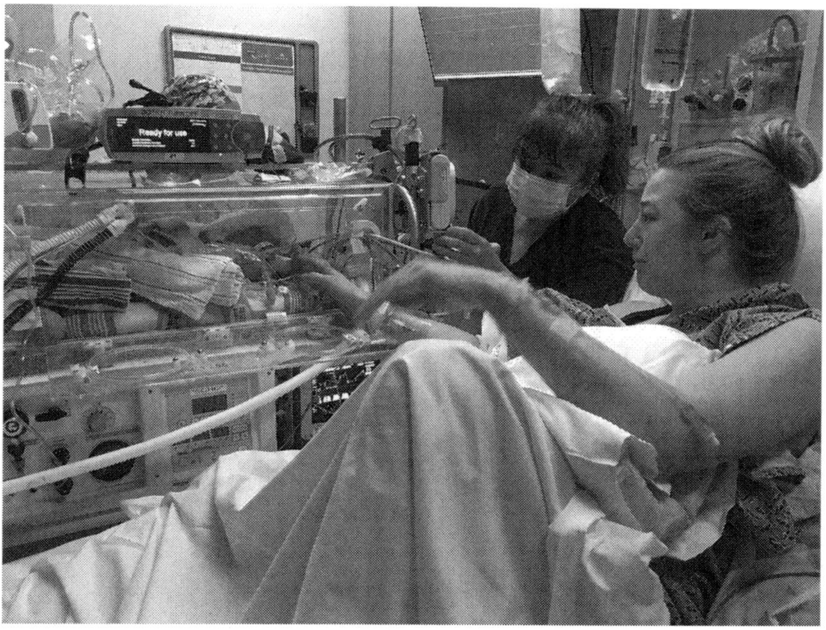

Meeting Scarlett for the first time before she was transferred to another hospital

work for us. Whether it was just talking into a microphone about hosting, alone in my room, as a distraction.

I can't control if my placenta ruptures, if my grandfather would be taken to a labour camp, if my great grandmother would have her land confiscated, or if my parents would have to leave everything behind. I can't guarantee a life that is totally free from hardship, but I can control whether or not I continue building a business I love, and if I choose to share what I've learned with other women who feel just as lost as I did before I discovered hosting.

I can decide that I do not want my family's sacrifices to be for naught. I never want what was confiscated from my great grandmother to be in vain, and today, the privilege of being able to own and invest in property is one I do not take lightly.

* * *

My mom and dad are both retired now, and hosting is a family business. My mom helps me with onboarding and designing new properties. My dad is our general contractor, and even got himself elected to HOA president to keep the condo association friendly to short-term rentals. Even my sister, who got her master's in data science, wrote her thesis on Airbnb pricing models. My husband is the best cheerleader and supports me in any new property we take on, or when I need him to get the kids out of the house so I can record the podcast.

My mom's first job in the US was as a house cleaner, working hard so that I could one day go to college and not have to clean houses. The truth is, after getting my business degree, I couldn't have been less fulfilled. Ironically enough, cleaning our units with my mom, in those busy winters, making every detail perfect for our guests, were some of the happiest times of my life. You'd better believe that when Violet and Scarlett are old enough, their first summer job will be driving to Big Bear to clean our short-term rentals. In the meantime, they'll be watching and learning from their mom what it means to be a hospitable host.

ABOUT THE AUTHOR

Natalie Palmer started hosting "by accident" in 2017, and soon found herself running a boutique vacation rental management business. She has since expanded her role as a host into helping others get started in the short-term rental industry. She is the co-founder of Level Up Your Listing Summit – a three-day women's STR summit, and is the host of _No Vacancy The Podcast_, which has quickly landed in the top 2% of podcasts worldwide. She is passionate about teaching others how to host stress-free, remotely, and make hosting fit into their lifestyle – not the other way around. Her courses have been taken by over 500 new and experienced hosts, and she works closely with Airbnb as an Ambassador.

She lives in Southern California with her husband and two young daughters, and never starts a day without a large iced coffee.

Links: bit.ly/hostwithnatalie

NOBLE CRAWFORD

A SECOND CHANCE AT LIFE TO HELP OTHERS AND GENERATE WEALTH

They were closing the blinds of the only window that provided me a glimpse into the intensive care unit hospital room as I was rushing down the hallway. With only a few yards left to reach the doorway, the last sight I can remember was the multiple nurses and doctors that stood bedside as they pulled the paddles out to shock her heart. "I'm sorry, sir, you can't be here. We need to let the doctors do their job." Those were the words that echoed in my head as the squealing noise of the defibrillator charging up pierced loudly. "Clear!" they shouted. They shut the ICU room door as they were applying the paddles to her chest.

In that moment, time stopped.

The day started about 4:30am with us checking into the hospital. The hospital advised us to arrive early. They'd scheduled the brain surgery for 6:30am and they wanted to allow enough time for paperwork and for her family to be with her beforehand. You see, she had a brain tumour the size of a golf ball. This explained the multiple headaches and small seizures she had been experiencing.

My hands shook as I signed "no fault" clauses and resuscitation orders, should things go south. Her family, my family and several friends gathered around to wish her well prior to being wheeled into surgery. My goal was to be the last one to whisper into her ear words of encouragement. Unfortunately, her relatives took up every second of time before they wheeled her off. I walked beside her gurney down the long hallway holding her hand. As I was gathering myself to speak life into her, the doctors began applying the gas to put her to sleep. By the time I had gained my composure enough to speak without a quiver in my voice, she was asleep. As they pulled her away, I couldn't hold back the tears. I had missed my opportunity to tell her how much I loved her!

The primary neurosurgeon said that the surgery should take about six to eight hours. Fourteen hours and two blood transfusions later, she was finally being moved to the ICU. Every visible part of her body was covered in tubes, wires, bandages and multiple machines moved in transit with her. She looked as though she had endured the biggest battle of her life.

The first forty-eight hours in ICU were the most critical. She experienced several unexplainable episodes of waking from her sleep and attempting to pull IVs and lines from her arms, neck and even her head. During those episodes, she kept saying, "It's hot! It's hot!" At the time, we had no idea what she was referring to. The nurses would give her something to calm her down and she would drift back off to sleep. This happened a handful of times.

Which brings us back to where the story began.

Thankfully, the doctors were able to resuscitate her after almost three minutes! As it turns out, she was allergic to morphine. She had been placed on a morphine drip immediately after surgery and it had been slowly causing her organs to shut down, effectively killing her from the inside out.

She remained in the hospital for the next couple of weeks. She was released on Christmas Eve that year. Thank God for her second chance! Our boys, thirteen, six and three at the time, needed their mother.

As a result of the surgery, she lost all her sense of smell and taste for the rest of her life. Unfortunately, the surgeons had to sever her olfactory nerve to completely remove the tumour. Then the hard work of recovery began. During this time, she had to relearn the simplest of tasks. She had to learn how to raise her spoon to her mouth, walk without assistance and speak without slurring.

At the time, I was working a W-2 job, as a commissioned sales rep. I had to make a decision to either stay at home and care for my wife or go back to work and keep grinding. I prioritised her well-being and elected to stay home and make her recovery my full-time job for the next six to eight weeks.

As she got to the point where she could manage her own self-care, I was called back into the office for a company sales meeting. In that meeting, I was berated by the CEO for my dismal sales numbers for the previous six weeks. This happened, despite the fact that everyone in the entire company knew what we were going through. I was humiliated, insulted and embarrassed.

In that moment, I made the decision to put myself in a position where I would never again be beholden to someone else's time!

I decided to grind it out at work for as long as it took in order to buy back my time freedom so that I could be there for my family whenever they needed me. Within five years, I closed a couple of huge deals, cashed out of my W-2 job and never looked back.

In that same year, I rebranded myself, launched my first podcast, worked on self-development and started a video marketing agency within the same industry. Because of the relationships I'd built, I was able to hit the ground running. I become a certified HubSpot agency. I quickly learned about MRR (monthly recurring revenue) and fell in love with it. The MRR model allows for a company to generate repeat revenue on a monthly basis over an extended period of time.

As a marketing agency, revenue was generated from project-based work and monthly recurring revenue from ongoing inbound marketing and video marketing. I was fortunate to work with some big brands like Samsung, Bose and others.

Despite the early success, I found myself working more as an

Noble Enjoying Life!

entrepreneur than I had been in my W-2 job. I had managed to do the one thing that I'd intended to avoid... create less time for myself and my family.

Fast forward three years and I was introduced to the concept of short-term rentals. My dad sent me a YouTube video and asked if I had heard about this new business model. It was brand new to me but, as it turns out, I recognised one of my former podcast guests, Jermaine Massey. Soon after, we attended a mastermind event in California where we were introduced to a couple of major players in the space, including Rebecca Slivka. We absorbed everything we could, came back to Texas, put our heads down and went to work.

Our introduction to short-term rentals was with the rental arbitrage method. Rental arbitrage is essentially leasing property and leveraging that property to use for short-term stays for your guests – with the owner's permission, of course. As I recall, our beginning was a bit rocky. We experienced a lot of rejection from property owners and landlords. However, after four to six months of persistence, we landed our first few doors. The rest, as they say, is history!

To date, we've been able to acquire a portfolio of both leased and owned assets and have the pleasure of helping other hosts scale their business using a very niche business model that generates significant, consistent, monthly recurring revenue. It's ironic how MRR showed up again!

For context, I have an extensive background working in the hospitality industry. On the heels of working in that industry for several years, I worked in the technology sector. In my last employed role, I worked across a number of verticals (corporate, healthcare, higher education, federal and military) whereby I had to design and sell systems into these sectors.

My background enabled me to learn the process of effectively prospecting and selling into all these verticals. More importantly, I participated in projects that included set-aside federal funds and grants. This gave me insight into the federal procurement process and how government contracts work. In addition, our company participated in military projects that require specific requirements to pursue.

During my tenure, I was able to learn the skillset of landing contract opportunities across the local, state and federal government. How does this translate into short-term rentals? The light bulb moment occurred when I thought to myself, "Why am I not using what I learned at my last job to go after contract opportunities within the short-term rental industry?" The process is the same. The only difference is the product or service. Game on!

I immediately started applying the strategies I'd learned to uncover opportunities for lodging and accommodations across multiple verticals. This one change to our business model exploded our revenue and continues to provide limitless opportunities. Imagine doing the upfront leg work one time and getting paid over and over again for your early efforts. This niche business model is like the gift that keeps on giving! Not to mention, it's guaranteed, consistent, long-term monthly revenue.

Here is a case study and also one of my favourite examples of one of the opportunities we've been able to take advantage of. I located a company that was holding a sizeable prime government defence contract. Under this contract, they are required to perform aviation related training, year round, for a six-year period. The trainees were working within the federal government, so they qualified for a special nightly rate.

Federal employees, military personnel, government contractors, etc., qualify for a nightly lodging per diem. This rate varies by city or postcode. You can look up this information for your area by searching the General Services Administration (GSA) website or Google "GSA lodging per diem and your zip code". The rates can vary by month or season.

At the time, the GSA rate for our area was $167 per night. We knew that the trainees were staying for two and four-week intervals. This was huge! As long as we could provide space at or below this rate, we'd be off to the races! The company holding the government contract historically used hotels to accommodate these groups.

After some upfront prospecting and good ole fashioned sales techniques were applied, we were able to get our company added to a list of extended stay and limited-service hotels to provide lodging for these men and women who were travelling to the area for their training and certification.

One group would stay for a two-week period. A second group would stay for a one-month period. Nine doors within a multi-family community are used to accommodate our clients. Five one-bedrooms and four two-bedrooms to be exact. Each one-bedroom where we host our thirty-day clients would turn over every month. Each two-bedroom, which accommodates our guests staying for two weeks, would turn over twice monthly.

If you're following the maths with me, then that means that for each one-bedroom unit priced at $167 per night, they generate $5,010 per month. With five units, that's $25,050 per month in gross revenue. Our rent is $1,450 per month plus a few hundred in expenses. That's over $3K per door in profit on autopilot!

This is where things get even better. Our two-bedroom, two-bath units house two trainees in two-week intervals. That means we're able to charge the GSA rate of $167 per night for both rooms in the same unit. That's monthly gross revenue of $10,020 per two-bedroom unit. We have four of these 2/2 units. Their combined gross revenue is $40,080. With rents around $1,800 monthly, you can see how the profit margins explode!

There you have it. Nine doors grossing over $65K in monthly revenue! This is just one case study of two different opportunities that we participate in with companies actively engaged in defence contracts. Aside from them being easy to clean and manage due to minimal turnovers, we also do not have to worry about pricing, occupancy, or seasonality. The biggest upside is that these are multi-year contracts! Do the work once. Reap the benefits for years!

We're currently operating forty-two doors. Our entire portfolio is comprised of direct booked clients with the exception of three properties. If direct bookings through government contracts is of interest to you, I have a twelve-month accelerator programme called GovCon Experience (govconexperience.com).

I'll share one more case study. As we all can remember, Covid wiped out a lot of bookings! It even caused a significant number of hosts to go completely out of business. We were fortunate in that we had already started implementing some direct book strategies; so, the impact of lost reservations was minimal. However, what we did experience was the total stoppage of new reservations. As a result, we doubled down on a couple of key verticals to generate bookings. One of which was higher education.

As Covid escalated, eventually we started to see colleges and universities close for the remainder of the school year. While this was not an issue for students who lived here in the US, it created a huge problem for international students who had to leave their dorms but could not fly back home due to airport closures. We saw the need and seized the opportunity.

I immediately started contacting student housing offices at local campuses where we had properties within a reasonable distance. They were eagerly looking to assist students with temporary placement and had even been in contact with hotels. In one city, we offered our three and four-bedroom townhouses as accommodations. We quickly realised that there was a specific demographic that was in dire need of help. We found that to be one of Asian females. They were not US citizens. They had no permanent US address. They were attending university here in the states but as misfortune would have it... they could not get back home.

Another interesting discovery was the fact that they had multiple friends who shared the same dilemma. As a result, we were able to convert a number of our three and four-bedroom townhouses from single reservation units to multi-guest units. We rented out the rooms instead of the entire property. It created a win-win-win scenario for the students, the college and for us. We went from little to no bookings for these units to full occupancy for months. Most important was the satisfaction we found in helping others.

While students worked great for us during Covid, we don't traditionally provide student housing beyond graduate level or medical students. However, we've since found a need for staff and faculty housing for tenured and visiting faculty, post-doctoral candidates, research assistants, etc.

I could go on and on with case studies in different verticals (i.e. healthcare, insurance, relocation, military, etc.). If you've read this far, I think you get the point. Direct bookings have enabled us to carve out a niche in the industry.

If short-term rentals is a space you're currently engaged in or if it's something you're considering, check out my podcast, Hospitality Cashflow (hospitalitycashflow.com). We're currently in season three and have an awesome list of industry influencers who have been on the show, with more coming! You can find it on Apple Podcast, Google Podcasts, Spotify and several other major podcast platforms.

If you're an experienced operator with multiple doors or doing a significant amount of revenue, I'm a participating coach alongside Kyle Stanley, Julie George, Mike Sjogren, TJ Tijani and Rachel Gainsbrugh in the 7 Figure STR Mastermind. Info at www.7figurestrmastermind.com

What does the future look like? We've recently entered the multi-family investing side of real estate. We've aligned ourselves with a general partner team that will allow us to execute our direct booking business model across a multitude of apartment communities. This is super exciting and provides an opportunity for

My family

us to accommodate a greater number of guests in different markets nationally. With 30+ day stays being required at more communities through rental arbitrage, and with regulations being mandated by cities around the country, this model is a game changer!

If anything I've written in this chapter resonates with you and you'd like to learn more about the services I offer with coaching or consulting, please connect with me. I'm always happy to provide value where I can.

Lastly, I'd like to leave you with my tips for success.

KNOW YOUR "WHY"

For me, it was having the time freedom to be there for my family, friends and those closest to me. Find your why. It's what will drive you when all else fails.

SET STRETCH GOALS

Get uncomfortable with some of your goals. Set some goals that are deliberately challenging. They may even feel impossible.

DEVELOP THE RIGHT MINDSET

You are what you ingest. Feed yourself positive, self-building, motivational, inspiring, helpful content. Be a reader. Listen to audiobooks and podcasts. Develop a morning routine. Practise visualisation and work on your mindset.

PROXIMITY EFFECT
Build and cultivate relationships. Network consistently. Never be the smartest person in the room. Leverage partnership opportunities. Always pour into someone else.

INVEST IN YOURSELF
Make an investment in self-improvement through a mentor. Start or scale your business by hiring a coach or purchasing a course. Attend masterminds with high-performing like-minded individuals.

TAKE MASSIVE ACTION
Nothing else matters if you don't take action! Be intentional with the activities that you dedicate your time to. Don't over-analyse. Don't procrastinate. Just do it!

Thank you so much to Jodie Stirling and Julie George for encouraging me to share my story with you. Special shout out to my fellow authors and a few of my industry friends, Jeremy, Veronica, Angela, Meron, Ramya, AJ, Almas, Adam, Jason, Titi and so many others. Thank you to my wife Elkie and my sons, Noble, Kenneth and Timothy.

I am honoured and grateful. Thank you for reading my chapter. See you at the top!

ABOUT THE AUTHOR

Noble is the principal and co-founder of a hospitality brand, a real estate investor and a consultant. Over the past six years, he has grown a portfolio of multiple doors across Texas consisting of owned assets and multi-family arbitrage units. He has recently started co-hosting for a high-profile client.

His diverse background spans several years in hospitality, technology, and sales and marketing. Noble has worked with brands such as Marriott, Hilton, IHG and more. He worked in various capacities including front desk, night audit, conference services, audio-visual production and technology.

Noble has recently entered the multi-family syndication space and is currently pursuing multiple opportunities in apartment ownership.

He currently coaches and mentors dozens of students in the short-term rental industry. He focuses his training on the topics of prospecting, sales and marketing, generating direct bookings within multiple B2B verticals, and securing local, state and government contracts.

Noble also consults for real estate investors, syndication teams, land developers and small business owners through his podcast and education agency, Hospitality Cashflow.

He is a husband to Elkie, and a proud father to three sons, Noble, Kenneth and Timothy.

Links: https://linktr.ee/noblecrawford

OMID TEHRANIRAD

BORN TO BE RAD!

I was born in Hollywood, which is a destination that fittingly produces movie stars! I am a product of two immigrants, who met in a most unlikely location, a secondary English class. My mother was of Colombian descent, and my father of Iranian descent. These two are very different cultures but they shared one thing in common, which was the love of being around people, and the ability to bring people together. That love had a heavy influence on my interests and mindset, which focused on building communities and being a hospitable host.

My early memories as a child involve being surrounded by a plethora of people at festivities. My parents would host lively parties that are reminiscent of the energy of a soccer stadium. You would see an abundance of food, hear the roar of conversation and see children of all ages running around. At the time, I thought it was normal to host constant parties. I later realised this blessing would build the foundation of my future calling. Hosting guests at my hideaway haus!

ASSIMILATING INTO THE MELTING POT

I never had formal training in hospitality school, but I developed an intuition to build relationships with people quickly. Being born in the melting pot of Southern California as a first-generation American was a blessing in disguise. I had to assimilate into the modern MTV generation while I also adapted to the many communities that were introduced to me. This ability to adapt and adopt different perspectives gave me insight on the common thread of what people enjoyed doing. There was an ironic simplicity of enjoyment within one's tribe.

I experienced the simplicity one meal at a time at my friends' dinner tables. I had friends from all over the world who were mostly first-generation immigrants like me. These experiences allowed me to gain insight from old-world values during the intimate moments of having a meal at home. The dinner table was a setting where I got to see the contrast and the commonalities between families. I was fascinated with etiquette, respect, how additional servings were requested, discussions about politics and so much more. It showed me what mattered to people.

Throughout my youth, I had the opportunity to travel. My mom worked for a major airline, cleaning planes, and we took advantage of her "standby" flight benefits. As a child, because of these benefits, I enjoyed the luxury of spending the summer in Cali, Colombia. Accommodations were very humble, and I had to learn and adapt to the food culture. Daily, I would enjoy a fresh cup of Colombian coffee as a five year old. The food and culture were super vibrant. Besides drinking coffee every morning, dancing to salsa music and storytelling, I learned people wanted a space to enjoy themselves. Everyone wanted their version of a hideaway haus!

THE MAGICAL KINGDOM OF DISNEYLAND

I remember growing up watching Disney movies like *The Lion King*. There was something magical about how I felt when I thought of the brand. For my first job, I yearned for the chance to be part of such an enchanting brand. I applied and they immediately wanted little old me to be part of Disney's outdoor vending team. This meant I was an interactive part of the guest experience. I couldn't have been any happier.

As I embarked on my Disney journey, I quickly learned about creating a magical experience for guests. People were coming from all over the world, spending their hard-earned money, to experience the same magical feeling that I had when I would think of Disney. It was ingrained in me to ensure that I was always smiling and that every action I took had an impact on someone's day. Disney called this "being on stage". As I observed families from all over the world, there was a common theme that I was getting familiar with from my personal experiences with others. People wanted a place they could be themselves and enjoy and forget about everything outside of that experience.

HOSTING HOUSE PARTIES TO WORKING A CORPORATE JOB

After I graduated college, I must have been in denial that I was now a working professional. All I wanted to do was have fun with my friends and family. This prompted bringing all my friends and family for any sort of event that I could celebrate. I would host parties regularly with the intent of creating the best memories. The way I would do this was by encouraging people to loosen up and be themselves the second they walked in the door. If you wanted to get in, you had to take a shot! One shot turned into two and, by the end of the night, everyone was sharing intimate stories and feelings with each other. You got to see more complex layers of people that were often hidden away. I wanted people to take away memories that we could always look back on. To this day, some of my friends talk about those special moments.

This carried over into the corporate world when I got into management. I wanted to build a strong community, create long-lasting relationships and have fun. I consistently constructed teams that were known for having exemplary performance in customer

Enjoy the process and seize the moment!

service, which was a result of building a strong community.

Eventually, I came across an opportunity to be a host for a short-term rental. At the time, it seemed like a fun passion project where I could blend all my previous experiences. Little did I know that this move would eventually replace my corporate job.

TINY HOMES IN JOSHUA TREE

Joshua Tree is an American national park in southeast California where two deserts meet. Each of these deserts has its own ecosystem and the characteristics are determined by the elevation. It is one of the most visited national parks in the country. When COVID hit, there was a growing demand to visit a national park that provided a raw experience in nature.

An opportunity presented itself for a tiny home new-build construction that was only 400 sq ft. I thought this home would be a great canvas to create a unique experience as it was different than anything that was on the market at the time. I took a leap of faith and began the process. Little did I know that there would be tremendous positive feedback generated by guests who would stay at my tiny homes.

Ultimately, the vision was for guests to have a place where they could have a sparkling desert landscape outdoor experience. You could have a small, efficient space that was well designed, with amenities beyond what you would have at home. This included a coffee bar, hammocks, TV and a hot tub, amongst other things. I wanted guests to enjoy luxury while unplugging from the craziness that the world brings. The intent was to create a memorable experience that a guest would never forget. If I can have a guest rave about their experience and desire to come back, I have done my job!

When you arrive in Joshua Tree, you immediately experience the beauty of Joshua trees all around. It is necessary to drive with your windows down and feel the refreshing air blow against your face. When the sun rises, you get to experience this orangey-red colour in the sky that is unforgettable. During the day, you can see the landscape and enjoy the incredible boulders that the national park has to offer. At sunset, you experience that orangey-red colour in the sky that is breathtaking.

Following the sunset, it is a must to grab some dinner at the JT Saloon, which makes you feel like you are in an old western movie. After having a drink, listening to some live music and indulging in some beverages, you are ready to go back to the luxury tiny home. You quickly get on your bathing suit and jump into the hot tub. You gaze at the shining stars. The stars illuminate so brightly that it puts you in a hypnotic state. By the time you snap out of it, you can also jump into a hammock and rock side to side. Once you are done, you come back to a luxurious bed, mattress and soft linens. You doze off from the relaxed state and begin dreaming about the beautiful experiences. You wake up and start your drip coffee, sit in a hammock outside and wait for the sunrise. The caffeine hits and your heart starts pumping a little faster, as you start seeing the orange and red colours in the sky. You start reflecting on becoming the best version of yourself that you've always wanted to be.

When a guest goes through the sequence above, I feel like I've done my job as a hospitable host. The guest has checked their worries at the door, and they are enjoying the present moment. They are in their hideaway haus!

MEETING X

A hideaway haus can be taken out of context for my most memorable guest whom I will call "X". At the time, I was a less seasoned host, and really valued keeping my occupancy as high as possible. This high occupancy was so important that, during the slow season, my strategy was to price below the typical market rates. My average daily rate for my 400 sq foot nineties-themed luxury tiny home was at $143/night at an 88% occupancy rate. When X came to visit my tiny home, he booked during the slow season, and it happened to be in the middle of the week. Guess what I had the property priced at? It was listed for $69. What a steal, and it became the gateway to a horror story!

X checked in to my property and went through the same welcome messaging that all my guests experience. I provided a welcome note and a luxury nineties-themed party packaged in my tiny home in Joshua Tree. During X's stay, I received only one communication sequence from him, which was at the beginning of his stay. He had a request for more towels and more paper towels, which was a little puzzling to me. For an overnight stay, this was not a typical request. I didn't think much of it at the time. I provided instructions on where to find the items he'd requested, as I wanted to make sure that he had a good experience. Then I thought to myself, *how many towels and paper towels does one human being actually need?* Well, that question was answered when my cleaner came to complete their routine cleaning.

I received a call from my frantic cleaner. She said she thought she'd arrived at a crime scene. There was a lot of blood on the towels and paper towels. There was trash everywhere, the sheets were on the floor. There was drug paraphernalia that included a crack pipe, a baggie with residue and a lighter left in the kitchen area. WOW!

Ironically, the story doesn't end there. Less than a month later, I had a guest booked at another one of my tiny homes. It was a similar scenario where we were in the middle of the slow season in the middle of the week. The property was priced below market

The most important things in the world are family and love!

rate and the guest had a profile with no reviews and no photo. Immediately after check-in, I received a call requesting extra towels and extra paper towels. I thought that sounded familiar. I decided to look at the external camera and it was X. He happened to be outside. I spoke through the speaker of my camera, and I directed it at X. I communicated that the police were on their way. I saw him scramble into the house to pick up his personal belongings, and he jumped into his car. I never saw him or heard from him again.

LESSONS LEARNED

As I reflect on the experience, I tried to make sense of what had happened. There are a few lessons that came out of it. First, I changed my pricing strategy during the slow season. I no longer price below the market. I realised that when I priced below the market, I wasn't attracting my target niche/customer. When working on a pricing strategy, ask yourself if the pricing strategy is consistent with your target market. Pricing can have an impact, as the guest that I attracted was price sensitive versus targeting a guest who was looking for an experience that I was offering. From a business standpoint, this also changed my perspective with targeting improvement around gross revenue numbers versus targeting occupancy. By doing so, it stayed aligned with being tactical around creating the best experience for guests. Lastly, look for patterns when it comes to the behaviour of guests. The identification of these patterns can help you better understand and anticipate the needs of the people who are visiting. Ultimately, you want the guest to have the best experience possible. The ultimate compliment is when a guest comes back or refers their friends and family.

What I've underestimated as a host is what a large impact I potentially have on someone else's life. Although as a host you have people come and go, you are forever a part of someone else's journey, and a part of their memory forever. I think about my most memorable STR stays, and the ones that stand out involve the host reaching out and picking up the phone to create a personalised experience. This is always in the back of my mind when it comes to setting the stage and setting appropriate expectations with operations.

HELPING OTHER HOSTS

Ed Mylett likes to say that you are best equipped to help the person you once were. It's super simple, pay it forward. I learned how to be a better host from an operational standpoint by leveraging the expertise of hosts who had more experience. This came in the form of podcasts, YouTube, shorts, conversations, meetups and virtual groups. There is no reason to reinvent the wheel.

The way to help other hosts is to set the standard for others to follow. I like to share various learnable experiences and be an advocate for my peers. I am fortunate I am a part of many Facebook groups, I am a host to the Find Your Freedom podcast and I create content that makes concepts fun and digestible. My goal is to inspire the next host who is thinking about making the leap of faith. There is a very strong community that is willing to help in the success that is bigger than yourself.

To conclude, you have an opportunity to leave a positive experience ingrained in someone's brain forever. You have a responsibility as a host to represent your brand but also to represent all hosts. By setting a high standard, you can touch a person's life one check-in at a time. Set up that hideaway haus!

ABOUT THE AUTHOR

Omid is the co-founder of Alpha Geek Capital, a high-performance coach and a podcast host. He helps aspiring real estate investors acquire short-term rentals through partnerships. In his short-term rentals, he creates a getaway experience consistent with his brand The Hideaway Haus. Omid's mantra is simple: check your worries at the door, and have a great time!

Having a great time stemmed from Omid's early and evolving influences. He grew up in a multicultural household that allowed him to thrive in the melting pot of Southern California. He travelled globally, always sought out the local and off-the-beaten-track experience, and he worked for Disney, which gave him perspective into so many communities. He realised people wanted a space where they could practise their version of self-care.

Omid has helped grow Alpha Geek Capital's STR portfolio to a 10+ million portfolio, which includes 20+ listings in multiple markets. Half of the portfolio includes themed tiny homes, which are adjacent to the national park of Joshua Tree. The goal with these tiny homes is to have modern luxury amenities where you can disconnect from the world and experience self-care. These tiny homes allow guests to stare at the captivating stars while sitting in a hot tub or a hammock.

As the co-host of the Find Your Freedom podcast, Omid interviews entrepreneurs to amplify their abundance mindset to inspire aspiring investors to seek out their dreams. Omid has been featured in numerous podcasts, including Bigger Pockets Rookie.

Omid lives in southern California with his wife of eleven years. He is also a father of three to Cyrus, Kian and Lucy. He loves to build communities and is an advocate for trying new experiences. He also coaches basketball and soccer in his local community.

Links: https://linktr.ee/omidtheradinvestor

REBECCA CRIBBIN

TWELVE LESSONS IN TWELVE YEARS

TWELVE LESSONS I'VE LEARNED BEING A WOMAN, A MOTHER, A PARTNER, A HOSPITABLE HOST AND A LEADER IN THE STRA MANAGEMENT INDUSTRY

The last twelve years have been a roller coaster for me, to say the least. I've worked my butt off, laughed a lot, cried a lot and learned some tough lessons along the way. In 2010, my children were nine and eleven, and I was a real estate agent with my own business selling and permanently renting property in the Southern Highlands of NSW in Australia. The opportunity arose to manage one lonely STR and, well, the rest is history.

Over those twelve years, my team have looked after more than 1,250 properties, taken 62,000 bookings with a booking value over $65million and helped nearly 50,000 people take fabulous holidays and create forever memories.

Being a woman, a mother, working with my husband and running a start-up business in a start-up industry all brought their own challenges. The song by Gloria Gaynor "I will survive" comes to mind.

Over these twelve years, I have also lost my mother, moved four times, renovated four houses, got divorced, had my heart broken, re-partnered and started four new businesses. One of my many mantras is: "if you want something done, give it to a busy person." I am proud to say I am busy, but things get done, there's no other option.

I would like to share with you just twelve of the many difficult lessons learned throughout this journey so far. I hope you can take advantage of my experiences and learnings, so you don't make the same mistakes I have.

1. Take the time now!

Now is the time to spend time with your family, children, partner and friends. You will never get this time back. You are in control of your business whether it's a monster like mine or you are looking after just your own STR property. Discipline your time and yourself to organise activities with your children (work the canteen, attend the sports carnival, take them for a milkshake or dinner, stand on the sideline at their Saturday morning sports cheering and embarrassing them), set up a regular date night with your partner and be the planner of family and friend gatherings. If you don't do it, it might not happen. Nothing is more important than this and that's why it needs to become your number one priority, from today. No excuses. Do it now!

2. Develop a thick skin quickly.

Please don't take anything in business personally. Yes, take the time to analyse how you or your team could have done it better; however, it's not personal, it's business. You will manage everything better if you stay unemotional and professional. We are so invested in our businesses, so naturally, it is hard to not take feedback to heart. It's human nature to be sensitive to criticism, even if it's constructive. Keep building your 'armour'. If you fail, don't be hard on yourself, it's tough and you may fail many times, but that's okay. Plan to manage it differently and better next time and don't judge

Rebecca Cribbin – ASTRA Conference – Gold Coast Queensland – 10+ ways to increase profit 2022 ASTRA Conference

yourself. No doubt, like most entrepreneurs, you are your worst critic. Be your best supporter. You've got this.

3. Be patient.

Everything takes time. Remember the tortoise and the hare in everything you do. Good things happen to those who wait. This applies in business and family life. Your children, your relationship and your business are always growing and learning, be patient with them too. Try to remember you are truly invested in all of them for the long game. I know you want it all now but be patient and focused and it will come.

4. Be genuinely helpful.

As a host and a property manager, we are forced to deal with all sorts of challenges at all times of the day and not necessarily when we have the time or are in the mood to do so. If you approach all your interactions with the intention of being genuinely helpful, then you will likely get a better outcome. We know that guests and property owners can be difficult, rude and even threatening. If you stay calm, talk softly and keep approaching each situation with a genuinely helpful stance, you are more likely to turn them around and work together towards a good outcome. Goodness knows, this is one of the hardest lessons learned that I have faced for twelve years and nearly 500,000 guests. Often, I struggled to follow my own advice. Remember, learn from your errors, reset and reengage the future conversations/situations differently.

5. If possible – work away from your home.

Without wanting to be stereotypical, if you work from home, mothering/fathering/parenting and housekeeping will often likely get in the way. If you can, work outside the home and by doing so your ROI will be greater with less non-work-related distractions. You can focus 100% on getting shit done. Try where possible to keep your work and home life separate, including conversations at the dinner table – especially if you work alongside a family member. Co-working opportunities are a dynamic way of accessing office spaces outside the home and they are now available everywhere, and are not overly expensive. Obviously, the recent pandemic has changed attitudes on working from home, but for me, I need the distinction. My preferred choice is work from my office and live in my home.

6. If possible – work away from your partner.

I spent the twenty years of my marriage working with my ex-husband Martin. We met at work, and we went on to work together in our real estate and then STR business. I still wonder if the pressures of working together might have taken their toll; the growth of our business and the pressures associated meant that we rarely found time for fun together or to talk about anything other than work – an easy habit to slip into when you are focused and busy, but also for me one that ended in divorce. Fortunately for us, Martin and I are still great friends, and he is still involved a little in the business we created together. Mind you, that's been hard work too. If you are blessed with choice, then my suggestion would be to choose to work separately. When you both get home from work, there will be plenty of opportunity to share your ups and downs without the added pressures of the business or work getting involved.

7. Take only calculated risks.

You are strong, independent and powerful and, with planning and forethought, a calculated risk can be worth it. Do the numbers, check the numbers, get a coach, be proactive in asking for help and advice before you jump in and check the numbers again. When you jump... jump fast and hard with all your commitment and effort. A risk without the planning and advice is just a gamble. We work too hard to gamble.

8. Recruit the best and outsource if necessary.

In the words of Richard Branson, who I was lucky enough to meet and have a one-on-one session with: "I always recruit people who are smarter than me." When you are recruiting give it the time it deserves (dedicate 100% of your attention to this worthy business transaction – this should take absolute priority), get help from a professional if you are not confident. Have a comprehensive role description with deliverables and targets. Try to find team members with industry experience, they are priceless, and be prepared to pay the market rate for those with skills but no industry experience. There have been many times when I have regretted not listening to the adage "pay peanuts, get monkeys". Recruit someone with different skills to yourself in your early days, they will be a balance to you and take the load off you. They can focus on the stuff that you aren't necessarily interested in or actioning directly.

Outsource to an expert if you need to. Know your hourly rate, what it costs the business to have you work in it, not what you pay yourself, but what the total revenue of the business is divided by the number of hours you work. After all, there is likely no business without you in it. If you can outsource something that you are not great at, don't like doing or that can be done at an hourly rate significantly less than yours, and you can do something revenue generating instead, then do it. Do your research, however, and be prepared to do a full handover. Outsourcing to the wrong person or organisation or neglecting to coach and train the outsource work is probably worse than not outsourcing at all.

9. Be a coach and delegator.

So now you have recruited the best, you need to work every day to keep them in your team. We all know it takes a lot more to recruit a team member than it does to keep one (in fact, the same applies with STR listings). Become a coach, teach your team everything you know and have learned, share your experiences, the good and bad. You are their best chance of success. Coach them and delegate to them with clear and concise guidelines so that next time you can hand over confidently. Give constructive feedback often and please don't put this off because you find it uncomfortable and confrontational – you will regret it. I most certainly do! Recently, someone told me to: "Confront the breach." It rings so true to me. As STR owners, managers and employers, we must do this every time, so things don't get out of control. We must communicate with our cleaners, linen suppliers or laundries, our property owners, our guests, our team members and ourselves. It's easy to ignore these breaches and keep the peace, but in my experience, in the long term it ends up worse. Complain or provide feedback whilst you are still happy, an easier journey to take for a positive outcome.

10. Book in time for you and holidays.

Our businesses are crazy, high pressure and 24/7. You will likely burn out if you don't take some time to yourself and the occasional holiday. Your family and relationships will suffer too if you are always looking after everyone else (that's our business, after all). Each week, book into your diary time to do something that you love and is relaxing for you. It can be as simple as time to read a good romantic novel in the park, through to self-care in the spa. Make time for yourself, you are worth it. Book a holiday at least every six months, a deserving break after such hard work. Going on holiday hasn't meant switching off completely for me in the last twelve years. I have taken lots of holidays, but I am always available and ON. However, there is something about being ON beside the pool or beach compared to being ON at my desk in the office. Book

Rebecca Cribbin Virgin Unite Entrepreneurs Pilanthropic tour of South Africa 2019

your break well in advance too, so you have something to plan for and look forward to.

11. Everything changes.

I must say that over the last twelve years, most of the work I have done to implement processes and ways of doing business hasn't lasted long. We work in an industry that is especially known for constant change. I guess it's relatively early in the product and industry lifecycle of STR and we can expect change to be a constant for some time to come. If you set yourself up to know that change is always imminent and do so with an open mind, you will be setting yourself up for success. The same can be said about our family and our relationships. If there is one mind muscle that needs to be trained and exercised in the STR and STR management industry, it's the ability to enjoy and take advantage of change.

12. 'If you fail to plan you plan to fail' and 'you can't manage what you don't measure'.

It is so important to allocate the necessary time to plan. I suggest that you consider formally planning and taking time out of your business to work on the business – to plan.

Do it annually (for a calendar year or financial year) and then every four months. Create a four-month sprint cycle. Post this, migrate to weekly and structure it to start before your week begins. And finally, daily, choose to do it at the end of the previous day or the beginning of the following day – whatever works best for you.

At this time, I suggest you also plan your physical health, mental health, wellness time, family time, getaways and holidays. If you plan, you are more likely to do and achieve. Book everything into a default diary. That should be your default for each week. Of course, you need to be flexible and respond to issues, however when you do, make sure that you move your defaults to ensure that you still fit everything in.

I have learned many other lessons during my life as a human, woman, mother, partner, business owner, host, friend and boss, and I look forward to sharing more with you all for many years into the future.

Cheers to you!

ABOUT THE AUTHOR

Rebecca Cribbin is a woman and mother first and, in addition to that, an accomplished STR property manager and team leader, award-winning industry advocate, published author and founder of multiple businesses.

Over the last twelve years, Rebecca's STR management business Holiday Rental Specialists has looked after 1,250 properties for busy investors, taken more than 60,000 bookings and helped nearly half a million guests create wonderful family and friend holiday memories. The team encourages owners to buy holiday rental properties in fabulous locations and present them beautifully so that guests rave about their experience and keep returning for more.

Rebecca's passionate approach and vast experience in this complicated and ever-changing industry is now culminating in a new venture, Holiday Rental Experts. Rebecca and her team provide coaching, training and consulting to guide STR managers to be more productive, more profitable and have more fun. They also help STR investors with a roadmap to short-term rental launch and success.

Steering a ship with a commitment to near perfect results, Rebecca identified the need for a true, accurate, detailed and informative guide for investors thinking about setting up a short-term rental, so in late 2022, Rebecca's first book *Ready, Set, Booked – Holiday Rental Success in 10 Simple Steps* was published.

Striving for best practice, whilst sharing her knowledge and working to achieve work-life balance is at the core of what Rebecca does. Rebecca works to travel and travels to work. One of her many mantras is "life's better on holidays" and she is incredibly excited and grateful to work amongst and be part of a community that focuses almost entirely on ensuring other people's lives are "better on holidays". Now that her children are adults, she can often be found travelling the world, sharing her stories on stage, whilst learning and collaborating with industry colleagues.

Links: https://linktr.ee/rebeccacribbin

ROSEMARIE TIPKA

HOSTING IN THE MOTHERHOOD

"Mrs Tipka? Your husband has been in a car accident. You need to get here immediately."

It was a rainy day in the fall of 2015. My husband Brian was on his way to a work conference when he was hit head-on by a driver who'd missed a curve in the road. I'd soon find out that the accident had actually happened hours earlier but, after suffering a severe concussion, Brian no longer remembered who he was. With his phone and wallet stowed away, it took hours for hospital employees to track down his identity and who to contact. In addition to his missing short-term memory, Brian broke his ribs, cracked his sternum and was left with broken bones pushing into his heart.

But he was alive. The darkly handsome guy I'd met at a college SCUBA diving class would live and heal. Our four kids at the time (now six) would grow up with their dad. And I'd still have the love of my life by my side.

In the days after the accident, Brian's memory slowly, eventually returned and we began processing what had really happened. Sitting next to his hospital bed, Brian reached for my hand and said, "I don't want to die on my way to a work conference. That can't be my story."

The defining moments of our lives are not always obvious when they happen. If it's a big event or crisis, survival mode kicks in and you're left just trying to get through to the next moment, hour, day, or week. It's only with the benefit of passing time that you can look back and say, "There! That moment. That's when the story started."

* * *

Hi, dear reader. My name is Rose Tipka. I am the founder of Your Family's Place, a vacation rental company nestled in the rolling hills of Ohio's Amish country. Along with my husband Brian, we own and manage a portfolio of rentals valued at over $2million. Your Family's Place offers pet-friendly, large homes spread across seventy-five private acres of 100-year-old oaks, winding hiking trails and peaceful ponds. We welcome multigenerational families and large groups looking for a place to relax and unwind. Our rentals tend to be the go-to place for family vacations, with many booking vacations year after year.

Our journey here hasn't been straight, easy, or even planned. It grew out of painful trials and powerful memories. But through it all, the foundation was laid for the family-centred life we always imagined.

Now, I wish I could say that day in the hospital was the start of our vacation rental company together... cue the music, life is beautiful! But life is more complicated than that. Brian needed a career change but wasn't sure what direction to take. I had left my career as a science teacher to take on caring for and home-schooling our children. But with four kids already, and the dream of more on the way, returning to the regular classroom was off the table. So, we started brainstorming. Brian had unique and specialised knowledge for his industry. Could he go and work for another company in the same field? It wasn't uncommon for industry lawyers to call him with questions, so what about becoming a lawyer, instead? Ultimately, each idea was scratched from the list because it didn't offer what we really wanted: a lifestyle that gave him more time with us.

And then it happened.

In the fall of 2017, I was extremely pregnant with our fifth child. If you've ever been pregnant, you know the kind of mental insanity that descends in those final weeks, and it also happened to be the hottest, muggiest autumn on record. A property came up for auction that caught Brian's eye. Keep in mind that we did not own real estate, apart from our own home, at this point. So, when he mentioned it, it was a hard no. I couldn't think about anything beyond being eight million years pregnant. The day of the auction came and went. I gave birth. The discussion was done, or so I thought.

Behind the scenes, our friend and real estate agent went to the auction. In shock, she called Brian, explaining that the bidding was less than half of what was predicted. So... he went for it. Five minutes later, she congratulated him on his winning bid. Knowing that I was focused on growing a human, he sat on the news for a while.

Six weeks later, we ran into our friend at a Christmas party, and she mentioned that the property was closing the next week.

"Wait, what property?" I asked, totally unaware of what was coming next.

But that's how we came to own our first rental property. And honestly? I wouldn't change a thing. My husband's instincts were spot on and, despite my initial reluctance, it turned out to be one of the best decisions for our family. Not only have we found the time freedom we've always hoped for, but we get a front row seat to the transformation and tender memories our properties create for others.

The property we bought wasn't perfect, but it was tailor-made for a vacation rental. With twenty wooded acres and two ponds, it was a little oasis away from the bustle of everyday life. The cabin that overlooked the water needed major renovation, but I already had the experience and a few local connections who could pull it together. The bigger question that loomed overhead was: who do we want to serve?

Founding a business that supports our family, and brings other families together, is deeply meaningful.

I'll get to that in a minute but first, you've got to understand some things about me.

Travel was woven into the fabric of our family's story. My grandmother had a large US map in her basement chock full of pushpins marking the places she'd visited. As a child, we spent many weekends camping, visiting new places and spending time together. It was never fancy, but it was always an adventure. When I became a teenager, my mother would invite my grandmother and aunt to join us for weekend getaways at a cabin in the woods. We'd spend it eating our favourite foods, swimming in the pool and beating each other at Rummy next to a roaring fire. At the time, I'm sure I didn't appreciate the importance of the memories being made, but those weekends held us together better than the same last name ever could. Today, I'd give anything to have another weekend with my grandmother – another case of clarity only coming with time.

In addition to the weekend getaways with my grandmother, our family took a week's summer vacation up to northern Michigan every year. We always stayed in the same location – a place where my mother vacationed as a child in the 1950s and the place where she brought her family. Thinking back on those memories often felt like eating every piece of Halloween candy but not getting a stomach ache – pure joy. I recently talked with my mother about how our week in Michigan was the highlight of my childhood. She told me that she worried that one year my sister and I would decide we were too "grown up" to go on the family vacation but, honestly, that thought never crossed my mind. Ever. Vacation was that important.

As time passed, we grew up, got married and had kids. We continued to gather together at the same place, year after year, until we were literally bursting at the seams. I had a new baby every other year, and my sister had two children of her own. Then, to add a whole new layer of complexity, we had dogs that we refused to leave at home. Have you ever tried to find a vacation rental for fourteen people and two dogs? I wish you luck.

So, just like that conversation with Brian in the hospital, we had arrived at another defining moment. There was no way I was going to give up the week in Michigan with my family, but finding places that would fit everyone and their dogs came few and far between.

"Relax," I told my family, "I've got this." And I built the very thing we needed.

Large families became our focus and Your Family's Place was born. We became our own customers expanding into new, larger properties, all while creating the vacation experience we wanted for ourselves. After all, who better to design a large-family vacation rental than a mom with a passenger van full of kids?

Our properties were designed for multigenerational families and large groups who wanted to feel like they were staying at their own family's vacation home. We took hospitality seriously, and worked hard to create personalised, welcoming experiences that would bring families back, year after year.

We didn't really know what we were doing initially, but with a focus on radical hospitality and making truly family-friendly accommodations, we built a thriving vacation rental business. In the time since we started, we've doubled our nightly booking fee and are often booked out a year in advance.

How did I do it? I'd love to tell you.

BECOME THE FAIRY GODMOTHER OF FAMILY VACATIONS

Making your guests feel at home starts with being a hospitable host. But that is a job which is both harder than it looks and easier than it seems. It's not enough to slap a "family friendly" label on your listing and call it a day. It requires thinking about the small details that can make a real difference for families.

Sometimes I think of myself as the Fairy Godmother of Family Vacations because it's my job to invisibly make our guests' vacation easy, enjoyable and relaxing in every way possible. By taking stressors away, our guests have more time to reconnect with the people who mean the most.

I'm all too aware that being a kid on vacation is way more fun than being the grown up on vacation. While my kiddos splash in the lake, I'm cleaning up lunch, planning the next meal, running a load of laundry, while gazing wistfully, yet regretfully, at the book I brought to read, thinking I would have all this extra time for fun.

So, I pay attention to the little things like making sure the kitchen is stocked with pantry essentials, so no one has to run out for a last-minute grocery trip. Or leaving a plate of fresh baked goods at every check-in, knowing that, after a long drive, hungry kids and parents will appreciate having something close at hand to snack on before they've even unpacked the car.

COMMUNICATE. COMMUNICATE. COMMUNICATE

First things first, and please take what I am going to share seriously, your guests are good people who want to have a great vacation. Unfortunately, many have had bad experiences and may feel skittish. As a host, the easiest thing you can do leading up to their stay is provide clear, friendly and reassuring communication. If you're a property manager with many units, their reservation may be one of hundreds you'll host that year. But to your guest, their stay is deeply personal. So please talk, message and email your guests in a way that reflects the importance of their stay, not the busyness of your own schedule.

Guest questions are never a bother, and you should always be available to help. Treating others with unconditional positive regard is laying the foundation for successful rentals with the right guests for years to come. After all, we know that repeat guests are the real goldmine of vacation rentals. One thing you have total control over is your communication. So, keep it respectful, friendly and professional.

HOW I COMMUNICATE WITH GUESTS

When a reservation comes in I send out two different communications. First, I record a personalised twenty-second video message and text it to the guest. In this message, I introduce myself and thank them for reserving the specific property for their dates. Then, I tell them that they can relax because we are going to take great care of their family. I let them know I am always available to answer any questions or help them have a wonderful vacation. That's it, twenty seconds and it's done.

The next step is a handwritten, personalised thank you note that I drop in the mail. In this note, I thank them for their reservation and ask if there is anything I can do to make their vacation relaxing.

WHY IT WORKS

If you have guests who book many months in advance, they may be paying a respectable deposit to secure their reservation. So put yourself in their shoes. Would you feel comfortable forking over a big payment and then not hear anything for months? That's fertile ground for buyers' remorse. These immediate, reassuring and personalised messages ward off guest anxiety and set the stage for the relaxing, enjoyable vacation your guests have been primed to have. None of this is hard to do, but it does take time and commitment.

CREATE FAMILY-FRIENDLY ACCOMMODATIONS THAT ARE ACTUALLY FAMILY-FRIENDLY

Special considerations need to be made when hosting families with children. As a mother of six, I feel some small authority on what "kid friendly" means. My first recommendation is not glamorous, and might not work for your company, but hear me out: being flexible with arrival and departure times can earn you a customer for life.

Have you ever been terrorised by a toddler whose nap time was disrupted? That's not the right way to start a vacation. What about travelling in a vehicle with a hangry teenager? I don't recommend it. As property managers, you have different levers to pull to please your guests. Consider how you can be flexible with check-in/out to improve your guests' experience.

KID-FRIENDLY INTERIOR DESIGN

The design of your vacation rental plays a big role in the comfort of your guests. During a survey of our past guests, we discovered that my "mom instinct" had inadvertently worked into the design in unpredictable ways. Our kids are in our rentals frequently, and they also can't keep their hands off things. So, there are no breakable decor items, or little knick-knacks that can be picked up, dropped, or misplaced. In my home, this is a matter of my own sanity, but in our vacation homes it was a small, yet important thing, that made parents feel at ease.

Staying in a Your Family's Place home feels like sticking your hand in the candy jar.

Speaking from experience, I know the abject terror of your child knocking something over and breaking fragile items. When one of my kids was young, we visited a museum with a collection of dresses worn by notable people. Despite my instructions to step back, my darling child hung his body over the barrier ropes in front of all the mannequins. In a split second, he fell, taking ropes and posts with him. His tumble set off a domino effect with the first mannequin falling into the second, the second into the third, all the way down the line. When the last one hit the ground, its head popped off and rolled away.

To this very day, I can still see them toppling over in slow motion. The horror. That was also the day I learned that museum security was nothing like the movies. Nobody came running. No alarms went off. It was just my family and a pile of mannequins. I collected the heads, righted them all, and dashed out of the room with screaming kids in tow. So do your families a favour, keep the breakable stuff somewhere else.

* * *

When I sat down to write this chapter, I wondered what I was meant to share with you. Now that you've got to know me a little better, you've probably picked up that being a mother is the most important part of my life. And yet being a mother, even six times over, did not limit what I could achieve. I learned that life presents you with struggles and may thrust you into positions that set your family on a new path. The reality is no one is coming to your rescue – you need to put on your own oxygen mask, strap your baby in a sling, and charge forward. If your partner is going through their own struggles, or you're a single parent doing it totally on your own, I want you to know that you have the talent and skills to make the life you always wanted.

In the summer of 2020, my husband left his desk job, and we started working on our company together. Now we are both home with our kids, living the life we always wanted. We had another baby in the autumn of 2020, completing our family. We did it, but also, I did it.

Being a mother is not a limited status. You can live a family and home-based life while also enjoying professional success. I still home-school our kiddos. Our work is scheduled into the week around our family activities. We make it work. You can as well.

ABOUT THE AUTHOR

Rose Tipka is the founder of Your Family's Place, a vacation rental company nestled in Ohio's Amish country. Owning and managing a collection of homes valued at over $2million, Your Family's Place offers pet-friendly, large homes spread across seventy-five private acres, welcoming multigenerational families and large groups travelling together.

With hundreds of five-star reviews, Rose and Your Family's Place is known for personalised hospitality, beautiful surroundings and for being like a home away from home.

Designed with nostalgic vacation memories in mind, families reconnect like the good old days, back before lives became too busy with jobs, technology and a phone that never stops buzzing. Whether sitting on the dock catching fish, hiking the trails in the woods, or going head-to-head over air hockey downstairs, there's something for everyone. Your Family's Place can't stop time but welcomes guests to slow down and reconnect with the people who are most important.

Your Family's Place's properties have been featured on Territory Supply's list of the best vacation rentals in Ohio. Rose has been featured in the *Cleveland Plain Dealer*, along with appearances on multiple hospitality podcasts including Boostly, Thanks for Visiting, Catch Up with the Karwells, Spilling the Tea on Airbnb, Get Paid for Your Pad, Superhog's Spotlight on Guest Experience, and Live Let Thrive.

Welcoming guests is a family affair. Rose can often be found chatting with guests, or prepping a property, with her six kids in tow. As a former high school science teacher, Rose also homeschools her crew. Museum visits, hours of reading aloud and star watching are family favourites. Her husband Brian, whom she met in a SCUBA class, is the CFO of Your Family's Place and the chief cookie taste tester. The most loved members of the family are their dog Velvet and their three cats Honey, Cojack and Marigold.

Links: https://linktr.ee/yourfamilysplace

RYAN DUFFY

TRADING TIME FOR MONEY

Most people, especially those with a spark of entrepreneurialism, have a shared collective dread of the phrase "nine to five". It has nothing to do with poor work ethic. In fact, I don't know of any successful self-proclaimed "entrepreneur" who works less than a fifty-hour week. The reasoning may be different for each person, but I believe it has to do with the desire for freedom. Early in my adult life, I found myself willingly trading time for money and not ever having enough of either.

In my early twenties, I landed a dream job. I became a Chicago fireman. Looking back at my time on the job, it still feels surreal. I was blessed to have a career that people made movies about. The job was a lot of fun and very fulfilling. It also had some great perks. One of which being the schedule. We worked a twenty-four-hour shift and then had the next forty-eight hours off. I quickly realised that with this sort of schedule, I could effectively work another full-time job to supplement my income. Sounded great in theory but in practice I found myself working endless hours with little savings to show for it.

Life started to move quickly, as it does. It felt like overnight, my

Our favourite summer pastime – Table Rock Lake

wife Shae and I went from being newlyweds to working multiple jobs and hardly seeing each other. A series of back injuries led to years of painkillers and ultimately ended my firefighting career. Shae and I were at a tipping point. We sold our home in Chicago to put some cash in the bank and moved our family into an apartment to figure out our next step.

A BIG MOVE

It wasn't too long after my first artificial disc replacement that we were down at Table Rock Lake to celebrate Independence Day. We had just spent the week playing in the water, riding ATVs through the woods, shooting guns and blowing up fireworks. It was so amazing that we didn't want to go back home to Chicago. Our son Gavin (three at the time) was in his element out in nature. The thought of taking him back to our basement apartment in the city seemed very unappealing.

The drive north seemed to take forever. Typically, we wouldn't have stopped for the night, but we were feeling a general sense of malaise at the idea of returning to the city and decided to stop outside of St. Louis for the night. Once we got settled into the hotel room, I pulled out my laptop and started browsing properties for sale near the lake where we had been and found one that caught my eye. It was a two-bed, three-bath A-frame with an unfinished basement on just over an acre, less than a mile from Cricket Creek Marina on Table Rock Lake. The photos weren't much to look at, but the house seemed to have enough square footage to grow into for a time. It was a two-minute drive to the water and they were asking $120k with $400 per year for property taxes! I told Shae I could deliver pizzas and cover that mortgage if I had to. We turned around and drove four hours back the next morning to see it. We moved in less than two months later.

WHO'S EVER HEARD OF OMAHA, ARKANSAS?

Shae had been working in real estate for a while in the Branson market and was starting to work with a number of clients that were vacation rental investors. She came home from work one night with a crazy idea. She proposed that we find a place to move our family to so that we could convert our home into a full-time short-term rental. She felt confident that, if we did, we could bring in over $30k a year in revenue. My immediate response was something along the lines of "bull**** no one has ever heard of Omaha, Arkansas!" Branson is an established vacation rental market. We don't live in Branson.

Shae made some really compelling arguments, though:

1. Our home was only a short twenty-minute drive from all of the major tourist attractions in town.
2. We had over an acre of land with privacy and separation from other homes (something most rentals in town can't offer).
3. The road we lived on ended less than a mile away at a full-service marina on Table Rock Lake.
4. (Here's the big one) Omaha currently had no restrictions on vacation rentals.

If you drive across the Missouri state line, just a few minutes north of us, you can't pick up just any single-family home and turn it into a short-term rental. There is a county permitting process that allows for some of this but, for the most part, if it's zoned residential, it's not going to happen.

We realised we were potentially sitting on a gold mine but we couldn't afford to buy another house for our family to live in. We ended up pitching the idea to some good friends of ours, Randy and Tammy (Randy was also my partner in the construction business), and asking for their help. There was a metal shop building just up the road from our house that had been on the market for a while. It wasn't much to look at, but it had a finished two-bed, three-bath apartment built into half of it with the other half being just a big open shop space. Our construction business was growing, and we could use the storage space for equipment and materials. They were totally on board! We went under contract for the shop house (shouse) and began preparing our home to become a rental. If it didn't pan out, we could move back into the house and put a different long-term renter in the shouse. It seemed like a pretty safe plan.

THIS IS A REAL BUSINESS

In 2019, our then seven-year-old Gavin was turning into a rock hound. The Ozarks area has some really cool geology (and even the only public diamond mine in the country). Trying to think of a name and theme for our STR, we turned to Gavin for suggestions, and he promptly decided it should be called The Crystal Cabin. It had a ring to it.

The Crystal Cabin went live in September 2019. Within a few weeks, we were booked up solidly through Christmas. We started this experiment hoping to gross $30-$40k per year but in reality it did $52k its first year! This wasn't a side gig to make a little extra money. This was a real business. Even after expenses, the income we were generating from renting out this now three-bed, three-bath house was replacing what I made swinging a hammer and required far less time once it was up and running. I decided to keep my home builder's licence active in case I needed it down the road, but I saw that I could make more money with my head than I could with my hands. I took my Missouri real estate licencing exam in November and went to work with Shae.

At the end of 2019, Shae's real estate business was really starting to take off after pounding the pavement for three years (literally, since she was door knocking to generate leads early on – even at one point being eight months pregnant with our second child!) and I got to help manage that workload while the cabin was cash flowing. One day, Shae got a lead on an off-market property that the owner was interested in selling. It was the house right next to the shouse we were living in, which was right down the road from our now cash-cow home we'd purchased to escape Chicago. A four-bed, three-bath house on an acre that checked a lot of the same boxes as our first rental property for $155k. This one needed some substantial work, though. The entire house needed remodelling inside and out, the yard was overgrown and it needed clearing to open up a view. This was going to be a complete gut job.

We had a conversation with our friends again and decided to partner up on the purchase. At this point, they were getting 25% of the revenue from The Crystal Cabin since they had backed us financially to buy the shouse. We would use the remaining cash flow from The Crystal Cabin to pay for the material needed to renovate what would be called The Ruby Retreat and we would save money on the labour by doing all of the work ourselves. It would take five months to get it done, but if it did as well as our first place, the cash-on-cash return assumptions were amazing. We'd have to get creative with the financing, though. We had just recently closed on the shouse and our debt to income was a little on the unfavourable side. We had some credit card debt from furnishing The Crystal Cabin and, while our income was starting to look better than it had in a long time, we were self-employed. The bank wants two years of returns if you're not a W2 employee.

FEBRUARY OF 2020

Things were moving along nicely. The real estate business was growing. The Crystal Cabin was starting to fill back up after our short off season in January and February. We even had a lot of the spring and summer starting to book up (and at rates that we thought were too good to be true). We had our 2019 tax returns done, paid down our debt enough to make the bank happy and we were ready to close on our next investment property.

THEN THE WORLD TURNED UPSIDE DOWN. REMEMBER COVID?

Two weeks before we were scheduled to close on The Ruby Retreat, everything ground to a halt. The Crystal Cabin lost $20,000 in bookings over the course of a week due to the lockdowns. The real estate industry froze as no one really knew what was going to happen. Then the state of Arkansas declared that there was to be a moratorium on vacation rental properties until this public health crisis could be resolved. They were even kind enough to put big flashing signage on the highway, right on the state line, where you turn to our neighbourhood to remind people that VACATION RENTALS ARE PROHIBITED IN ARKANSAS! Airbnb (following local ordinance) blacked out our booking calendar **indefinitely**. Apparently, hotels were safe but the private home we had that was hundreds of feet away from the nearest neighbour and professionally cleaned and disinfected between guests was dangerous...

MULTIPLE EXIT STRATEGIES

This became a very scary time to follow through with acquiring another mortgage. Our income was reliant on the real estate industry, which became extremely questionable, and we had no idea if and when we would be able to run The Ruby Retreat as a vacation rental. The saving grace for us was the fact that it would be a perfectly great option for a long-term rental. We knew that with being this close to Branson and Table Rock Lake yet with an acre of land as a single-family home, we would always have demand. With that reassuring thought, we moved forward with the purchase. We would spend the next six months remodelling the Ruby. We knocked down two fireplaces, painted the cabinets, redid flooring, new counters, new plumbing and lighting fixtures, new siding and the list goes on. It was a gut job then we had to furnish it. Here comes my brilliant wife once again with her connection to the owner of an estate sale business. We were able to furnish it with high quality furniture for a fraction of the cost.

Helpful hint: pick up seasonal and Christmas decorations throughout the year at garage and estate sales.

REINVESTING PROCEEDS

With a successful Crystal Cabin (grossed over $80k in 2021) and Ruby Retreat (grossed $70k in nine months in 2021), us and our friends were undergoing major changes in life circumstances. They bought an awesome homestead an hour away and we acquired twenty-seven acres near us to build a house on. We both needed a cash injection to move to our next chapters and it was a seller's market like no one had seen in decades. We sold The Crystal Cabin for $350k! Next up we sold The Ruby Retreat for $412k! The windfall from these properties has been life-changing. The funny thing is neither could appraise for anywhere near what they sold for! The list price was due to the fact that these were fully furnished, turnkey vacation rentals with gross revenue beyond anything in the nearby Branson market. It keeps getting better. Remember we lived in The Crystal Cabin? Yeah, well, we lived in it for two out of the previous five years at the time of the sale. What does that mean for our $200k profit from the sale of The Crystal Cabin? NO CAPITAL

Surrounded by natural beauty

GAINS tax. We also sold The Ruby Retreat close to the same time and after the 50/50 split with our friends, we had another $125k but that one we needed to use a 1031 Exchange in order to avoid capital gains. All this translates to us having to buy more property. But where? Well, we realised that we'd discovered the Mecca of emerging markets just twenty minutes outside of an established STR market that had restrictions. However, because we were in a rural area, there was not much to buy at any given time. How could we acquire more property in this opportunity area?!

ON TO THE NEXT

I spent months writing letters, scouring the county tax map for the names of vacant land in our area and trying to see if anyone was interested in selling. If we couldn't find another house, we'd build one. Finally, after countless letters, Christmas cards and phone calls, I got a bite. Someone wanted to sell a few acres of land right next to the entrance to the state park campground and marina. He happened to tell us his neighbour who lived in the house up the hill wanted to sell as well. We ended up using our 1031 Exchange money to put $125K down on the $190k purchase price of a four-bed, three-bath house on one and a half acres. The amount of remodelling this one needed was staggering. The house itself and the finishes weren't the worst. It was the layout! We ended up relocating an interior staircase, relocating the front door, moving the kitchen, adding a fourth bathroom into the basement, which required cutting into a concrete slab, new roof, new deck and the list goes on. How could we afford this?! We paid nothing out of pocket. We put in such a big down payment (thanks to the sale of The Ruby Retreat) that the bank felt comfortable floating us more money with that house as collateral (HELOC). I should also mention at this point we had built a very good relationship with a local bank that could see what we were doing and saw that we were investing in an emerging market.

THE NOW

As of December 2022, we are building our dream home. After a decade of designing for other people, Shae finally gets to design one for us on what will be a million-dollar estate on twenty-seven acres overlooking our beloved Table Rock Lake. We have restarted our construction business with a focus on unique custom vacation rental builds. We currently have three homes in progress with four more breaking ground next month. We have partnered up with some investors and are building a high-end treehouse resort in our beautiful area of unrestricted bliss just south of a thriving STR market. This is all built on creative, well-researched ideas, risk taking, good friends and family who believed in us.

LESSONS

#1 Buy real estate and be flexible

The greatest physical asset you have is your house. Owning a home can be the quickest path to wealth generation. Learn the value of sweat equity and make smart investments into your property. If you see rapid appreciation in value, you can reappraise and pull out funds or sell and move on if you see a greater opportunity. Don't think you have to stay in one place forever.

#2 Have multiple exit strategies

Can I flip it? Can I STR it? Can I LTR it? If all else fails, can I move into it?

I'm sure a lot of people will argue with me on this point but it's how we assess all our personal deals prior to acquisition.

#3 Be creative

We couldn't have broken into this industry when we did without the help of friends and thinking outside the box. Find a way to house hack, seek trusted partners and improve your skills to be able to bring greater value to yourself and others.

#4 Vacation rentals are work

Don't let anyone fool you into thinking you can buy a property, put it online, sit back and drink a margarita. To make money at it you have to be willing to put in the work. You don't have to physically do it yourself, but you do have to make sure systems are implemented, you have the right help in place and you maintain quality control.

#5 Have a direct booking system

Building your business solely reliant on third-party OTAs (online travel agencies like Airbnb) is like building your house on someone else's land. If they change the rules, you could be SOL.

Have faith.
Love on your family and your neighbours.
Be a good steward of the land.
God bless.

ABOUT THE AUTHOR

Ryan Duffy is a professional recreationalist residing in the Ozark Mountains just outside Branson, Missouri. Following a series of back injuries sustained during his career as a Chicago firefighter, Ryan (along with his incredibly talented and beautiful wife Shae) decided to give up his urban jungle in pursuit of star-filled skies, lake life and a quieter country setting to raise his family. His firm Duffy Homes Realty assists clients in the sale and acquisition of investment properties as well as offering guidance on the development of their land.

In the autumn of 2019, Ryan and Shae founded Ozark Mountain Vacations, which has grown into a collection of short-term rental properties and five-star management in Omaha, Arkansas near Table Rock Lake. While most Branson area accommodations are crowded into large condo or resort settings, Ozark Mountain Vacations breaks the mould by offering individual single-family homes on larger lots with private amenities. This enables guests to reconnect with nature and each other while still being just a short drive from major area attractions.

Ryan has been a licenced home builder since 2017. Through their construction business Duffy Homes LLC, Ryan and Shae are creating purpose-built developments focused on preserving the look, feel and values that drew them to the Ozarks. The Duffys pride themselves on supporting others in their investment journey and emphasise the transformational nature of smart real estate investment for individual families and communities as a whole.

Links: https://linktr.ee/duffyhomes

RYAN LUKE

EFFICIENT HOSPITALITY: WHAT YOU'RE PROBABLY NOT PRIORITISING AS A SHORT-TERM RENTAL HOST

HOSPITALITY IN AN HOUR OF NEED

In the late hours of an autumn day in the Northeast of England, a woman viciously tapped at her phone screen, despite the creeping numbness in her fingers.

She was desperate for help.

With her was her young son, no more than two, maybe three years old, and a barely packed suitcase.

This woman had just escaped from one of the most terrifying situations of her life. An abusive partner, who was threatening her and her son's well-being, while they had no family nor friends to turn to.

The survivors needed a safe place to stay – and fast. The woman was afraid to get the authorities involved straight away, so she contacted a number of hotels and short-term rental companies instead. Unfortunately, it was all to no avail.

As the sun began to set into the night sky, the woman's resolve dwindled. But she summoned the strength to contact one more short-term rental provider; and to her enormous relief, they said: *"Of course. We can get you checked in tonight."*

That company happened to be Luke Stays.

And the woman, a guest whom I'll never forget.

AN INSIDER'S VIEW, WITHOUT THE FLUFF

Over the years, I've been labelled as money-obsessed, selfish and obnoxious.

You see, there's a real (negative) stereotype that's associated with wealthy STR business owners who make regular trips to the Middle East.

This is often with little regard to the excruciating amount of hard work that these very business owners put in behind-the-scenes.

I haven't always been so forthcoming in my admission of criticism from others. But being a hospitality entrepreneur gives you thick skin. It has to. Otherwise, the industry will chew you up and spit you back out like a flavourless stick of gum.

The criticism used to frustrate the hell out of me in my early days of business. But now, I look back at the global empire I've built and, more importantly, the people my team and I have been able to help, and I'm left with nothing but gratitude and pride.

I'm delighted to say that the woman who contacted Luke Stays in her hour of need is in a safe and healthy place now, along with her son. I can't possibly claim that we're entirely responsible for turning her life around – however, we *are* a part of her story now. And a significant part at that.

To me, this is the absolute pinnacle of being hospitable.

It's funny because if you were to look at my business from the outside, you wouldn't immediately think of it as a "do good brand" that gives back to the wider community. But this is the precise problem with the world, our industry and society at large. People have become very surface level and this naturally bleeds into standards of hospitality, too.

Honestly, it's an epidemic.

Those who are willing to look past the bullsh*t and delve deep into the details are few and far between.

But I've always been a straight-talking person (maybe it's the Geordie in me). So, you can count on me to share with you exactly what I think it takes to be a "hospitable host", while also telling you what *not* to do – unless you want to fail epically.

In saying all the above, I should probably start by telling you a little bit about myself and how I got here.

AN UNLIKELY HOSPITABLE HOST

Just after I turned thirty-four, I came to the realisation that I needed a pension. The problem was, I had nothing in place to secure this, nor any kind of long-term financial protection for myself and my family.

I despised the thought of the "regular means" that people would conform to, to fund their pension pot. As a bit of an anarchist since childhood, I had no intention of working my arse off at the expense of my own contentment, then retiring by the time there'd barely be any life left to live.

So, I started looking for a way to create residual income; and that unwillingly became a full-time hustle. The days seemed longer back then. I remember sitting on the couch in our living room for weeks on end, as a thick fog of depression would envelop me. I had tried and failed with many other business initiatives; and the light at the end of the tunnel was beginning to seem dimmer and dimmer.

I toyed with the idea of property, having heard that it turned many people into self-made millionaires; but I hadn't a clue of how to begin. Eventually, the light-bulb moment occurred at a Grant Cardone sales conference (of all places), where I saw a young man on stage speaking about deal sourcing. Looking back at it now, I'd say that moment changed the entire trajectory of my life.

In a nutshell, the young entrepreneur on stage was explaining

Off to the match with Newcastle's biggest fans

how he would "package up" property deals and sell them for up to 10k profit. I watched him open-mouthed and immediately thought, *I can do that, too.* And that's pretty much when Luke Stays was born.

The first deal I did was a lease option deal. I funded a "mini refurb" for a small apartment on my credit card thinking it'd be instant, easy money. That was the first of my *many* mistakes as a business owner.

Following the refurb and over a dozen property viewings, I couldn't for the life of me get it rented out. It was a nightmare. I'd just invested a load of money that I didn't actually have "on a whim" and essentially put myself at the risk of losing it all. Would this now turn into another fuck up, to add to my existing string of failures?

Now, this was all happening during a time when the Airbnb landscape was booming. A new way of travel had emerged, and the industry was rife with money-making opportunities. It's funny to think that, back then, I had no idea what serviced accommodation and the short-term rental industry even was. The idea of opening up your home to allow guests to stay in it on a nightly basis was unknown to me, and I was completely oblivious to the fact that thousands of other property hosts were leveraging this opportunity.

A friend enlightened me about what he was doing with one of his properties at The Quayside in Newcastle. He was renting it out on Airbnb for £200 a night.

Shit, I thought.

I instantly realised what I needed to do.

That same day, I drove up to IKEA and bought furniture with guest satisfaction in mind, even though I'd done no prior training nor professional work in the short-term rental industry. I set my apartment up with the new furniture and listed it as an STR – and that resulted in over £3,500 worth of bookings in the space of just forty-eight hours.

And so, I did the same thing again.

And again, and again.

Until I was hooked.

In the early days of scaling the business with more properties under my belt, I learnt that the better service I provided to my guests (and their specific needs), the more I could grow.

So, I began to put the correct systems and processes in place and dominated the market in the Northeast of England first. This would often involve targeting weekenders across tourist areas, and marketing to day-to-day contractors during what would traditionally be "off peak season".

The latter enabled me to gradually build a sustainable STR business that didn't suffer from "empty calendar syndrome" like many of my competitors. This was purely down to me understanding the psychology of my guests; knowing exactly what they needed, and when.

By 2020, when many hospitality businesses were heading for a nose-dive because of the pandemic, I kept my entrepreneurial hat firmly on and executed the same STR strategy in Dubai, a city that I've always felt incredibly connected to.

I was now operating short-term rental models for some of the most luxurious properties in the world – the only thing that had changed was the needs of those specific guests, to which I always ensured the business adapted.

Thanks to this model, a hell of a lot of consistency and guest-focused hospitality, Luke Stays now has a fully-fledged team of cleaners, sales directors, accountants, and marketers, as well as a portfolio of investors who recognise the lucrative benefits of serviced accommodation.

The company itself controls over £90m worth of property and, as a team, we have enormous goals that we're determined to reach by 2024. I'd say the most fulfilling part of my "job" is that I now also work with a growing team of franchisees, who started off as aspiring property business owners just like me, and are currently changing their lives because of the Luke Stays brand and the serviced accommodation model.

Being hospitable pays off. In more ways than one.

START WITH EFFICIENCY, NOT EMOTION

It seems cliché to say but the global short-term rental industry is like a close-knit family. While there are hundreds of thousands of STR professionals scattered across various parts of the world, we share commonalities among us, and each try to do good by the industry and the people we serve, in our own respective ways.

Just as you'd find in any family setup, our industry is rich with different characters and personality types. For example, I have quite the reputation of being logical, process-driven and fast-paced when it comes to business. This would be an accurate analysis of my personality, as these are definitely some of my strongest skills.

The thing is, for many years, I'd convinced myself that perhaps I wasn't "hospitable" enough, because I didn't fit into the traditional mould of wearing my heart on my sleeve.

Of course, I have emotions just like any other human being, but I pursue efficiency and tangible results more than anything else in my line of work. That's the stuff that gets me motivated. That's the stuff I bounce out of bed for every morning.

But I was wrong. Efficiency, systems and processes is an

enormous part of being hospitable – and being healthily content overall.

In fact, psychologists have discovered via countless studies that organisation and efficiency boosts our mental well-being and happiness levels, dramatically. So, being process-driven and translating that same energy when providing a service to your guests can absolutely make you a better host.

What you must understand is that human beings are biologically wired to seek out familiarity. This means, when you create a "service blueprint" as an STR host and continually deliver against the high standards you've set for yourself, your guests will start noticing a pattern in your brand and service behaviour. This inherently makes their brain release more oxytocin (otherwise known as the "love drug"), which increases feelings of trust, reliability and emotional loyalty.

Many short-term rental hosts get so caught up in the bespoke and "creative" part of the guest experience that they dismiss processes altogether. Don't get me wrong, those creative personal touches are an absolute necessity when it comes to being a memorable host, but you can't possibly add artistic detail to a broken canvas.

Get the basics right first and build on that gradually.

When I share the story about the young woman who escaped the abuse of her husband with her son, people always comment on how emotionally attuned and empathetic our brand is. And while this is correct, because we would never dream of seeing another human being in pain, empathy alone means fuck all if you don't have the systems in place to do anything about it.

The reason we were able to be hospitable to that woman's urgent needs was because the team at Luke Stays has always run like a well-oiled machine.

We had the *systems* in place to take her call.

We had the *systems* in place to check her into a short-term rental property as soon as possible.

We had the *systems* in place to guarantee that this guest would be 100% safe, thanks to our I-PRAC accreditation.

In retrospect, I could fill up an entire book with the countless number of mistakes I've made as a short-term rental host, let alone a chapter. But in the interest of keeping things digestible, I'll pinpoint the one thing that I wish I'd done differently at the beginning of my entrepreneurship.

As somebody who has always been focused on "results", there was a point in my business journey when I became consumed with the idea of scaling as quickly as possible. We were seeing incredible things off the back of the effort we were putting into Luke Stays, and I was determined to double, triple, *quadruple* our property portfolio within a matter of months.

However, life should always be about finding a happy medium.

This is something I'd completely lost sight of during my "aggressive growth" stage. I'd realised that I was great at closing deals, but the sheer speed at which we were moving meant that I was letting the quality of our properties and general service standards slip. Had I not noticed this at the time I did, I could have done some serious damage to the reputation of a company that I'd poured my blood, sweat and tears into.

While having the right team, systems and processes in place will surely help you scale faster, don't let it cloud your perspective on the importance of maintaining quality. Growth in the short-term rental industry is only ever good when you're in keeping with service standards, and that's why the best hosts are those who achieve the perfect balance between efficiency and clear attention-to-detail.

I've since branched out into the world of serviced accommodation interior design with an in-house design team that specially kits our properties out for the perfect guest experience. We've also created a seamless direct booking process on the new Luke Stays website (by working with professional web developers, copywriters and designers), and have introduced a new StayCover feature that's automatically added to every direct booking. It's a bit

Spending time with some of my awesome franchisees during our monthly meet-up sessions

like Airbnb's AirCover, but way better and in the sole interest of our guests.

Realising your mistakes and fixing them with innovative solutions that are backed with logic and intelligence is vital when it comes to being hospitable, in every sense of the word. Don't ever skimp on the details like I nearly did, as it'll cost you far more than just your reputation.

MY (ORGANISED) DEFINITION OF "HOSPITABLE"

The good thing about efficiency is that it's a habit that can be learned over a period of time, if you're dedicated enough.

While your impression of me might be largely to do with grand holidays, luxury stays and numerous podcast appearances, I spend an *enormous* amount of time giving back to an industry that's helped me so much. I understand, firsthand, the struggles of being an aspiring business owner with little-to-no direction; and I guess my take on the importance of hospitality runs through in my act of service to others.

Our growing (free) Facebook community is an open table for anybody to join and learn about becoming successful and hospitable short-term rental hosts. The group regularly features live interviews with other industry experts, heaps of organic and valuable content, and trending topic discussions. At the core of hospitality is the relationships we build with other people, after all, and I'm proud of how our community enables this.

Of course, the Facebook group is not the only place where I share free industry advice and guidance. My LinkedIn profile (also home to my growing LinkedIn newsletter), Instagram and massively engaged TikTok channel always gives away the latest tips in being the best short-term rental host you can be, while also throwing in how you can continue to scale your business.

To date, I've worked with hundreds of aspiring short-term rental hosts on a one-to-one or group coaching basis, and given them all the tools and guidance they need to thrive in this industry. This, as well as our rapidly growing franchise community – which has now gone international – is based on the back of my experiences and failures, so that I can help other hosts avoid the mistakes I once suffered from.

I may not be a poet, a visual artist, and it's unlikely that you'll find a heart-shaped canvas on the wall of one of my properties, but the consistency and sheer hard work that I've put into understanding my guests and tending to their needs – no matter how big or small – puts me in a good place to call myself a hospitable host, I think.

Never underestimate the power of organisation, reliability and efficiency that's not up for compromise. Often, it's what your guests crave most.

ABOUT THE AUTHOR

Few professionals – if any – have achieved the height of success that Ryan reached during just the first seven months of his journey in the industry. Within this short timeframe, Ryan managed to acquire the first twenty-one properties for his portfolio. This unbelievable milestone turned out to be a sign of the times because, despite his lack of experience, the entrepreneur continued to thrive from then on.

Whether it was down to his long-drawn experience in competitive sports, or the fact that he resented the thought of being enslaved by a soulless job, Ryan went on to expand his portfolio to a staggering 350 properties (across the world), many of which he successfully operated as short-term rentals.

The rapid success of Ryan's business Luke Stays led him to set up headquarters in Dubai, while also giving back to the industry in numerous ways.

Not only has Ryan recruited over 100 team members (in-house and freelancers) as a result of his growing businesses, his franchise model has given other aspiring STR business owners the tools, mentorship and resources to scale their own companies. To date, Luke Stays has changed the lives of numerous business owners, and is officially recognised as the industry's most trusted short-term rental brand.

While Ryan controls in excess of £90m of property across thirty-four worldwide locations, and has enormous plans of growth by 2024, you will rarely see him turning down the opportunity to support other entrepreneurs who face the same struggles as he once did, making Ryan Luke the industry's most well-versed, no-nonsense and selflessly hospitable professional.

Links: https://linktr.ee/Officialryanluke

SARAH ORCHARD

THE WRITING WAS ON THE WALL

Have you ever felt that you had to do something so strongly? Even if other people thought you were a bit bonkers?

So, there Ade and I were, sitting in the bar of a quaint beamed country house hotel on the 19th of September 2016. We were tired, having driven 130 miles after work from Surrey to the Wye Valley, perched on the border of Wales.

We were also feeling rather anxious. What were we thinking?! Why did we agree to do this?

As we sat in the dimly lit, cosy bar, I read a message scribbled on the chalkboard:

"Sometimes the smallest step in the right direction
ends up being the biggest step of your life.
Tip toe if you must,
but take the step."
– Anon

I couldn't believe it.

It was a sign we were doing the right thing and finally starting our journey to make it happen.

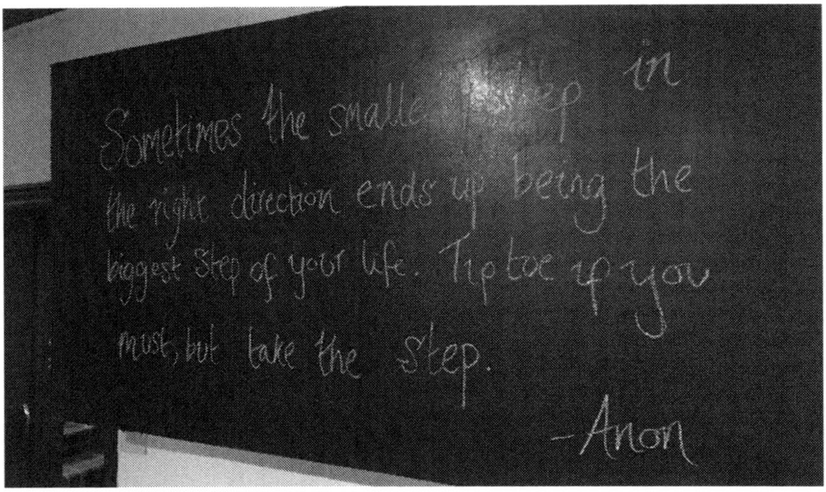

The writing was most certainly on the wall!

It felt like someone knew and had written that just for us.

How weird when I think back to it now, but I so needed that message on that evening to bolster my spirits and determination to make our vision a reality.

You see, our mad dream was to build a glamping treehouse in our own woods.

And we were sitting in that hotel on that particular evening to film the next day with the BBC One TV show *Escape to the Country*. They were helping us to find our dream home to build our new glamping business and start a new life in the Wye Valley, located in Gloucestershire, UK.

At that point, we had been house hunting for two and a half years. We'd seen twenty-three properties and struggled to find anything in our budget that fitted the bill. You see, we had a rather long list of requirements. Doesn't everyone with a new home?

Our long-distance house-hunting trips were taking their toll. Not to mention our pocket too, with a couple of speeding tickets!

Ade had been away on a business trip for his corporate job. I was chatting to a friend who happened to live in Gloucestershire, and she could see we really were desperate to get started with our dream project in the Wye Valley.

"Why don't you apply to be on *Escape to the Country* then?" piped up Dee.

There was a long pause on the phone from my end. "Because Ade will kill me! He is shy and said he never wants to go on telly and that show." You see, it had crossed my mind and I had asked at least once before!

"Well," she said, "he's not here at the moment, so I think you should just do it!"

I said, "I'll think about it!"

Later that evening, I found the online application form on the BBC website and sent it off. Thinking no more of it. They wouldn't pick us anyway!

Two days later, I got a call to say they wanted us to appear on the show.

Big gulp. Eek! Now I would have to tell Ade what I had done.

The air was somewhat 'blue' when I told him what I had done and even more so when I said they were coming to film in just three days' time at our house.

Crikey, that was quick. No going back now...

Going on the TV show was life changing for us. It was that small step in the right direction, for sure. And it was, in fact, the biggest step of our life together.

We both enjoyed the filming experience. Even Ade admitted he actually enjoyed it. The film crew were great fun and made the entire process really relaxed and enjoyable. They stayed in touch with us, and Jonnie Irwin and the production team have revisited us not once (as usual) but twice to catch up on our progress. They were suitably impressed with our visions, determination and what we had created.

We moved into our new home in the stunning Wye Valley on the 26th of April 2017.

FAST FORWARD ALMOST THREE YEARS...

We launched our glamping treehouse called *The Hudnalls Hideout* on the 14th of February 2020. I'd be lying if I said it was plain sailing. Truthfully, it was quite the opposite.

The planning application process was stressful, complex and laborious. We live in an Area of Outstanding Natural Beauty (AONB) and next to a Site of Special Scientific Interest (SSSI) – an ancient deciduous woodland called The Hudnalls National Nature Reserve – which our business is aptly named after. These areas in the UK are highly protected to preserve the natural landscape, ancient woodland and its native inhabitants. In our immediate area, there are highly protected bat species and rare dormice.

The A-frame structure we chose to build is also rather unique (the first of its kind in the UK) and, weighing in at fifty-five tonnes and $38m^2$, it is large too! There is probably a good reason why nobody else had chosen to build an A-frame treehouse before! It took eight months to build with a team of five men, in the wettest winter the locals could ever remember. Just our luck! But little did we know then that much worse was to come...

The COVID-19 pandemic hit the world and shut us down on the 23rd of March 2020, only five weeks after our long-awaited launch day. Ade and I had some pretty dark days in that first week after lockdown one hit the UK. We shed many tears and had many sleepless nights.

We had come here with a dream. It had taken us almost five years to get this far. And now it seemed it was stopped in its tracks before it had even got going.

I know we felt like many hosts around the world did too. Shocked, scared, sad and a little lost without our guests to fuss over.

But if you want something badly enough, you keep going, right? And we did.

Was it worth it? Hell yes.

Launching and promoting the Hideout has been the most enjoyable experience of my thirty-year marketing career. It was hugely satisfying. I finally got to market my own holiday business. Not just other people's.

The Hideout has had such a wonderful guest reaction and

much media acclaim. It has been featured in *Condé Nast Traveller*, *Lonely Planet*, *BA High Life*, *Wanderlust* magazine, *The Times* and *The Stylist*, to name but a few. In 2021, it also featured on Channel 4 TV's *Extraordinary Escapes* with Sandi Toksvig. Sandi brought TV chef extraordinaire Prue Leith to stay with her, and they both loved the treehouse experience.

I knew from the beginning that I didn't want to pay commission and had the marketing expertise myself to successfully promote our new venture. So, we went 100% direct from the get-go. I built a website and created an email waitlist of over 500 people. Therefore, when we did launch, we got off to a flying start with fifty bookings in the first nineteen days. Our goal in year one was to achieve an 80% occupancy rate. However, despite the pandemic, we achieved an occupancy rate of 96% from launch. The Hideout is now booked solid back-to-back for an average of six-to-nine months in advance.

FRESH-FACED HOSTS (AND A BIT NAÏVE, IF I'M HONEST)

Ade and I were new to hosting. My parents had a B&B in a rather run-down UK seaside resort when I was a teenager, and I helped my mum by waiting on tables in the summer holidays. Still, we had never run our own hospitality business.

I'm not sure anything can truly prepare you for being a host. Dealing with the general public can be challenging at times. And, if I'm brutally honest, also a little hurtful when guests treat your property with disrespect or cause careless damage.

The key thing is you do need to like people. Many people say this. But you REALLY need to like people, as they can try the patience of a saint! Everyone in this book will be a testament to the fact that 95% of guests are a delight, but the 5% who aren't really do test your metal!

So, my advice to anyone looking to start on this short-term rental adventure is to ask yourself: do you really like dealing with people?

You are never truly ‘off duty’ and guests can be highly demanding.

Ade now works in the business full-time. However, we have help with grounds maintenance, the changeover cleaning and outsource the laundry to a commercial company, as we have a rural septic tank that wouldn’t like the volume of laundry involved with three changeovers every week, fifty-two weeks of the year.

I run my marketing business GET FULLY BOOKED to help fellow hosts full time, but I do all the guest extra sourcing and fulfilment, and all the marketing for the treehouse. There is a lot involved in running a short-term rental. Even one unit can be very time-consuming. Changeovers can be time sapping when things get broken or fail unexpectedly, even if you have spares of absolutely everything possible (or you thought you did!).

HOW TO KEEP YOUR SANITY!

As new hosts who had been on such a drawn-out journey to create our dream glamping business, it can take over your life. It is easy to slip into talking about your new venture 24/7.

We are a husband-and-wife team living and working onsite, so it can be really unhealthy for your relationship to talk about the business all the time. To start with, we slipped into that trap big time. We felt like we could never switch off. Our lives had become a bit obsessive about the Hideout and nothing else to the detriment of our social life and hobbies. I think the impact of the pandemic lockdowns didn’t help that intensity to be honest.

I was talking to a business coach about my marketing business, and she asked me if Ade and I had business meetings. Ade and I had come from successful corporate careers, so meetings were not a new thing to us by any stretch of the imagination. Still, we didn’t have formal meetings for the Hideout. What she suggested was so simple but so easy to overlook. She said, “As directors, don’t you have a weekly board or operations meeting?” Bingo! I felt silly for not seeing such an obvious solution. We had a business that we

Sarah and Adrian Orchard
– the creators of the award-winning The Hudnalls Hideout

weren't really treating like a proper business in this one aspect. We now have a weekly operations meeting with a set agenda that we always work through. We don't make extra work by doing formal minutes, but we agree actions and note our individual tasks to move the business forward. This means we know we have a fixed time to chat through business ideas and actions, so talking about the treehouse doesn't sneak into EVERY evening over dinner. It's vital to have time to switch off from your business.

SO, WHAT HAS MADE OUR SHORT-TERM RENTAL SUCH A MASSIVE SUCCESS?

Many of the people I help with their marketing ask me this question all the time. They want to know what "formula" we use. And it's a simple one:

MARKETING, MARKETING, AND THEN EVEN MORE MARKETING!

Many hosts start out with the mantra, "I have built it, and they will come." They have lovingly created their short-term rental business and have been so preoccupied with that all-consuming process that they lost sight of the fact that nobody even knows they exist. Hence why the likes of Airbnb, Booking.com, Vrbo, etc., have a stranglehold on many starting out. Don't get me wrong, they have a place, and if you feel you will not have the time or energy to learn how to market your own STR then you can certainly use an agent like these to be your hired marketing muscle.

But The Hideout and my hundreds of one-to-one clients prove it is totally feasible to market and succeed in going it alone.

So, you have decided to market your short-term rental yourself. What next?

I strongly believe that a differentiated branded guest experience is the primary factor in our success.

In planning our treetop paradise, we spent a lot of time reviewing competitors. This started with lining up some visits through Canopy & Stars to visit two treehouses and chat with the owners. These early visits were so insightful and gave us lots of ideas and sight of the pitfalls that might lie ahead for us.

Having found our location and the area of the country we wanted to start our search in, we spent many hours doing online research. Looking at competitor websites and what they offered on paper. Attending trade exhibitions also helped our fact-finding and building our business case to know that our new venture was viable.

I feel there's another key factor that has also contributed hugely to our success – research stays! We did many research stays and compiled a detailed outline of every aspect of our customer experience. From the website, booking process and pre-arrival emails, through to arrival and details in the accommodation to enhance our stay. We stayed in different types of structures, from tipis and yurts to quirky cottages, cabins and treehouses. This helped us to narrow down the rental type we wanted to set up.

Guests always comment on our attention to detail and the fact "you can see the love and care that has gone into it" and "you've thought of absolutely everything". In our research stays, we noted things that were great to have or perhaps even missing from our visits. All the details and extras that make your stay relaxing, and a smooth and comforting experience.

Another tip is you MUST stay in your own accommodation. It is amazing how many hosts don't actually do this. Often because in your rush to launch and get guests in, it's just too full-on and busy to actually have it finished and ready in time. However, you need to "sleep" in your guest's shoes and road-test your stay experience from start to finish. We also had a set of trial guests to give us unbiased and frank feedback before we had our first paying guests in the Hideout. This was really useful, as the feedback pointed out some things we had overlooked.

The night we opened the Hideout, we had a major winter storm hit, called Storm Dennis (hey, like we needed more bad weather?!), with very high winds and torrential icy cold rain, so no guests had actually booked for Valentine's night. I imagine the prospect of spending a significant amount of money to stay for a very wet and windy weekend probably wasn't that appealing. Funny that! So Ade and I headed down to the treehouse to road-test our creation for the first time. We had spent the previous four weeks doing all the final back-breaking landscaping to banish the shin-deep mud and manually carrying every piece of furniture and item down to the middle of the woods. One day, I walked 28,000 steps. It had been a long haul to get this far, and now we were hit by a nasty storm to cap off eight months of constant rain during the build. Surely we would get a break at some point? It really felt like things were not on our side. It wasn't a relaxing, romantic evening in our new creation. We collapsed into bed. Exhausted.

Little did we know it at the time of that first opening night that lockdown one would give us a few more unexpected chances to stay in our creation. These stays added to our pre-opening stay and really helped to fine-tune and perfect the guest experience. It was silly little things that we had overlooked, and it helped to iron out any small faults and make the guest experience that much better.

Guests notice the attention and thought that has gone into the guest experience. They have time to savour the experience, and they notice EVERYTHING!

Never overlook those little details. And don't be afraid to do things a little differently too. It all counts in making you stand out.

WHAT MAKES THE HARD WORK ALL WORTHWHILE?

I won't lie to you; running a hospitality business can rarely be described as a "side hustle". It's easy to underestimate exactly what is involved in being a hospitable and successful host.

The Hideout is a romantic and unique experience, so we tend to get guests staying with us for life's little special occasions, from birthdays and anniversaries to proposals and mini-moons! One of the things I personally enjoy so much is adding extras and surprise touches for guests who are celebrating with us. There is something wonderful about creating a memory at that moment in time in someone else's life through the hosting experience. It might sound like a cliché, but it really is priceless. That feeling and memory helps keep you up and motivated when you have challenging or disrespectful guests. Every host you hear say that is not exaggerating. It really does.

When we have a proposal stay booked, I am like a nervous partner popping the question myself, making sure everything is perfect and adding in little extras like fresh rose petals scattered in and around the outdoor bath, upgrading their complimentary Prosecco to champagne, and adding silk rose petals to the unique loft bed in the treehouse mezzanine bedroom. We wait, with bated breath, to see if they said "yes". An extraordinary thing to be able to be part of. We have had our first engaged couples now married and starting their life journey together. That is something so incredibly special to know we played a part of it.

One set of guests we are welcoming back in 2023 for their third stay. That has to be the biggest compliment. To have guests choose to return time and time again, when they have so many amazing holiday choices out there. Another set of guests came for their second visit and wrote in our guestbook that "The best just got better". That was such a compliment as we strive to keep adding to the Hideout experience, adding in new touches and features for guests to ensure that we give them a reason to return. From adding an enhanced covered outdoor dining area with a DeliVita wood-fired oven, to our latest creations, The Lookout Bar and Larder in the summer of 2021 – a private bar and honesty shop for just the guests to use – and a new Woodland Sauna experience in January 2023.

MY FINAL THOUGHTS

Always keep pace with the market trends and never stop caring about each and every guest experience with you. Enjoy the hosting adventure!

ABOUT THE AUTHOR

Sarah Orchard is the co-owner of the UK's most sought-after treehouse retreat experience, The Hudnalls Hideout.

This luxury one-of-a-kind A-frame treehouse is set deep in the heart of the Wye Valley Area of Outstanding Natural Beauty in Gloucestershire (UK). It offers a romantic adults-only 'perched paradise' where guests can kick back, relax and sleep in the treetops immersed in nature.

Sarah and her husband, Adrian, found their ideal location to build their dream project through the popular UK property hunt television show BBC1's *Escape to The Country*. After a long two-and-a-half-year search looking at twenty-three properties, with the much-needed help from the show, they finally found the perfect spot for their short-term rental build.

With no road access, the treehouse was painstakingly hand-crafted in-situ over eight months and is perched high in the tree canopy with chic interiors, an outdoor copper bath on a wrap-around deck and a totally secluded woodland location.

The treehouse opened on the 14th of February 2020, and Sarah has achieved a 100% direct booked occupancy rate of 96% from launch, despite the global Covid pandemic. The Hideout has a waitlist and is fully booked around twelve months in advance.

Sarah Orchard is also an award-winning visibility expert. She helps fellow short-term rental hosts confidently move from being invisible online to maximum visibility, web traffic and more direct bookings. She is the founder of get-fully-booked.com and the creator of her unique seven-step proven marketing system, designed to show short-term rental hosts and hospitality businesses how to get fully booked with ease.

Links: https://linktr.ee/sarahorchard

VINCI SEVILLA

ALL I WANT IS NOTHING MORE, TO HEAR YOU KNOCKING ON MY DOOR

I want to share with you two very personal and life-changing stories that reflect some of my most memorable experiences during my journey...

as a hospitable host...
as a husband...
as a father...
as a business owner...
and as a person.

The reason I share these two stories with you is twofold:

1. It gives me a chance to show you my WHY. My family is my WHY. They are WHY I do all of this. They are my motivation, my inspiration, my everything. I encourage you to find your WHY before starting your journey.
2. Hosting is more than just about getting a house, furnishing it, and throwing in a smart door lock. It's about the people. Keep that in mind if you want to start in this hospitality business. It will be your guiding light, your north star, in many difficult situations.

And before I forget: my name is Vinci Sevilla Jr.

I hope you like my poems and my stories.

* * *

NEWBORN BUSINESS

I am a new dad and a hospitable host too.
Running an Airbnb, my days are full and true.

I'll juggle it all, with love and care,
For my family and my guests, I'll always be there.

But amidst the hustle and bustle,
My little one remains my top puzzle.

It may be tough, but I wouldn't have it any other way,
I am blessed, to live and work, every single day.

– Vinci Sevilla Jr

* * *

As I sit here, typing away on my laptop, I can't help but feel a sense of excitement and nervousness as I relive that morning of the 22nd of September 2021. It was the morning I became a dad.

My wife and I were sitting up in bed in our home in Riverside, California, getting ready to give birth to our first child.

It's a momentous occasion, one that we'd been preparing for over the past nine months.

But even as we geared up for this new chapter in our lives, I couldn't help but feel a bit overwhelmed.

You see, we'd just started our first STR (short-term rental) Airbnb business three months before, and while my wife's pregnancy had been relatively smooth sailing, running a successful STR business requires a lot of time and effort.

In fact, we had guests checking in that very same day.

As the contractions started to pick up in intensity, my wife and I made our way to the hospital.

The drive was a blur of nerves and excitement, and before I knew it, we found ourselves in the labour and delivery room and our baby girl was on the way.

I had never been this anxious in my life and I fervently whispered prayer after prayer for a safe and healthy delivery.

The next few hours were a blur of activity as our baby made her way into the world. I stood by my wife's side every step of the way, holding her hand, and offering whatever support and encouragement I could.

As soon as our beautiful baby daughter was born, it was like everything else in the world fell away. All my worries about my work, our STR business, about meeting guests' expectations and keeping everything running smoothly, disappeared in an instant.

All that mattered was this beautiful, perfect little girl in my arms.

But as much as I wanted to stay in this bubble of new parenthood, the real world doesn't stop.

I had guests arriving at both of our STR properties in just a few hours, and I had to make sure everything was ready for them. One of the properties had a leak and another had a clogged sink.

Luckily, one of the best things I ever did when starting our STR business was to hire an amazing team that were our 'boots on the ground'.

Sleep deprived, I checked in on my sleeping newborn daughter and my amazing wife who deserved every bit of rest she was taking, and called up my team to ensure they had everything they needed to prepare for our incoming guests. They quickly resolved everything, and I breathed a sigh of relief.

Business was running.

Wife was resting.

My beautiful child was sleeping.

Life, at this moment, was absolutely bliss.

My daughter's name is Serenity. Serenity means peace. Let me tell you, those first few months, she did not give us much serenity.

My FAMILY is my WHY.
What's yours?

Every day seemed to blend into one long, exhausting blur. I was constantly juggling my full-time job, the needs of my family and the needs of my business.

It was a delicate balance, and one that often left me feeling drained and burnt out. My wife, Patricia, throughout this entire time, has been my rock and, without her support, we never would have been able to make it through. It's not easy, but we were determined to make it work.

As the days passed and my wife and daughter got stronger, I started to get a better handle on things.

I figured out a system for managing my short-term rentals while also taking care of my family, and things started to feel a bit more manageable.

I learned to delegate tasks and prioritise my time. I also started to embrace the moments of chaos and unpredictability, seeing them as opportunities to grow and learn.

Technology was my best friend and automating my processes and systems completely changed my business. At this point, two months after Serenity was born, we were able to pick up a third property and, with the automated systems in place, I only spent an average of ten minutes a day on our business.

But even as I started to feel more confident in my role as a husband, father and new business owner, I never lost sight of the most important things: my wife and daughter.

My little girl was my constant source of joy and inspiration. She was the reason we kept going when everything else seemed impossible.

My family is my everything, and I'm grateful for every moment I get to spend with them.

As I look back on those early days of fatherhood and entrepreneurship, I am grateful for the lessons I learned and the growth I experienced.

It wasn't always easy, but it was worth it.

In the end, I think the experience of balancing my newborn and my business has only made me a better person.

I've learned to be more organised and efficient, to prioritise the things that matter most, and to appreciate the little moments in life.

And, most importantly, I've learned that no matter how busy or hectic things get, the love and support of my family will always see me through.

* * *

THE STORM AND THE HOST

There was a hospitable host, so kind and true,
Who welcomed a guest, when the storm was due.

The power went out, in the middle of the night,
But the host was there, to make everything all right.

As the storm raged on, and the night grew late,
The host remained vigilant, and never did hesitate.

To comfort and care, for his guest in need,
A hospitable host, indeed.

When the storm passed, and the skies were clear,
The guests left with a smile, and a heart full of cheer.

– Vinci Sevilla Jr

* * *

When the world welcomed the 2022 New Year, snow was falling gently from the sky and the air was crisp and cold.

It was a typical winter day at the Creek-Side Cabin, our first short-term rental in the Great Smoky Mountains of Tennessee.

I had just finished preparing my cabin for the arrival of my next set of guests when my phone vibrated.

Buzzz.

I received a weather notification: a massive snowstorm was headed our way and was expected to bring with it heavy snow and strong winds.

Less than twenty-four hours later, the wind was howling and snow was falling heavily, accumulating rapidly on the ground.

As the storm raged on, the power in the area went out, plunging the entire region into darkness.

I knew I had to act fast if I wanted to keep my guests safe and warm. I spoke with the power company and there was no estimated time for restoration.

Luckily, our cabin ran on propane for heat, and we had access to a backup generator for power. I quickly gathered blankets, flashlights and any other supplies we could find, and set them out for my guests to use.

Buzzz. Buzzz. Buzzz.

I received multiple notifications on my phone.

All my incoming guests for the next two weeks had just cancelled their trip.

While some hosts have a strict no-refund cancellation policy for trips so close to their start date, this was one of the worst snowstorms the region had seen in years.

As a hospitable host, some of the biggest values we stand by in our business is honesty, integrity and safety for our guests. We were happy to provide full refunds for all our guest cancellations.

Buzzz. I received another phone notification.

It was a booking inquiry from someone trying to book my cabin that very same day.

For their privacy, let's call this guest Mike.

Mike and his family were on their way out of the mountains when the storm came upon them, and they needed to find a place to stay. Roads were closed and all the hotels and cabins nearby were out of power or heat.

Mike asked if our cabin had any power or heat. They were parked at a petrol station a couple of miles away with no power and were desperately looking for shelter. Luckily, their phone still had service somehow and they were able to see my cabin listing pop up on Airbnb.

With our small generator and a half-empty propane tank, my cabin was the only one within miles that had adequate heat and power. I knew that many other guests and travellers were probably stranded and in need of shelter. Without hesitation, I made the decision to open up my cabin to anyone who needed a place to stay.

I quickly told Mike our situation and welcomed them to shelter at our cabin.

I also spoke with Airbnb and Vrbo and told them that if there were other guests that needed a place to stay from the storm, we would be happy to shelter them at no charge as long as our small but mighty power generator and heat was available.

As the storm raged on, more and more people began to seek shelter in my cabin. Some were travellers who had been stranded on the road, while others were local residents who had been caught off guard by the sudden and severe weather and needed a place to shelter for a few hours.

Despite the chaos and uncertainty, I did everything I could to make sure my guests were comfortable and taken care of. Some of the guests had food and began sharing with others around our fireplace while others provided blankets and warm clothing to those who needed it.

Eventually, the storm passed, and the power was partially restored. Some guests were able to return to their homes, and others found residence elsewhere.

Mike and his family stayed in our cabin for the rest of the week.

They, too, eventually left, but not before thanking us for our kindness and generosity during such a difficult time.

As the power was slowly restored, and the snow-covered city began to come back to life, I couldn't help but feel a sense of pride and accomplishment.

I had opened my home to complete strangers and had done everything in my power to keep them safe and comfortable.

Generosity and kindness had brought people together and created a sense of community in the midst of a difficult and trying situation.

And in the end, that was all that mattered.

Buzzz.

REFLECTION

Isn't it funny, how God brings you to certain places in your life you never thought you'd be?

Where are you right now?

At this moment in time, reading or listening to this, where are you in your life today, and how much has it changed in the past year?

Whether you switched jobs, moved elsewhere, fell in love, fell out of love, met a new friend, or did something scary or new, your past self may be quite surprised where you've ended up.

Go on, take a few moments and reflect on this.

Ridiculous, right?

If you'd told me last year that I would start my first short-term rental and grow a completely new business into a national portfolio with properties located in some of the most popular holiday spots across the United States, while coaching and educating others on how to replicate the exact same process I use, and then invited to co-author this book alongside some of the greatest hosts and minds of the short-term rental industry, I would have laughed in disbelief.

I'll tell you this, though: no matter what happens, the good or the bad, God is good.

Serenity Sevilla, our pride and joy.

Family and friends ask me all the time, "How did you overcome starting something completely new, like running a short-term rental or Airbnb business?"

I typically like to explain how I overcome my fear of starting something new by using the 'windscreen and the rearview mirror' metaphor.

All cars have a windscreen and a rearview mirror.

Typically, the windscreen is approximately 80% bigger than the rearview mirror.

In a sense, we should look forward through the windscreen at the road upon which we are driving for the majority of the journey. However, it's important to occasionally glance in the rearview mirror. It's impossible to drive looking only through the rearview mirror.

We have small rearview mirrors and very large front windscreens because what happened in the past isn't nearly as important as what happens in the future.

In short, where we are going is more significant than where we have been.

MY REARVIEW MIRROR

From the start of our hosting journey in June 2021 to December 2022, we've hosted over 3,427 (and counting) guests, friends and families for gatherings, weddings, reunions, funerals, sporting events, social media influencers, engagement proposals, holidays, post-pandemic Covid reunions, as well as the Make A Wish foundation, Boy and Girl Scout troops of America, and so much more.

In eighteen months, we brought in over $400k+ in bookings, across six amazing properties in some of the most popular holiday spots covering three states within the United States.

So, what's next?

MY WINDSCREEN

I have a goal to positively influence as many people as I can through this amazing short-term rental industry around the world. Like many other hosts, I recognise that this is an industry where anyone can succeed, regardless of their previous experience or skill set. I hope to continue to support, motivate and inspire others to replicate the same success that I have had in pursuit of their financial freedom journey.

My wife and I will continue to grow our business so that we can continue to live a life of abundance that allows us to help our family, friends and community.

ONE LAST THING

If there's one last piece of advice you can take from all of this, I hope you take this:

Many people used to say to me: knowledge is power. Over time, I've learned that isn't true. I believe that the *application* of knowledge is power. You can listen to all the podcasts and YouTube videos in the world, or read all the books you want, but until you actually apply that knowledge, until you actually start, you'll never grow.

Also, if you haven't already noticed, I love writing poetry. You can find a poem I wrote, dedicated to all the hospitable hosts around the world, in the front of this book.

ABOUT THE AUTHOR

*"'You miss 100% of the shots you don't take. – Wayne Gretzky' –
Michael Scott"
– VINCI SEVILLA JR*

Vinci Sevilla Jr is an active real estate investor and entrepreneur holding a portfolio valued in excess of $22.5M consisting of long-term rentals, short-term rentals and large multi-family. Vinci lives and works in Southern California and has worn many hats in his professional career, starting off as an engineer, management and as a senior adviser to one of the top energy utility companies in the nation. Aside from his W2 nine-to-five job, Vinci is the founder and CEO of Getaway Haus, a technology and data-driven real estate investment and management firm. Their national portfolio specialises in top tier short-term rentals that currently operates in California, Tennessee and West Virginia, and is actively expanding across the US. Vinci is also the co-founder of NVST Capital, where they take on large multi-family syndications and help investors maximise their returns.

Besides advising energy utility corporations and running his successful business, Vinci is a seasoned keynote speaker and thought leader in promoting STEM (science, technology, engineering and mathematics) to young minority students in underprivileged areas. He has a passion for educating those in personal finance and loves to share his knowledge in real estate investing. Vinci is also active in establishing local real estate investing communities where building wealth and financial freedom are at the core.

Vinci's greatest accomplishment and his WHY is his family.

He and his wife, Patricia, just had their first child, Serenity, turn one year old in September 2022. Patricia was barely five months pregnant when she and Vinci began setting up their first short-term rental together. They had no idea how much this path would change their life forever.

Links: https://linktr.ee/vinci_sevilla_jr

WEI YANG

DISCOVERING THE PERFECT FIT: THE JOURNEY OF GROWTH THROUGH DISCOMFORT

Like many immigrant tales with humble beginnings, I came to the US with nothing but the clothes on my back and lint in my pocket. Admittedly, I was only eight, but I knew the move to the other side of the planet, leaving everything familiar, was not an easy choice. Like most immigrants seeking a better future, a spark was lit, and I became a hustler ever since.

As a child growing up in the United States, I faced many challenges, particularly since I did not speak the language and found it difficult to comprehend why my school considered "hot dogs" as an acceptable food to serve children. Despite these struggles, we were fortunate enough to reside in a traditional home, which my grandparents paid for by selling everything they had back in Taiwan to move us to the suburbs of Maryland. The three generations, including my brother and I, all lived together under one roof as a family of six. However, due to both my parents working tirelessly and my dad taking on a second job on the weekends, "vacations" pretty much disappeared from our lexicon during those earlier immigrant years.

The closest we got to a family vacation was when my dad

bought a new Mercury Sable five years after we settled; this would be our first vehicle that could comfortably seat all six of us at the same time. To celebrate, my dad decided to take one weekend off from his convenience store gig to do something together with the whole family. I was so ecstatic for a change in routine that I started planning for this outing immediately.

"Oooh! Can we go to Pennsylvania? There's a huge model train display I want to see, and it's also close to a chocolate theme park!"

My dad didn't want to disappoint his firstborn son, so naturally he agreed. With the entire family packed in a car one early Saturday morning, we were finally taking our first official family vacation since moving to the States; destination Hershey Park! After hours of driving, fumbling with paper maps and enjoying the mountainous scenery of the Appalachians, we arrived. For a kid who loves chocolate and disliked every other form of candy, especially candy corn (not relevant, just wanted you to know), Hershey Park would be my Holy Land. I still remember driving on the road alongside the park and seeing the roller coaster from the road, smelling the chocolate in the air, listening to kids screaming in pure joy, eating mounds of candy, swimming and diving gracefully into pools of velvety chocolate.

In truth, I have no idea what goes on in Hershey Park and, to this date, I still can't bring myself back to find out. My head was out of the window as we pulled closer to heaven's gate, only to see that we were now pulling away from our destination just as fast as we had arrived. What in the world was going on? Why were we not heading into the Good Place?

"I thought we are going to Hershey Park?!"

"Yes, we came but we have to keep driving so we can make it home before it gets too dark."

I don't know if my parents were trying to raise a supervillain, or if they just enjoyed burning gasoline, but this pattern of "almost vacations" would happen a few more times in my childhood and, every single time, they got me good. Looking back, I do wish there were more memories of our family enjoying time together versus everyone just struggling in parallel trying to make it in the States.

I'm sure everyone did their best, but I do wonder how many of life's moments I missed because we were too focused on making a living instead of just living. If you're still wondering, I never did make it to that model train museum either. Chugga chugga no choo.

Although I missed out on family vacations in my adolescent years, I do have very fond memories of personal vacations as an adult. Luckily for everyone, I did not turn into a supervillain. Most of my trips, whether domestic or international, expanded my world view, and I also came to appreciate how special large friend groups and extended family vacations can be. The trips that take a year to coordinate and plan, months to reserve and a week to experience rejuvenated my soul. It didn't matter if we stayed at the best house on the block or if I was connecting with a seven-month-old or seventy-year-old; simply having the environment and the opportunity to escape the grind and explore together was enough to help me find centre again. This is also why being a host is so rewarding because we get to create opportunities like this for others.

THE LONG WINDY ROAD TO REAL ESTATE

Being a host was not something I dreamed about. As a technology savvy young adult chasing the American dream in not one, but two dot com booms really skewed my perception of what is possible. The sky is no longer the limit, it's become a place where people store their selfies and where businesses with a great idea can turn a few lines of code into million-dollar SaaS (software as a service) solutions. Who needs real estate when money is raining from all these clouds? From college through my twenties, I spent about a decade in various start-ups, learning everything from UX design, code to building systems and product management.

Through this phase of my life, I also saw my parents struggle with their real estate investment (REI). It wasn't that the purchase or their ideas were bad, but their language barrier really prevented them from reaching the investment's full potential. To me, REI

Joe, Jessy, Soojin & Wei
– the best part of running STRs is meeting other like-minded STR owners

(real estate investing) with LTR seemed like a lot of work for very little reward. Whatever "profit" they saw at the end of the year always seemed to funnel back to maintenance or repairs in preparation for the next tenant. I just didn't understand the point of it, especially when stocks and crypto seemed to be a much more passive investment.

I personally did not invest in real estate, again choosing to chase those SaaS clouds and trying to make it rain. However, I did buy a condo as our primary just a couple of years before the 2008 crash and yes, it was upside down for many years to follow. It took ten whole years for the property to get back to the price I had paid for it, at which point, I quickly exited.

Real estate had left a very sour taste in my mouth as an investment vehicle, but as it turned out, my inability to take flight with REI was limited to my mindset from observing my environment. That all changed in 2017 when I met Soojin, who was not only all in on real estate investing, but she also showed me how it can be done profitably and effortlessly.

When we started dating, Soojin was just starting her journey into real estate investing. I knew something was different when our date night discussions were more about future investments than the latest movie that was out. I watched as she saved for her second investment home and, in the span of three years, turning that into a portfolio of over twenty homes. Not only was she able to leverage her growth, she also had an uncanny ability to screen and pick great tenants; *a tenant whisperer*, if you will. I can't even count the number of times she would get the keys to a new purchase, hold an open house, and sign a tenant by the end of the same weekend. It was certainly a one-eighty from my parents' experience in real estate and, while I was still not fully convinced, ultimately it was her conviction that "this is the way" and her proven results that changed my stance on REI.

THE STR PIVOT

When my parents finally got rid of their Maryland rental in 2020, we decided it would be a good idea to reinvest the funds into properties in Georgia, where I reside. Now that REI was on my radar, I expected to outperform my parents combining Soojin's knack with tenants with my experience setting up systems and running businesses. In February 2021, after months of searching, Soojin and I picked up an off-market two-bedroom, two-bath from a distressed seller. We were able to acquire this metro Atlanta property in a transitional neighbourhood for just shy of $150k.

This property with the huge fenced-in yard at best would rent between $1800 to $2000 a month, which by LTR standards is a great performer when measured against the 1% rule. Unfortunately (or very fortunately), the world was still a year into the global pandemic and, while travel restrictions had loosened, the federal eviction moratorium was still in place. It seemed like every day on social media landlords were venting about non-paying tenants and how unreasonable it was that the government gave renters a break, but not homeowners. On the flip side, some tenants would gloat about living rent free in both their homes and in their landlords' minds; it was crazy town! My main concern was to make sure we were careful about this investment and that we weren't handing over a newly renovated home to a squatter. After some thought, I suggested we pivot away from standard rentals and try our hands at short-term rentals, not realising how this one simple change would completely alter how we did business going forward.

Setting up the Airbnb required another $14,000 in design and furnishings. While we didn't know if the extra expenses would pay off in the middle of the pandemic, we did enjoy putting our personalities and special touches into the home and providing the space where our guests could create memorable moments. Regardless of the results, I was proud of our team's effort and the ability to pivot when needed. Luckily for us, the effort rewarded us with a consistent $5,000 per month revenue, far outperforming the long-term rental homes in our portfolio.

It would take us a few more months to learn the intricacies of the business, deal with strange edge cases, scale to multiple units, hire and fire help, take on co-hosting clients, systemise our processes and change our operations from reactive landlords responding to issues to proactive hospitable hosts helping our guests celebrate memorable moments. As you read this, I am very excited about the future of SuperSTR Experiences Co., and I can't wait to see how we will evolve the company into the next phase. If you are just starting your journey and want to link up, please feel free to reach out! We are always happy to chat and support, which leads us to the next section.

I WISH I KNEW...

Hosting comes with numerous sets of challenges but seeing happy guests and knowing you helped them create memorable moments provides a lot of reward and satisfaction as well. Below are some of the things we did right, and some things I wish I had known when we started.

1. **Figure out who you want to serve.** COVID has changed how we work, how we use our living spaces and how we vacation. Depending on where and how you start your STR journey, your first property may be best for travelling professionals, or it may be better suited for a vacationing family that also works remotely. Understanding the strengths of your area, your house, your guest avatar and designing the space accordingly to fit can help you increase your nightly rates and occupancy rates. Make sure you take these things into consideration when starting out.
2. **Education is key!** Like all new ventures, your chances of success skyrockets when you have a mentor to help you hit the ground running. When we first dabbled in short-term rentals, my team and I signed up for Mike Sjogren's Mastermind course. This was a huge investment for us, but it turned out to be one of the best decisions we made earlier on. We saved ourselves months of trial and error with our first rental and avoided death by a thousand cuts by learning best practices from Mike's course and fellow mastermind members.

   Like most of you jumping into this, we still clocked in at our W2s and we didn't have the luxury of time to figure it all out the hard way. However, within six months of our first guest check-in, our revenue had far exceeded our educational investment, and this wouldn't have been possible if we chose to not invest in education or ourselves.

   We still strive for continuous improvement and, even today, participate in multiple bootcamps and masterminds. Not only are we keeping up with industry trends, but we also love meeting and making new friends with like-minded entrepreneurs. I really wish I had accessed groups like this when I was running my earlier start-ups; it would've made a huge difference having the mentors and support groups to help keep my business objectives straight.
3. **Collect rental agreements (and security deposits!)** As a

new host, one of the calls you don't want to get is from your neighbour telling you there's a rave at the STR you just dropped $100k on. Parties got so bad in many areas that many cities started requiring permits to operate and create other rules to discourage running Airbnbs. I'm here to tell you things like this can be prevented if you set up your listing asking guests to sign a rental agreement and collect security deposits. Sure, there may still be the occasional guest who will behave badly, but if you screen accordingly and let them know ahead of time that the deposit will be forfeited when a party is detected, they will think twice about booking your place for a pop-up party.

4. **Nurture your relationships!** You may think you need to pay the highest rate to get the most reliable cleaner or best handyman, but the truth is, relationships is what drives this hospitality business. Besides pay, show your appreciation through other means as well. Make sure your staff are happy and make sure their families are good; sweat the small stuff! You can't buy loyalty, but you can earn it. I promise your hospitable nature will pay off in dividends.
5. **Focus on quality!** While economy of scale will certainly help with many aspects of this business (e.g., hiring cleaners, buying supplies, etc.), it is also important to learn the ins and outs of being a hospitable host and focus on quality before attempting to scale. There is no shortage of problems to solve in this space but making sure you have a solid, documented process and a well-trained team in place will save you a lot of headaches when growing your business.
6. **Stay on brand.** Be true to yourself, understand your worth and stay on brand. As a new host, you will undoubtably want to chase after every opportunity that presents itself. Sometimes this may mean you accept guests who ask for discounts upfront and later become your biggest headache. Sometimes this means hiring less than stellar cleaners or handymen because you are in a bind; or worse, holding on to them because you're desperate. It may also mean you want to take on untrusting or micromanaging

Wei and his daughter Cara; future RE owner/operator

investors who won't be a great partner because you think you're willing to bend over backwards to accommodate, though nothing will ever be good enough. My advice is, don't do it.

In each of the above examples, you will end up spending most of your time and effort troubleshooting the relationships and the reward wouldn't be much better than if you had just not engaged at all. It's not worth the headache. Focus on the opportunities that match you for you.

7. **Who Not How**. Are we able to recommend another book inside this book? The premise of *Who Not How* by Dan Sullivan is to ask yourself *who* can help you solve a problem versus how you can solve the problem at hand. If you got into STRs with the intention to scale, understand your weaknesses or the parts you don't enjoy and delegate them out. The only way to go far is to go together with great partners and supportive teams.
8. **Start with the exit in mind**. If you're serious about using STRs as the vehicle to fund early retirement or to build generational wealth, treat this venture like a business and not a hobby. Whether you are looking to run one unit, one hotel or you have your sights set on bigger goals, you should always start with the exit in mind. Like all businesses, you want to design it to be attractive for your exit strategy and have it self-sustain without you as the bottleneck or you as the only revenue-generating piece. Learn the steps but fire yourself from as many roles in the business as you can so you can focus on the growth of the business.
9. **Keep your accounting straight.** Along with the previous tip,

one of the best things you should do in this (or any) business is to keep the business accounting separate from your own. As a hospitality manager, there are many expenses you can deduct that have to do with the furnishing and operations of running your STRs. If you are also the owner of the investment home(s), there are additional tax strategies like cost segregation that can further reduce your tax liabilities. Learn what they are and see if they make sense for your operation.

10. **Take action!** The worst action is inaction. Done is better than perfect. You either succeed or you learn. It doesn't matter if you're hosting as an owner, co-hosting for others, or even running STRs through arbitrage, the best way to learn is by doing, so in addition to reading our stories, make sure you set some time aside to act. This book is full of action takers, and you, yes YOU, may just be in the next one we read about.

ABOUT THE AUTHOR

Wei Yang is a serial entrepreneur with twenty-five years of experience in product management, a job where he anticipates customer needs and creates solutions that are loved. Although he has extensive experience catering to users, it wasn't until the pandemic that he combined his knack for delighting users with hosting guests.

Before short-term rentals, Wei saw firsthand the struggles his immigrant parents had managing long-term rentals. With poor cash flow, high-maintenance tenants and "profits" that seemed to always funnel back to repairs, Wei believed rental properties were unnecessarily difficult.

It wasn't until December of 2017 when Wei met Soojin, who spoke highly of real estate investments (REI) and showed him the steps, he understood the ability of investment properties to build generational wealth. As it turns out, not limiting yourself to one belief (i.e. real estate is not worth the trouble) opens new doors, literally!

Fast forward to April 2021 when landlords across the US were contending with the COVID-19 eviction moratorium, Wei pushed for a pivot in their investment strategy that would ultimately change their trajectory for how they approach REI. For the price of household essentials and a splash of southern hospitality, Wei and his partners would turn an $1,800/month rental into a $5,000/month short-term rental and avoid worrying about evictions for non-paying tenants.

Wei and Soojin now own and operate SuperSTR, a luxury short-term rental management and consulting company with a focus on memorable guest experiences. In the two years since their first guest, the company grew to seven properties, hosting over 500 stays, including ninety-four pups and 1,521 guests. Wei has also been featured on short-term rental podcasts and continues to grow their consulting business, helping interested investors get into short-term rentals. More importantly, Wei is excited to leave a legacy for his daughter Cara, helping her get a head start on her real estate investment journey.

Links: https://linktr.ee/superstr

WIL SLICKERS

HOSPITALITY SAVED MY LIFE

Growing up, I struggled to fit in. I come from a family with seven siblings. I am the seventh of seven with a twin brother with Down's syndrome and five older sisters. I share this because it helps set some context on my upbringing. I was friends with everyone, but I didn't have a core group of friends I could rely on. Growing up, I thought that was okay and that I was happy to call everyone my friend, not knowing how much more important it was to just have a few really close friends, especially in my earlier years. In high school, I know now that I was more alone than I ever thought I was. In reality, I wasn't close with my family. My dad and I didn't get along well at the time, and I always felt like I was off in my own world while still trying to be a part of everyone else's. This led me to making some poor choices, including experimenting with drugs, and I started stealing things when I could because I was the kid that was "under the radar". I started to become depressed and felt like I didn't have any direction in life. I was very lost, confused, and in the pain of loneliness I was drowning in emotions that I didn't know how to process properly.

After high school, I made even more poor choices and those choices ended up catching up with me, which then made me end up homeless just after graduating. I lived out of my car, a little Geo Metro, and started a part-time job shovelling horse manure twice a day for $100 a week for a family I actually kind of knew growing up but didn't really connect with until the end of high school through a friend who was trying to help me out. I eventually ended up living on site in a trailer/camper that had no water and barely any power. I was so lost and didn't know how to change my situation. I was barely living off food stamps and that $100 dollars per week. To this day, though, I can say that the family who helped me through all of that is one of the reasons I am alive today. They truly helped me as I was figuring out my next path in life.

I had a heartfelt conversation with Mark, the father of the family who let me stay on site, about setting intentional time aside to write out a plan for what I wanted my life to look like in a year, two years, three years, and so on. And to be honest, I had no clue what I wanted my life to look like a week from then. All I knew was that I didn't want to go to bed hungry every night and wonder how I was going to afford to get petrol money so I could make it to a job interview without my car running out before I got there. That conversation with Mark left a permanent mark on my life and I don't think there is a day that goes by where I don't think about that special moment. That was the first time I felt like someone was being intentional about the words they spoke to me. He even cooked me a meal prior to having that conversation. Something I will never forget.

Months after that conversation with Mark, I decided to join the Army National Guard. I knew I needed something to help turn my life around and, after that conversation, the army was the best solution I could think of at the time. The army helped me gain discipline and self-respect that I'd never had before. I went from barely weighing 115lbs to 160lbs in a matter of four months during the Army Basics Training and AIT (Advanced Individual Training) and, honestly, was in the best shape of my life. This truly helped in so many ways. For once, I wasn't looked at as the skinny short kid from Stanwood, Washington, but I was finally Wil Slickers, the

Amplifying Voices Through Audio

guy who started over and was proving himself to the world. The homeless kid who struggled with drugs and depression turned into a fit, confident and driven man starting a new chapter.

A few months after coming home and working, I started to see my mental health go downward once again. As I was staying in shape, I became easily persuaded and slipped back into the party lifestyle I had once left. Partying and living for the weekend was a cycle I had the hardest time escaping. Eventually, it had got so bad that I attempted to commit suicide. This was after I had moved to Spokane Washington, a five-hour drive from where I grew up. Being in a new city with new people was great in theory but I was emotionally unprepared to be alone and in my own head for so long. So, I turned to the only thing I knew, drinking and partying, the worst things to do when you have thoughts about ending your life. My childhood friend, Alex, was living a couple of blocks away from my apartment, and on the night I was going to end my life, he showed up just in time.

From what felt like years later of trying to get myself out of this darkness, I tried to start my own chauffeur company when Uber had just started to become a thing, but it didn't work out. I ended up closing that business exactly one year after opening it, but I had got my first taste of entrepreneurship. A few short days after closing that business, I ended up applying for a job at a Marriott Autograph Collection hotel, where I'd picked up some chauffeur clients once, and was hired on the spot.

I will never forget that interview. I had these suites from when I was doing the chauffeur company and realised that I could use them at this fancy four-diamond hotel. During my interview with the front desk manager, he asked me two really important questions that I didn't think were as important at the time. He asked me first how I was with technology. I told him an honest answer and said it was something I would need help with and that this would be my first time working at a hotel, but I was confident I could pick it up quickly. To give you some context about this hotel, it has over 700 rooms. For a first-time hotel job, and this one being in the Autograph Collection with Marriott meant that there was no hotel exactly like it. It had all the perks of a Marriott property but was owned by a very wealthy individual. This was a big deal and very intimidating for me at the time. His second question was how was I with people. And again, with an honest answer, I told him that I was great with people and loved them.

After a few intense days of training, I started to get the job a bit more. After three or four months on the job, I fell in love with the hospitality industry and knew that this was where I belonged. I learned so much at that Marriott property and wanted to grow in leadership positions but, in all honesty, that hotel was so big and the managers at the time were very comfortable being in their positions, leaving it very hard for me to move up. I spent two years at that Marriott before moving to the Oregon Coast to work for an independent hotel group. I became a fine dining restaurant manager and eventually left to become an assistant general manager at a different hotel in the area due to some leadership transitions that were happening with the previous group.

While on the Oregon Coast, I started my own podcast called

Slick Talk: The Hospitality Podcast. I was honestly just very bored and still had somewhat of an entrepreneurial itch from my chauffeur days. The podcast became a way for me to talk about what I was learning at my job or, as it's known today, interviewing industry leading experts who I could learn from. I was having so much fun and started to get some really good traction with the show. I was getting emails every day from people wanting to be a guest on the show. My natural curiosity must have been the reason why people were tuning in and then wanting to be on the show. My guests and I were having these really high-level conversations that someone in my position may never have had if it wasn't for the medium of podcasting. And I can say to this day that I am actually good friends with the majority of them.

One very intense and busy summer on the Oregon Coast later, I started getting more and more exposed to the vacation rental sector of the industry. Either podcast listeners from the vacation rental industry were talking about the podcast, asking to be on it, or I was seeing how vacation home management was solving problems I faced in my hotel days. And a lot of people may not know this but my parents were how I got into vacation rental management. They have a two-bedroom and two-bath apartment above their garage and asked me about this thing called Airbnb. My show became so time-consuming that it was all I could think about while also obsessing about vacation rentals. At the time, this scared the shit out of me because I knew I could take it full time. But I had doubts from my past entrepreneurial failures.

Well, that all changed once I had this idea of doing a vacation rental series on the podcast. A ten-episode series where I was interviewing the best minds in the industry at the time and it caught on like wildfire. I was then approached by sponsors. I had never been paid to podcast before that and felt like I'd walked into a gold mine. But how was I supposed to know how to price these sponsorships? After talking to some of the sponsors, I ended up making almost $10,000 on this ten-episode series and, from that moment forward, I told myself I had to take the show full time.

The 27th of December 2019 was my last day as a hotel manager. I had put in three weeks' notice and I never looked back. Oh, and did I mention I started a luxury management company for vacation homes? Because I did. This helped my podcast take off and gain a wider audience. I eventually left this company and partnership during COVID. I will share a little more on this later. But in 2021, I had co-founded a new property management company called Recreation Rentals, which focused solely on experiential hospitality, and I am still part of it today with my co-founder, Adam Knight, who was actually one of my first industry guests on the podcast.

Just as things were starting to take off in early 2020, the COVID-19 pandemic hit. I was almost forced to start over again with the monetisation on my podcast and was eventually activated to the army to help run testing sites throughout the whole Washington state. In the beginning, I was honestly a little scared and upset because I had worked so damn hard to take the podcast full time. I had just tasted the freedom of self-sustaining entrepreneurship and then it was gone in the blink of an eye. Despite all the challenges and moments of doubt, I pushed through and continued to run my podcast again in April of 2020. After my six-year term in the Army National Guard was up and I was taken off orders for COVID, I was discharged and went back to full-time podcasting and running my vacation rental business.

In September of 2020, Michael Goldin – founder of Storied – joined me on Slick Talk and we had such a great conversation that he asked me, "We should do that again more often, any chances of making that happen?" Shortly after a mutual feeling and agreement, he and I launched a podcast and morning news show called Good Morning Hospitality.

Now, let's fast forward a little bit because, in October 2021, I went to my first industry conference called the Vacation Rental Management Association International Conference – or VRMA International for short. It was held in San Antonio, TX, and finally, I was going to meet everyone I had connected with online the previous few years in person. My first day at the conference, I was surrounded by industry podcasters and even sponsors all asking me similar questions from a podcasting standpoint or wanting to spend advertising money on my show. As excited as I was, I thought I had capped myself out on revenue for my main podcast. This was one of the best realisations because the perfect timing had just happened for me to have one of the best ideas of my life.

On the 1st of December 2021, I launched Hospitality.FM, the industry's biggest podcast network for hospitality. We started with six podcasts that we were producing (or editing) and I had hired my first employee, Claire, who has become one of my most trusted people in the business. We now work with and manage over thirty industry podcasts in all verticals of hospitality.

As you've read to this point in my chapter, you can see that where I started this story to where we're ending it has been a pretty big jump. From attempting suicide to multi-entrepreneur in hospitality. A complete one-eighty-degree turn around of my life. What wasn't fully covered in this chapter is the amount of work, not only I had to put into my businesses, but the amount of work and time that went into discovering who I am and how I can live a life in complete honesty with what I want and need.

One thing or lesson I can say I am very happy that I learned during these last two years or so is that the more I live my life on my own terms and less on the expectations of others in my life, like family, friends and even colleagues, the happier I have become. That realisation didn't come easy but I am so glad it made itself known in my life.

To end this chapter the same way I started it, *hospitality saved my life* because it gave me a sense of purpose and direction. It allowed me to connect with people and create a sense of community that I had been missing for more years of my life than I can count. The hospitality industry gave me the opportunity to take my experiences, good and bad, and use them to help others in and outside of hospitality. I am now able to provide a platform for people to share their stories and experiences in their rawest forms.

Looking back on my journey as I have been figuring out how to write it on the pages of this chapter, I am grateful for the struggles and challenges that I faced. They have made me who I am today and have given me the strength and determination to succeed in the hospitality industry and anything else I put my mind to. This industry and experience allowed me to process losses and wins in the weirdest way but also in the way I actually needed.

Hospitality truly saved my life, and I am forever grateful for it, and I hope my story gives you inspiration to go above and beyond your own expectations for your life and journey in this industry and in the relationships around you.

ABOUT THE AUTHOR

Wil Slickers is the founder of Hospitality.FM, the biggest hospitality podcast network in the world, while also being the co-founder of Recreation Vacation Rentals with a property portfolio of ten homes from Washington State, Florida, Pennsylvania and other states coming soon. He got his start in the industry by working at a Marriott Autograph Collection hotel with over 700 rooms and eventually became a hotel manager prior to becoming a full-time podcaster, launching Hospitality.FM and Recreation Rentals. As seen on season two of Office Hours with David Meltzer, featured as one of the Top 50 Influencers in Global Hospitality Awards, Top 20 Influencers in Vacation Rental Technology, and quoted as an industry expert in the Hospitality Industry Report by Hostfully. Wil Slickers is based in Denver Colorado as a single entrepreneur in hospitality and is the "fun uncle" of twelve nieces and nephews.

Links: https://poplme.co/hash/CHfyfoBG/2/share

MARK SIMPSON

After being in hospitality for most of my thirty-nine years on this planet, I have a story or two to share.

In the first edition of *Hospitable Hosts*, I explained how our family saved a guest's life!

When Jodie asked if I wanted to come back for the second edition, I knew exactly what I wanted to put down, as it is not only a brilliant story, it sits nicely with what I do now for my career as founder of Boostly, where I give hosts the tactics and tips to boost their bookings.

This story involves a balloon, a six-year-old girl and a unicorn.

To best tell this tale, I need to start at the beginning.

My family's hospitality business was based in Scarborough, UK. It was a fourteen-bedroom guesthouse with three holiday cottages as well as a tearoom and restaurant. Every year, we would welcome thousands of guests through our doors. Our niche was families, with children of all ages loving our friendly farm animals and fields to roam through.

My role in the business was to attract as many guests as possible and to ensure they booked directly. I loved to experiment with many forms of marketing, from Facebook to Snapchat to email to direct mail. Some experiments failed, and some experiments were a massive success. There was one that stood out as a massive success, and that is what I wanted to share with you in my chapter. If you're a host reading this, I hope it inspires you in what you could potentially do for your business.

Before I continue, I need to add a disclaimer here. Otherwise, she will kill me.

This idea was my wife's (Laura Nicholson Simpson).

In 2016, everyone was focusing on online advertising. Facebook and Google Ads were becoming very popular. Fewer businesses were focusing on offline marketing as businesses pivoted to online. With that, it left a massive gap in the market.

When everyone zigs, you zag.

We had just conducted a massive survey on the guests who had visited us over the past two years. We had printed off all our reporting tools from our property management software tool and the goal was to work out which 20% of locations brought in 80% of our guests. Initially, the idea was to run newspaper and radio ads in that 20% of locations.

After spending hours putting in the work and research, we discovered that most of our guests lived less than two hours' drive from where we were located. It was surprising to me, as I'd assumed it would be further.

Laura then came up with an idea of how we could do something different from the traditional marketing ideas. She explained that when she was a child growing up in South Africa, she had found a balloon with a note attached to the bottom of the string. She said that we could do something similar, seeing that the majority of our guests lived less than two hours away from where we were based. It was the perfect enhancement area. The note would contain a voucher for a fully comped three-night stay with us on the farm. It was a genius idea and one we could easily implement.

Laura found a company that sold biodegradable balloons and, within a few days, it was ready to go. We made sure the winds were blowing away from the coastline and off it went.

A few weeks past and there was no phone call. We had placed our number at the bottom of the note so anyone who found the balloon could redeem their prize. I was about to place this experiment in the pile of failed ones, when all of a sudden, the phone rang.

There was a lady on the other end of the phone who explained that her daughter had found a balloon with a note on the end of a piece of string. They hadn't wanted to call the number because her partner thought it was a scam at first!

After putting her mind at rest and assuring her it wasn't a scam, we were able to sort a date when the family could come and redeem their stay. They lived a few hours away, which amazed me at how far the balloon had travelled.

Just as the phone conversation was ending, with a very excitable young mum, she mentioned that it was perfect timing as it was her daughter's sixth birthday and she loved farm animals and horses. She joked that her favourite animal was a unicorn. My wife heard this remark and, without batting an eyelid, loaded up the computer and beamed as she showed me what was on her laptop screen.

A few weeks passed and the lovely family arrived to check-in. It turned out that the mum had a bit of a following on social media and was also a blogger. She had been posting on social media about the balloon, the prize and her upcoming holiday to the farm.

Upon arrival, we showed the family and the young girl to their bedroom. Laura had been busy making the room extra special for the girl's arrival. After hearing it was her sixth birthday and her love of unicorns, she had bought a stuffed unicorn toy on the internet as a gift for the little girl and had left it on her bed for when she'd checked in.

The girl squealed with excitement as she not only saw her room but also her new toy.

As we left the family to check-in, I went to go and check emails and any notifications online. The mum had posted an update on her Facebook page and tagged us in.

What resulted was a mountain of comments and messages to reply to from friends or followers of the mum who wanted to know more about our accommodation. They had seen her posts about the prize, the balloon and what we had done for her daughter.

Not only that, the local press had seen what we had done and I had an email from the journalist who wanted to come down and interview the girl, the family and us.

An idea that cost us less than £20 and took us only five minutes to put together resulted in massive exposure, a feature in the local newspaper and a mountain of direct bookings.

The little girl came back to see us for her seventh and eighth birthdays.

It was a beautiful experiment that was firmly placed in the successful pile.

Links: www.boostly.co.uk

SCAN HERE!

HOSPITABLE HOSTS BOOK PARTNERS

hostgpo

They say that the key to success is often found outside of one's comfort zone. For me, an attorney turned vacation rental entrepreneur, this certainly rings true.

When I first heard about lease arbitrage in the short-term rental (STR) industry, I was immediately intrigued. I had been practising law for several years, but I had always been fascinated by the hospitality industry and loved to travel. In fact, I had just come back from a trip to Copenhagen where I stayed in a stunning vacation rental in the middle of Nørrebro – a hip part of town that has no hotels in it. So, in 2014, when I learned you could make money by renting a house, furnishing it, and creating a vacation rental experience for others to enjoy, I decided to get uncomfortable, give it a shot and leased the home directly across the street from where I lived.

As an attorney, I was used to (1) tracking every minute of my day (billing by the minute) and (2) being an egomaniacal overachiever. I was hyper-aware of how I spent my time. I would wake up early, work a full day as a lawyer, and then do the heavy vacation rental work at night – with some sporadic guest messaging from my phone during coffee breaks and from the water cooler. It was a lot of work, often fourteen-hour days between the two, but I enjoyed it, and it gave me a taste of being my own boss – where "the sky was the limit".

Those gruelling months, full of long days, started to take their toll. I was used to valuing my opinion and trusting my gut, but in the vacation rental industry, I had to learn to be humble and learn from my (many) mistakes. I can recall a specific "red pill" moment for me, when I accidentally ripped my suit trousers while trying to assemble a coffee table late at night – I was out of my comfort zone and clearly doing things wrong. I had lost track of valuing my time, was stretching myself too thin, and was trying to solve problems with brute force rather than intellect.

Back then, there was no vacation rental community and very little industry education material. Fortunately, I stumbled upon a great business partner who coached me through those months of my STR journey... and helped me buy a new pair of slacks.

I took a step back to reflect, and then took a leap of faith to hang up the suit altogether, and I am glad I did. I have since managed over 250 vacation rental units, from super-luxury mansions in Malibu to cabins in the woods, and have had tens of thousands, if not hundreds of thousands, of guests with plenty of crazy vacation rental stories (from drug busts to corrupt cops, from checking in A-list celebrities to cooking dinner with a family of nine from Laos). Even though I started in 2014, which was already 3.0 or even 4.0 in the evolution of the modern vacation rental industry, it still feels like it was the Wild West compared to today.

As the vacation rental community continues to grow, I have tried to pass on the lessons I had learned and to lift others up on their own paths. One of my biggest lessons, which has become the focus of my career now, is educating folks on how to furnish a vacation rental home. In the beginning, I would often pick up items off the high street or buy things from big box stores like Ikea. I quickly realised that this approach was not sustainable. Low-quality sheets and pillows got guest complaints and buying cheap furniture from big box stores ended up costing me more time and money in the long run because I had to replace them frequently.

While online shopping can be a good alternative, it also has its challenges. There are so many options that it can be overwhelming, and many people end up buying off-brand items that they don't know anything about. I also went through a phase of buying from unknown online brands, but it often felt like playing roulette, with no guarantee of the quality of the items I was purchasing.

There was one day in particular that changed it all. I was at an Ikea with my team of sixteen people, and we ended up with forty-eight shopping carts full of items to check out. Uncomfortable. The checkout alone took three hours, and when I asked for a discount, the woman just laughed and said it wasn't even close to enough for a "volume" discount. The whole experience was a nightmare and didn't end there; we still had to build the furniture. When one of our many U-hauls got into a fender bender, it was the final straw. I swore to myself that I would never do it again.

After one of the craziest forty-eight hours of my life, I knew there had to be a better solution. I co-founded HostGPO to provide a curated selection of high-quality, durable furnishings and supplies for vacation rental owners. By leveraging the buying power of a group, we are able to offer better prices and take the hassle out of sourcing and setting up vacation rental units. Our 50+ vendor partnerships were made so HostGPO members always get better rates than the standard trade discount or through other wholesale clubs.

As a host myself, I understand that there's more to running a vacation rental business than just buying furniture, linens and supplies. That's why HostGPO has also partnered with service-based companies in areas such as insurance, dynamic pricing software, welcome guides and more to provide our members with a complete package of support.

Looking back at my journey, I can confidently say that stepping out of my comfort zone has made that zone bigger. By stepping out of my comfort zone, I have built a successful business managing hundreds of vacation rental units, and I have founded a company that represents hundreds of thousands of units and am able to help other hosts grow and succeed. I keep pushing myself every day to get even further outside. It was a wild ride, but I am grateful for every experience and every lesson learned along the way. For anyone thinking about taking a leap of faith – relish the discomfort! You never know where it might lead you.

Jeff Iloulian, Co-founder

www.hostgpo.com

Autohost is an intelligent screening platform for hospitality, providing a scalable and automated process to vet guests, verify identities, and prevent fraud using machine learning and behavioural checks. The platform helps operators comply with regulations, prevent abuse and keep properties safe. Autohost automates ID collection and verification, biometric scans, background and credit checks, damage waivers and security deposit collection. Using relevant and objective data points, Autohost minimises chargebacks and avoids discrimination, enhancing the guest experience with a streamlined digital check-in process. With Trust and Safety handled, Autohost empowers fast-growing operators to focus on inventory growth and scalable expansion.

www.autohost.ai

At Cash Street Technology LLC, we firmly believe that financial education serves as the solution to many of the world's problems. We offer financial education through mentorship, educational courses, couples' wealth and health retreats, mastermind meet-ups, associations and business resources necessary to succeed in life, business and the real estate industry. Andrew and Meghan's strong background in financial management, real estate, entrepreneurship and leadership skills, combined with their dedication to making a positive impact on the world through their continued philanthropic efforts, make them an asset to any couple, individual, or organisation. Spending one-on-one time with this dynamic duo will help you gain expertise and experience.

www.cashstreettech.com

Boostly

www.boostly.co.uk

bnbamplify

www.bnbamplify.com

operto

www.operto.com

ESTELLE

Keeber

www.immortalmonkey.co.uk

SUPERHOG

www.superhog.com

INVS

INVESTED TALENT

www.investedtalent.com

Thank you for reading *Hospitable Hosts 2.* If you've got something positive out of the book, please review it on Amazon.

Join our community: www.hospitablehosts.com

Follow our journey on Instagram: @hospitablehostsbook

SCAN ME

Nashville

Australia